Henley-on-Thames
town, trade and river

An England's Past for Everyone paperback

Other titles in this series

Bolsover: Castle, Town and Colliery

Bristol: Ethnic Minorities and the City 1000-2001

Burford: Buildings and People in a Cotswold Town

Codford: Wool and War in Wiltshire

Cornwall and the Coast: Mousehole and Newlyn

Cornwall and the Cross: Christianity 500-1560

Exmoor: The Making of an English Upland

Ledbury: A Market Town and its Tudor Heritage

The Medway Valley: A Kent Landscape Transformed

Parham: A Sussex House and its Restoration

Sunderland and its Origins: Monks to Mariners

In association with the VCH Oxfordshire Trust, Oxfordshire County Council and Oxford University Library Services.

Henley-on-Thames
town, trade and river

SIMON TOWNLEY

with contributions from Ruth Gibson,
Geoffrey Tyack, and Antonia Catchpole

Phillimore

First published 2009

A Victoria County History publication
Published by Phillimore & Co. Ltd, Madam Green Farm Business Centre, Oving, Chichester, West Sussex, England in association with the Institute of Historical Research at the University of London.
www.phillimore.co.uk

ISBN 978-1-86077-554-3

British Library Cataloguing in Publication Data. A cataloguing record for this book is available from the British Library.

Typeset in Humanist 521 and Minion

We wish particularly to thank the following EPE and VCH staff for their efforts during the production of this volume:

John Beckett – Director of the Victoria County History
Matthew Bristow – Historic Environment Research Manager
Sarah Byrne – Production Assistant
Catherine Cavanagh – Project Manager
Jessica Davies – Publications Manager
Skye Dillon – Education and Skills Manager
Nafisa Gaffar – Finance and Contracts Officer
Mel Hackett – Communications Manager
Nick Hall – Administrator
Dmitri Nemchenko – Web Manager
Alan Thacker – Executive Editor of the Victoria County History
Elizabeth Williamson – Architectural Editor of the Victoria County History

Printed and bound in Great Britain

Cover image: Henley's waterfront in 2008. (University of London)
Back cover image: Henley from the Wargrave road by Jan Siberechts (1698) – detail showing a barge passing through Marsh lock. (Courtesy of The River & Rowing Museum, Henley-on-Thames)

Contents

List of Panels:

Foreword

I defy anyone to sit at the river's edge under a willow and not feel the stress and cares of the day being washed downstream. Sometimes after a slow journey down Remenham Hill, where the road is cut deep into the chalk hillside like a special gateway to Henley, I see people leaning over the bridge and looking up the Regatta course to the green swell of the Chilterns at Hambledon, and I know they'll be feeling calm and happy. 'The river glideth at its own sweet will' even 65 miles upstream from Westminster, here in this prettiest of market towns, and those of us lucky enough to live nearby are happy to share its secrets.

One of the great joys is to look at the buildings above the shops, whose roof-lines tell a story of a town steeped in history – there are all types of structure from timber-framed Tudor to brick and flint, there are courtyards with glimpses of secret gardens and an excellent pub on every corner. Henley-on-Thames has nestled in this bend in the river for nearly a millennium; it is a town that has grown from serfdom to Starbucks, that has moved effortlessly from river trade (beechwood, corn, malt) to river recreation (the Regatta, the festival, boating holidays).

And the people we see in the streets are as varied as the buildings – among those who have loved the town are the late John Mortimer and George Harrison, and you can still see the likes of Jeremy Paxman, David Gilmour and Jeremy Irons strolling around on market days. Laid to rest in St Mary's beautiful churchyard is Dusty Springfield, her grave always dressed with the flowers of her fans. Sir Bulstrode Whitelocke, who owned Henley in the 17th century, described the river as 'a good neighbour' to the town. In my view they are a marriage made in heaven.

Don't visit Henley without this book – it will allow you to discover and then rediscover all the beauty and variety of the town, its history and its hidden treasures.

Simon Williams

Preface

Set amidst the rolling tree-covered slopes of the south-west Chilterns at a picturesque bend in the Thames, Henley is probably best known for its graceful 18th-century bridge, and above all for its annual Royal Regatta. The Regatta reflects Henley's 19th-century emergence as an inland resort and fashionable social centre; but the town's relationship with the river and the surrounding landscape is much older and much more varied. This book traces the history of the town and river over time, from Henley's origins as a planned medieval market town and inland port shipping grain to London, through to its present-day role as a small service, tourist and commuting centre.

The research has been a collective effort, carried out under the auspices of the Victoria County History's England's Past for Everyone project (EPE). EPE is a series of self-contained local-history projects supported by the Heritage Lottery Fund, combining the work of professional historians with that of local volunteer groups and other contributors, and encompassing paperback publication, web resources, and school projects.

For Henley, much of the basic archival work was undertaken by Oxfordshire VCH staff: Simon Townley, Robert Peberdy and Antonia Catchpole, with Mark Page and Stephen Mileson working on surrounding rural areas. This is also feeding into a main-series VCH volume on the Henley area, to be published in the near future. Robert Peberdy kindly gave access to his unpublished PhD thesis on medieval Henley (listed in the bibliography), on which Chapter 4 draws heavily. Research into buildings was commissioned from Ruth Gibson and Geoffrey Tyack (who respectively drafted the sections on medieval and later buildings), with additional work by Nicholas Cooper. VCH and EPE staff in London (listed at the front of this book) have helped in innumerable ways.

But this has also been a community project, benefiting from the work of volunteers and local historians in Henley and elsewhere. Since 2007 a Henley Census Group (set up for EPE) has been transcribing 19th-century censuses for parts of the town, and is busy relating entries to the buildings themselves. A Probate Group set up for an earlier EPE project is transcribing wills and other probate documents and helping to analyse the material, co-ordinated by Barbara Allison. The work of both groups will be made available on the EPE Explore website (www.englandspastforeveryone.org.uk), alongside additional material from the project. Members of the long-standing Henley Archaeological and Historical Group have been unfailingly generous in sharing their research and their wide local knowledge, among them Ann Cottingham, Hilary Fisher, Roger Kendal, and Peter Anderson. Valerie Alasia summarised the Henley entries from 19th-century newspapers, John Bailey made available his work on the history of Henley sport, and Derek Toms took additional buildings photographs. Numerous other people have given access to buildings or to documentary and photographic material, while Laura Wortley generously shared her ongoing research into Jan Siberechts' Henley paintings. David Clark and members of the Oxfordshire Buildings Record helped with building recording at the *Old White Hart* and elsewhere.

Equally important has been the support of Henley River & Rowing Museum, whose staff (both past and present) gave access to their collections, answered endless queries, and helped publicise the project by including us in their lecture series. Particular thanks are due to Jane Bowen, Eloise Morton, Suzie Tilbury, Valerie Wardlaw, and the museum's chief executive Paul Mainds, who has been unfailingly enthusiastic. The River & Rowing Museum was also the educational partner in our schools project, working with pupils from Mabel Prichard Special Needs School in Oxford to investigate buildings and the river in both Henley and Burford. That part of the project was delivered by Valerie Wardlaw and Jill Hutchinson of the River & Rowing Museum, and by Nicole Smith and her colleagues at Mabel Prichard. Educational materials from the schools projects in Oxfordshire and elsewhere are available on the EPE website.

As always, thanks are due to the staff of numerous libraries and archives: in particular Oxfordshire Record Office, Oxfordshire Studies, the Bodleian Library, Henley Library, Berkshire Record Office, Gloucestershire Record Office, and The National Archives. Dan Miles of the Oxford Dendrochronology Laboratory undertook tree-ring dating of several Henley buildings, and Cath D'Alton drew the maps.

Finally, the project would not have been possible without support in funding or in kind from the following bodies, to which (along with the Heritage Lottery Fund) warm thanks are expressed: Oxfordshire County Council (core staff funding); the VCH Oxfordshire Trust (staff and partnership funding); the Bodleian Library and Oxford University Library Services (accommodation and research materials); and the History Faculty of Oxford University. The Marc Fitch Fund and the Oxfordshire Architectural and Historical Society contributed to the cost of dendrochronological dating.

Simon Townley
County Editor and EPE Team Leader, VCH Oxfordshire

Angel

Chapter 1 Henley in Time and Place

Figure 1 A classic view of Henley and its 18th-century bridge (completed in 1786). The impressive church reflects the town's late medieval prosperity, based on the river trade with London. Just visible on the right is the red-brick façade of the *Red Lion*, one of the town's major 18th-century coaching inns.

For many people, mention of Henley will summon up idealised images of the annual Royal Regatta: blazers and boaters, skiffs and houseboats, strawberries on the lawn. It is an image reinforced by countless photographs of the Regatta in its Edwardian heyday, and for those unfamiliar with the town is likely to awaken either a strong nostalgia and attraction or – for some – an equally strong aversion.

The Regatta has been a prominent feature of Henley life since the 1830s, a symbol of (and a major contributory factor to) its 19th-century emergence as an inland resort and a centre of genteel tourism. But the town's relationship with the river and the surrounding Chilterns landscape is much older and more complex. Originating as a medieval planned town in probably the late 12th century, Henley first rose to prominence as a market centre and inland port, funnelling grain and fuel drawn from a wide hinterland into the expanding metropolis of London, and channelling luxuries, fish and other goods in the opposite direction. From the 16th century the capital's demand for malt stimulated a local malting industry, and from the late 17th century its position on the main overland routes between London and the west turned it into an important coaching town, bringing in a new fashionable elite, and cementing its emerging role as a social as well as market centre for the surrounding countryside. From that period date many of the town's characteristic Georgian houses and frontages, visible symptoms of its 18th-century prosperity.

Binding all this together was the Thames, valued equally as a crucial transport corridor for heavy London barge traffic, and as a crowning element in the south-west Chilterns' much admired scenic beauty – a combination which from at least the 17th century attracted prosperous merchants, professionals and aristocracy to the town and its surrounding wooded slopes. The attractions were summarised in lyrical fashion in the 1650s by Sir Bulstrode Whitelocke, a lawyer, landowner and Parliamentarian who owned Henley and Fawley manors:

> These hills are richly adorned with pleasant woods and groves, consisting for the most part of beech which crown the tops of the hills; and [at] the foot of them gently glides the River Thames, offering to carry their burdens (which are not small) of

> wood and corn to their chief city, London, which he doth, and returns money and other necessary commodities in exchange for them. Indeed he is a good neighbour, enriching this country by his navigableness, and allowing them sufficient meadow for their hay, and store of salmons, trouts, pikes, perches, eels and other good fish for their provisions. He hastens not by a quick though clear and sweet stream through this country, but gravely keeps on his way, delighted with his flowery banks, and the bending groves saluting him.

Figure 2 The county of Oxfordshire in the SE of England.

With the dawn of the railway age Henley seemed, for a time, to have lost its golden touch, as railway competition undermined the centuries-old primacy of the Thames river trade, and the town's initial failure to secure a branch line left it isolated, for the first time in its history, from the most important transport routes. But with the opening of the Henley branch in 1857 the town was able to capitalise on its burgeoning reputation as a resort and social centre – a reputation inextricably linked with the development of the annual Regatta, which was established in 1839 as a conscious attempt to draw trade and visitors to a place still reeling from the collapse of the coaching and river trades. By the 1890s over 34,000 visitors a year (including royalty and the most fashionable elements of society) regularly attended 'this world-celebrated water picnic', winning this small Oxfordshire market town of still under 6,000 people an international reputation.[1]

The following chapters explore all those aspects of Henley's history, beginning with its medieval origins, and concluding with its continuing role as a small service town and tourist centre at the dawn of the 21st century. Through all the changes flows the connecting thread of the Thames, and the story is consequently

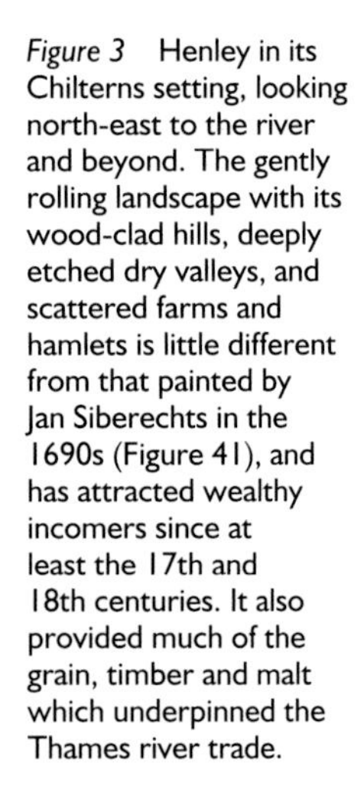

Figure 3 Henley in its Chilterns setting, looking north-east to the river and beyond. The gently rolling landscape with its wood-clad hills, deeply etched dry valleys, and scattered farms and hamlets is little different from that painted by Jan Siberechts in the 1690s (Figure 41), and has attracted wealthy incomers since at least the 17th and 18th centuries. It also provided much of the grain, timber and malt which underpinned the Thames river trade.

one not only of the town itself but of the changing life of the river, and of how developments in river use and navigation affected Henley from the Middle Ages to the canal age and beyond. At each stage, despite the sometimes glittering social surface, Henley has also remained a working town, its inhabitants engaged not only in the river trade but in the crafts, manufactures and sale of agricultural goods typical of any small market town. This, too, forms part of the story, from the fishmongers, leather workers and innkeepers of the Middle Ages to the departure of Brakspears' Brewery in 2002.

THE CHILTERNS SETTING

First, though, what of the town's surroundings? If Henley's most obvious characteristic is as a riverside town, just as important is its setting within the south-west Chilterns – a geographical shorthand which encompasses much more than just a line of chalk hills running from near Hitchin in Hertfordshire to near Goring in Oxfordshire. Even now the Chilterns comprise a distinct and uniquely attractive landscape, one of scattered farms and hamlets set among steep-sided slopes, small uneven plateaux and deeply etched dry valleys, and clothed for the most part in a mixture of woodland, wood pasture and small irregular fields (Figure 3). The pattern is an ancient one, even though the precise outlines of the woodland have ebbed and flowed over time, and the current dominance of beech wood may go back no further than the 16th or 17th centuries. Medieval estate records point already to mixed cereal-based agriculture based on pasture, wood and grain, while the Tudor traveller John Leland drew attention in the 1530s to the abundance of corn and wood in the Henley area. Daniel Defoe, writing 190 years later, reckoned that the beech woods of the Buckinghamshire Chilterns grew 'more plentifully than in any other part of England'. Equally distinctive are the area's buildings, a reflection (as always) of local geology and resources. The prevalence of medieval timber-framing in an area with so much woodland is unsurprising, but what gives the Chilterns so much of its character is the use of flint and brick. Across much of the area the underlying chalk is covered by patches of gravel, sand, and clay-with-flints, which stimulated an extensive brick-making industry around Nettlebed long before the dictates of fashion turned places like Henley and Marlow into predominantly brick-built towns in the late 17th and 18th centuries.[2]

No less than the river, the agricultural potential of the Chilterns and of the Oxfordshire vale beyond provided a key to Henley's success. From the Middle Ages the dominant economic force

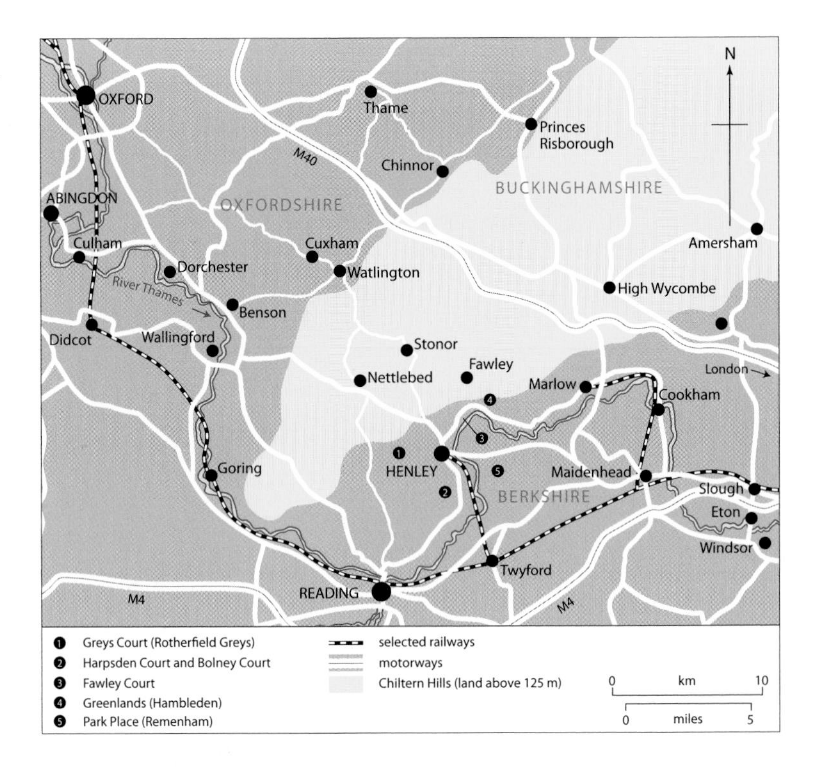

Figure 4 Henley in its setting, showing present-day roads and selected railway links.

in the Chilterns and beyond was the expanding city of London, whose growing population needed fuel and food. Until the railway age both were funnelled along the Thames corridor from a vast and varied hinterland, in which the Chilterns' mixed agriculture played a central role. Medieval accounts show the extent to which estates within easy reach of the Thames (Cuxham, for instance) geared their production for the London market, shipping grain through Henley on a regular basis. Firewood (for industrial as well as domestic use) followed a similar pattern as late as the 17th and 18th centuries, when the diarist Samuel Pepys mused on the advantages of burning beechwood (bought at Henley) on his fire, and Defoe listed the woods' numerous additional uses, 'without which London would be put to more difficulty than for anything of its kind in the nation'. Livestock farming, typical of the Chilterns' mixed sheep-corn husbandry, also left its mark, not least in the late 15th century when Henley briefly became a trans-shipment point for raw wool, traded not only through London but through Southampton by wealthy Henley merchants such as John Elmes (Chapter 3). Like all small market towns, Henley remained deeply enmeshed in the agricultural economy until modern times, its annual fairs and weekly Thursday market providing vibrant social and trading occasions for farmers and townspeople well into the 19th and 20th centuries.[3]

If the Chilterns' agricultural resources were crucial to Henley's success, no less important (at least from the 17th and 18th centuries) were the area's visual attractions. Bulstrode Whitelocke's lyrical description has already been quoted, and from the 18th century rapturous accounts of Henley's idyllic riverside setting among rolling tree-covered hills became commonplace. Approaching Henley from Maidenhead in 1782 the German traveller Karl Moritz stopped off to rest by a milestone, 'to enjoy one of the most delightful prospects':

> Close before me rose a soft hill, full of green cornfields, fenced with quick-hedges, and the top of it was encircled with a wood. At some little distance, in a large semicircle, one green hill rose after another, all around me, gently raising themselves aloft from the banks of the Thames, and on which woods, meadows, arable lands, and villages were interspersed in the greatest and most beautiful variety; whilst at their foot the Thames meandered, in most picturesque windings, among villages, gentlemen's seats, and green vales.

Later travel writers agreed, and by the 1840s *Lewis's Topographical Dictionary* was noting how the surrounding hills and 'lofty beech-woods' were 'interspersed with elegant villas' of prosperous middle-class incomers – a process which accelerated considerably with the opening of the railway, and which has continued to the present day. The former Beatle George Harrison

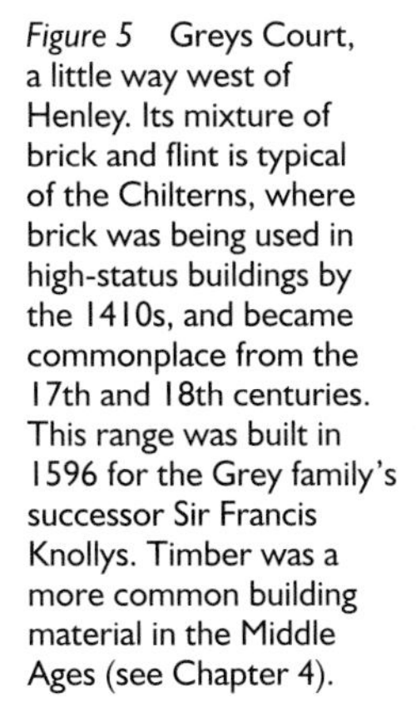

Figure 5 Greys Court, a little way west of Henley. Its mixture of brick and flint is typical of the Chilterns, where brick was being used in high-status buildings by the 1410s, and became commonplace from the 17th and 18th centuries. This range was built in 1596 for the Grey family's successor Sir Francis Knollys. Timber was a more common building material in the Middle Ages (see Chapter 4).

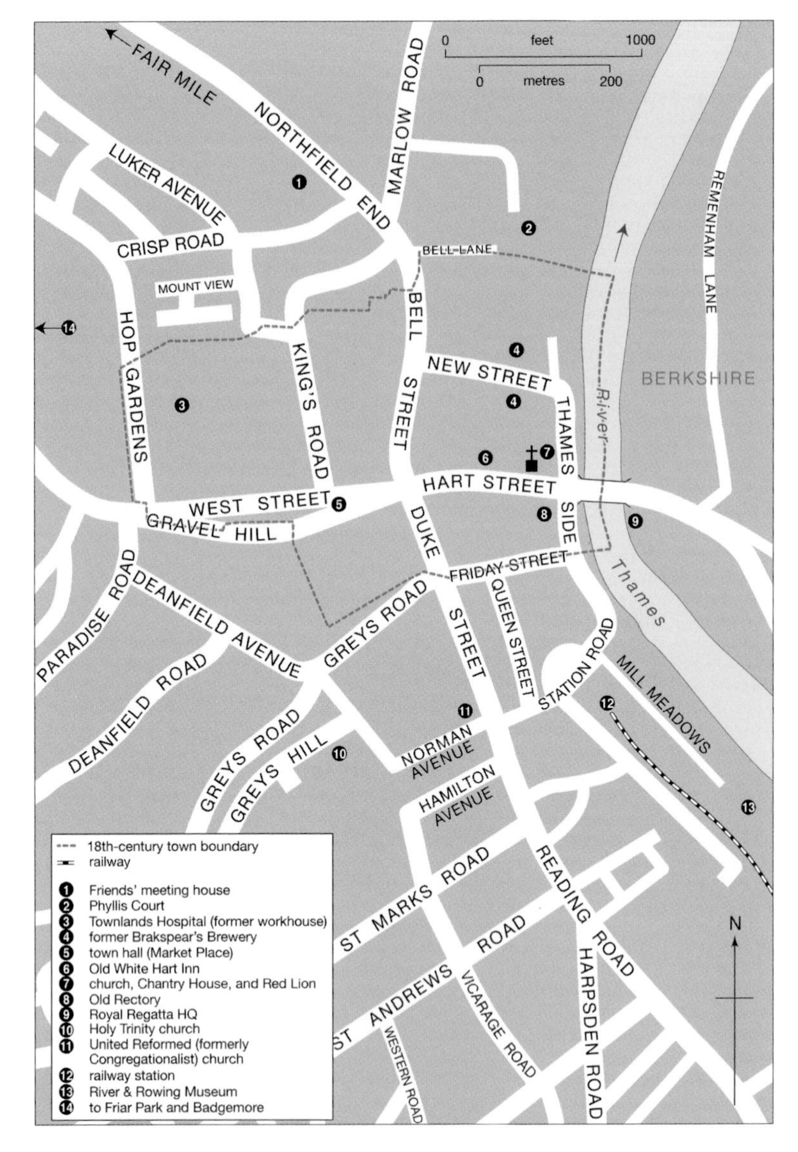

Figure 6 Henley's streets: a simplified plan showing key buildings. The red outline shows the town boundary as it existed until 1892, though by then many of the southern suburbs had already been built up (see Chapter 9).

was following a long tradition when he acquired Friar Park (a pleasingly bizarre and eclectic country house on Henley's western edge) in 1971, the house itself having been built as a country retreat in the 1890s by the successful London lawyer Frank Crisp. As late as 1993 a local planning report – not a literary form generally associated with lyrical enthusiasm – characterised Henley as 'one of the most delightful and visited of all the towns along the River Thames', its 'attractive townscape and historic buildings' enhanced by 'a rural backcloth of exceptional scenic quality'.[4]

Combined with the pull of London, one final impact of the Chilterns setting was the extent to which Henley, perched on the very edge of Oxfordshire near its intersection with Buckinghamshire and Berkshire, has always looked eastwards to the capital rather than north-westwards to the county town or the Midlands. True, even in the Middle Ages its trading hinterland stretched across the Chilterns escarpment to encompass such places as Benson and Ewelme, while its position on some of the country's most important west-east routes (by road as well as by river) ensured that links with Oxford and beyond remained an important feature of its social and economic life. Nonetheless, as one historian and former resident put it in 1989, 'even today the inhabitants have little to do with the county town, and to most of them Banbury is *terra incognita*'.[5]

TOWN AND RIVER

Through this landscape snakes the majestic curve of the middle and lower Thames, running from its disputed Gloucestershire source to London and the Thames estuary beyond. A dominant feature from time immemorial, the river has long been associated with ritual and myth: a recent book calls it a 'sacred river' comparable with the Ganges, and however fanciful some of the associations the sculpted personifications of 'Tamesis' and 'Isis' which grace the 18th-century Henley bridge (Figure 79) show its continuing hold over the imagination. More prosaically, within recorded history it has served as barrier and boundary, as a power-source for the numerous water mills which once lined its banks, as a source of food, and more recently as a source of recreation.[6]

All those uses are mentioned in the following chapters; but the river's most significant role, certainly for Henley, was as a transport corridor. Long before Henley's creation as a planned town the Thames was a major transport artery, and by the 13th century the new town was fully participating in the growing river trade with London. By 1300 navigational problems upstream (discussed in Chapter 3) were turning it into the highest point for regular commercial river traffic – the basis of its lucrative medieval role as a trans-shipment point for goods passing to and from the capital, which were habitually transferred from cart to boat (and vice versa) at Henley with its numerous riverside granaries. Even after the reopening of the upper river in the 16th and 17th centuries London's continually growing demands ensured Henley's continuance as a major inland port, frequented by 'bargemen or watermen ... transporting ... malt, wood and other goods'. The pattern continued until the advent of the railway, prompting the final slow demise of commercial river traffic on the Thames in the 19th and early 20th centuries.

Figure 7 The extra-ordinary crush of pleasure boats at Henley Royal Regatta, photographed in 1898. By then the event benefited significantly from the railway (extended to Henley in 1857), attracting over 35,000 visitors a year, and bringing substantial economic benefits to the town.

That demise ended a millennium or more of continuous history, which in various ways helped mould the Chilterns landscape and the pattern of towns, villages and settlements which we see today. Like many Thames-side towns, Henley developed as it did because of its prime position on the road and river network in relation to London; while the development of the rural villages and estates within its hinterland was similarly conditioned by their proximity to the Thames highway, and to a major inland port.

Such factors were already important by the 13th century, and may have been among the potential benefits weighed by the king and his advisers when the idea of establishing a new planned town at Henley was first mooted in (probably) the late 12th century. The medieval town and river trade will be looked at shortly; but first, how and why did the medieval planned town of Henley come into being?

Chapter 2 The Birth of Henley

Figure 8 Planned medieval towns like Henley were laid out on the initiative of enterprising lords, who commissioned specialist surveyors. In this 14th-century drawing a king directs a master mason, who holds a set square and dividers. Henley itself was a royal estate, and the new town was laid out on royal authority, possibly by Henry II in the late 12th century.

For many people, the creation of new towns is probably associated with 20th-century planning initiatives and suburban garden cities. In fact, the period between the 11th and 13th centuries saw the deliberate creation of large numbers of planned new towns across England and Europe. This was a time of expanding trade and commerce, rising population, and increasingly sophisticated markets, of which medieval 'new towns' were both a symptom and a cause. The majority were founded by enterprising secular or ecclesiastical lords, who hoped to increase their profits by attracting merchants and craftsmen and stimulating trade.[7]

Henley fits firmly into this category. The town's basic plan, with its large wedge-shaped market place, its regular street plan grouped around a central crossroads, and its long, regular house (or burgage) plots running back from the street frontages, makes it abundantly clear that this is a planned medieval town of familiar type. By 1250 it was a flourishing market town participating in the expanding river trade, and though the date and circumstances of its creation are not fully clear, almost certainly it was laid out on royal initiative, most likely in the later 12th century.

For very little of this do we have unequivocal evidence. Written sources for Henley survive in significant numbers only from the 13th or 14th centuries when the town was long established, and what archaeology there has been has so far unearthed very little about how and when it was laid out and what preceded it. As with so many medieval towns, therefore, the following account is partly conjecture, based on careful consideration of the town's layout and of the fragmentary written evidence which survives. Future archaeology may clarify the detail and the chronology, though it is unlikely to alter the broad overall picture.

BEFORE THE TOWN

Medieval 'new towns' were by definition new creations. But not all were laid out on vacant sites, and none were set into an entirely empty or undeveloped landscape. How much is known about the area around Henley before the town's creation?

Among the most important factors determining settlement are roads. The Fair Mile preserves the line of a major Roman road from Dorchester, which must have crossed the river at Henley, and perhaps connected with roads to Verulamium (now St Albans), Silchester and London. Its presence helps explain a sizeable 2nd-century Roman building excavated west of Bell Street, which may or may not imply a small Roman settlement. Almost certainly the road remained an important route into the Anglo-Saxon period, though where it originally crossed the river is unclear. Possibly it branched eastwards through what are now the grounds of Phyllis Court, fording the river to run up the opposite bank along the line of modern field boundaries. Alternatively the Fair Mile could have continued to the site of the present bridge (Figure 9), which was probably an early crossing point long before the bridge was built. There may, in fact, have been two or more fords. Either way, Henley was almost certainly the site of a major crossing point from a very early date.[8]

From the late Anglo-Saxon period, written evidence takes us a little further. In the 8th century the Henley area belonged to the king as part of a vast royal estate centred on Benson, some 10 miles away across the Chilterns. By the time of Domesday Book in 1086 much of this estate (including Bix, Badgemore, and the Rotherfields) had been granted to neighbouring local lords, but the Crown hung onto

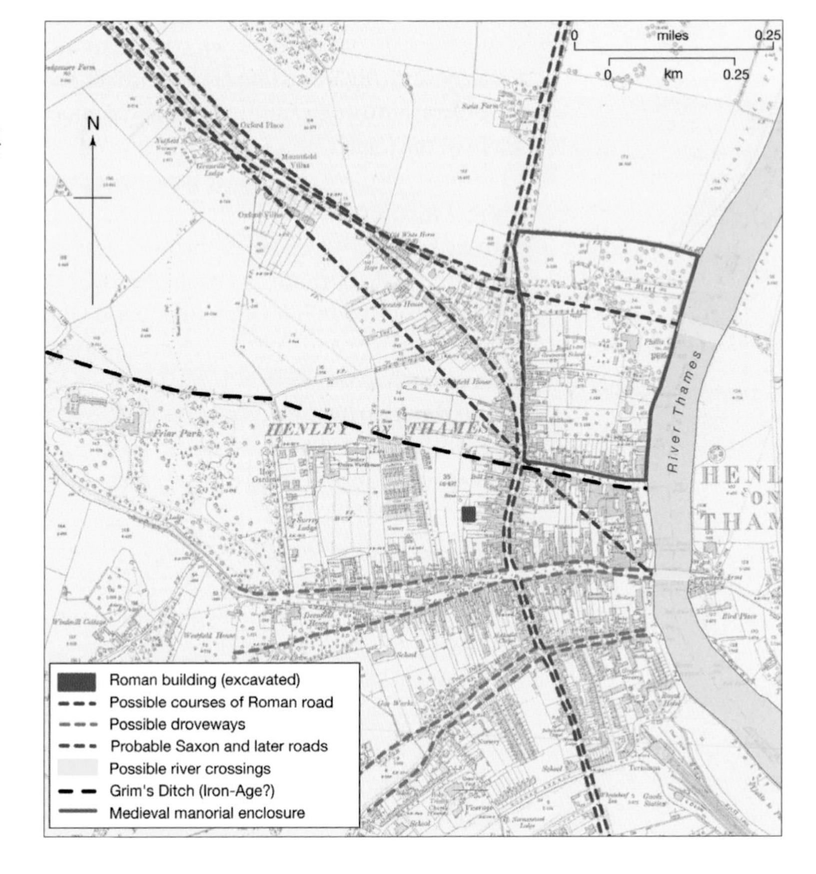

Figure 9 A conjectural reconstruction of pre-urban Henley, showing some of the features which may have conditioned the shape of the planned town.

the area around Henley itself, which remained a detached outlier of the Benson estate into the 13th century. The boundaries of this residual royal estate are not recorded, but like the later parish of Henley it probably ran from the low-lying meadows by the river up to the valuable woodland and wood pasture of the Chilterns hills. The place name Henley means '(at the) high wood pasture', and presumably it was the area's agricultural resources, combined with the river crossing, which persuaded the Crown to retain control over Henley, even though in the 12th century it was sometimes leased or granted to powerful noblemen or royal servants for fixed periods.[9]

How the 11th- and 12th-century estate at Henley was organised is not recorded. Probably there was a small rural settlement, which may have been obliterated when the planned town was laid out. If so it may lie under the modern town, where fragments of late 11th- or early 12th-century pottery have been found. The church's location certainly seems to predate the town's creation, since the dimensions of the medieval churchyard bore no relation to the highly regular plots of the planned medieval town to its west (below). By the mid-12th century and possibly much earlier there appears to have also been a small royal lodge or manor house on the site of Phyllis Court and the area to its south, known later as Countess Garden (Figures 9–10 and 23). The first written evidence dates from the early 13th century, but King Stephen issued a royal charter at Henley in 1142, and from the 1150s Henry II may have used it as an occasional stopping-off point on journeys between London and his residences at Benson or Woodstock. For the rest of the time it perhaps provided a base for bailiffs and farm staff running the residual royal estate. Other features of the pre-urban Henley landscape are similarly hinted at in the modern layout. The wide wedge-shape of West Street, Gravel Hill and Hart Street looks strongly reminiscent of an ancient droveway, perhaps for funnelling livestock from pastures on the west towards the river – the neighbouring parish's name of Rotherfield means 'open grazing for cattle', and describes the mid-Saxon landscape. If so, this was a pre-existing feature taken over into the later town plan. A second droveway may be preserved in the line of Greys Road and Friday Street, while the intersecting north–south road from Reading to Marlow and London almost certainly existed by the late Saxon period.

And yet the pre-urban estate may not have been entirely agricultural. In the angle between the Fair Mile and the manorial enclosure is a large triangular area, now built on, but in origin probably a large triangular green at the manor house entrance. If so, not only would it have created a grand vista to the house, it may also have provided a forum for trading: an embryonic, unofficial market typical of many future towns.[10]

THE CREATION OF THE TOWN

A Royal Foundation?

Some time before the early 13th century a planned town and market place were laid out south of the royal lodge or manor house. The written evidence is suggestive. In 1177–8 Benson manor (including Henley) fell back into royal hands after a lease of 20 years, and the Crown took its agricultural management back in hand. The following year Henry II set aside an unspecified amount of land at Henley 'for making his new buildings', for which the sheriff's annual account for the Henley estate records a rent allowance of 2s. 6d. (i.e. the land no longer yielded this income because it was used for other purposes). Conceivably this refers to urban development, though given the small sum involved it more likely reflects expansion or rebuilding of the royal manor house. Around the same date, an impressive new bridge appears to have been built or rebuilt at the end of what is now Hart Street, possibly in stone (Panel 1) – a major investment which is unlikely to have been undertaken in isolation. None of this proves that the town was created at the same time, but the concentration of activity is striking, not least because Henry II is known as a founder of new towns. His borough of New Woodstock was being laid out at the gates of Woodstock park at just about this time.

For Henry to have created a new town at Henley in the 1170s would certainly make sense. The economy was expanding during the renewed stability which following the civil wars of the mid-12th century, and a significant number of towns seem to have been created or expanded during the period. Locally, trade along the river appears to have been flourishing in response to increased demand from London (see Chapter 3), and Henley may have participated in it. The grant of an annual fair between 1199 and 1204 (when the manor was briefly held by the great Norman lord Robert de Harcourt) does not necessarily imply urban status, but may nonetheless reflect an attempt to capitalise on the town's early success. By the 1260s Henley had a guild merchant (a corporate body of leading traders and craftsmen) headed by a warden, which was already accumulating a small amount of corporate town property. From then on, its development as an urban centre closely involved with the Thames river trade becomes increasingly visible.[11]

So far as the town's origins are concerned, this is as far as the documents take us. But further hints are contained in the town's layout, before an increase in written documentation puts us on slightly firmer ground from the late 13th and early 14th centuries.

Analysing the Town

Medieval towns like Henley were planned with meticulous regularity, with house-plots of specific dimensions laid out along new or existing streets and market places. The plot boundaries have often remained remarkably stable, so that measuring their size and shape can help us judge which parts of a town formed part of the original layout, and which (with different dimensions) were possibly added later. Until tested by archaeology or confirmed by documents the results can only ever be conjectural, though over the last 50 years the technique has grown increasingly sophisticated as the body of towns for comparison has grown larger.[12]

In Henley, the plot layout suggests that the first phase of the new town comprised a wedge of land along what is now Market Place and Hart Street (both called High Street in the Middle Ages). Possibly it was laid out around an existing droveway as suggested above, which would have provided both a natural axis and a wide enough space for stalls and trading. Long narrow house plots were laid out to its north

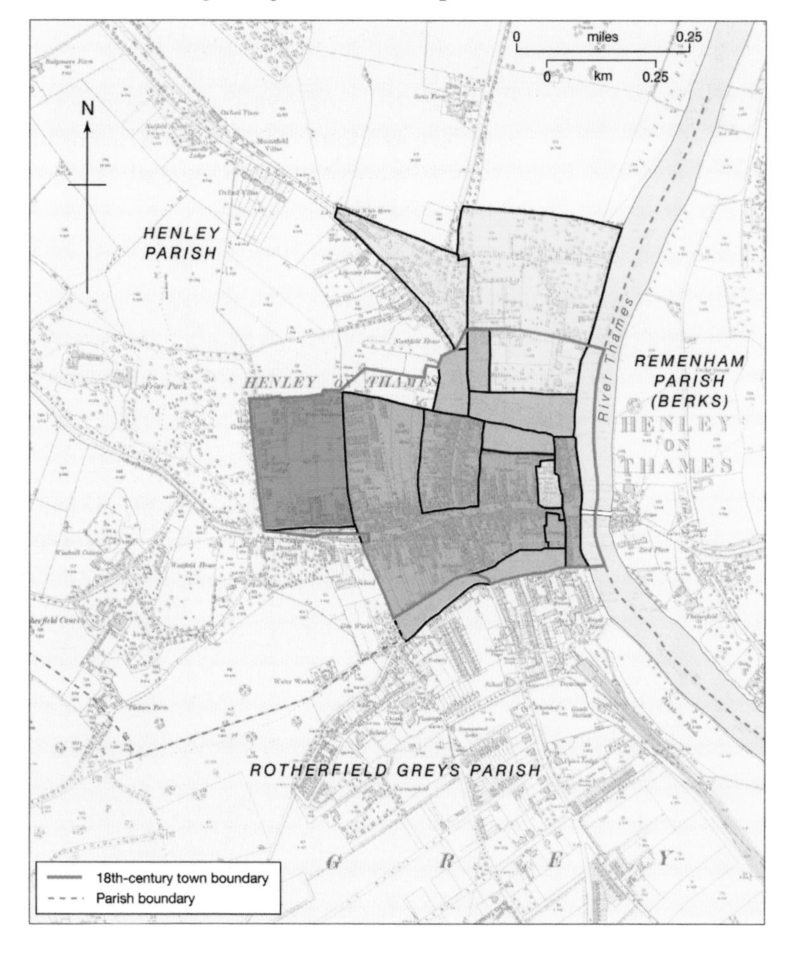

Figure 10 A conjectural reconstruction of Henley's medieval development, based on analysis of the town plan. The yellow areas (rectangular manorial centre, adjoining triangular green, and church site) may have pre-dated the planned town, with a rural settlement nearby. The orange area (Bell Street, Hart Street, market place and waterfront) represent the first stage of the planned town, probably in the late 12th century; the green areas (Friday Street, New Street, and the northern parts of Bell Street) reflect its gradual expansion over the next 150 years or more. The blue area was part of Hen Field, brought into the town before the 18th century (Figure 23). The base map shows the town in 1899.

PANEL 1

Henley's Medieval Bridge

Figure A *This arch (now hidden in the cellar of the* Angel Inn*), with its stone voussoirs and shuttered flint, probably formed the medieval bridge's western abutment.*

Henley's existing bridge was completed in 1786, replacing a dilapidated predecessor along its south side (see Chapter 7). The earlier bridge existed by 1225, and physical remains suggest that it was built in stone around the 1170s, perhaps when the planned town was laid out. By the 16th century the main span was of timber. As no medieval descriptions survive, the bridge's original structure has to be pieced together from architectural fragments, occasional written references, and later paintings.

Archaeological and Written Evidence

Though nothing remains of the medieval bridge's main part, two stone arches from each end survive underground, abutting the modern bridge (Figures A–B). One (on the Berkshire side) was discovered during building work for the new Henley Royal Regatta headquarters in 1984; the other survives in the cellars of the *Angel on the Bridge*. The vaults are of shuttered flint with stone (ashlar) dressings, and their style, which included diagonal tooling in the stonework, suggests a late 12th-century date.

This does not prove that the entire bridge was of stone, since paintings of the 1690s show stone arches at either end of the timber structure. In the 1980s, however, a large masonry block with similar diagonal tooling was found on the riverbed in midstream, implying that the bridge had a continuous span of stone arches. If so, it collapsed before the 1530s when the Tudor antiquary John Leland said it

Figure B *The edge of the medieval bridge arch excavated on the Berkshire bank in 1984, showing its alignment with the arch embedded in the cellars of the* Angel Inn *(the tall white building opposite). (Photo: Ann Cottingham)*

was 'all of timber', though he suspected that 'it was [formerly] of stone, as the foundations show at low water'. Repairs mentioned in the 15th century could have been in timber or stone.

The Siberechts paintings (Figure C)

The best evidence for the 17th-century bridge comes from Jan Siberechts' paintings of Henley (Figure C). These show a timber structure linking the stone arches, its roadway protected by wooden rails. On the Berkshire side the bridge was approached by a short embanked causeway, probably the 'clappers' (or clapper-bridge) mentioned in the early 16th century. The road on the town side must have been similarly built up to connect with the tall bridge, and the shallow, almost segmental, arch in the cellar of the *Angel* is probably part of that construction, set back from the river's edge and so not shown in the painting. The visible arch by the water's edge was much taller, and was probably part of the original stone span. It appears to have been demolished when the *Angel's* cellar was built or extended, leaving flint walling from its mutilated western pier within the cellar.

Bridge Buildings

Siberechts showed several buildings adjoining the bridge, one of them built out into the water on stilts. Medieval deeds paint a similar picture: in 1354 a granary had a cellar built into the bridge arch, presumably much like the *Angel*. The adjoining chapel of St Anne (mentioned from 1405) was associated with a bridge hermit, who collected alms from passing travellers towards the upkeep of the chapel, bridge and highway. This was a common medieval arrangement, although in Henley most repair-funds came from town properties given by leading inhabitants (see Chapter 4) – an indication of the bridge's crucial importance to the town.

Figure C *Detail from Jan Siberechts's painting of Henley from the Wargrave Road in 1698, showing the timber bridge demolished around 1785. (Courtesy of the River & Rowing Museum, Henley)*

Further Reading: South Midlands Archaeology, 15 (1985), 77–9; 16 (1986), 101; 19 (1989), 52; Oxfordshire Historic Environment Record, PRN 2215; Briers, refs at 239; Leland, J, *Itinerary*, ed. Toulmin Smith, V, 71.

Figure 11 Henley market place in 1880, looking west to the late 18th-century town hall (on the site of a former market house). The market's wide wedge-shape may perpetuate the line of an ancient droveway for cattle, which ran to an early river crossing. The buildings on either side still occupy the long burgage plots laid out at the town's creation. The 18th-century obelisk (removed in 1885 and now located at Mill Meadows) stood near the site of a medieval market cross, mentioned in 1308.

and south in the usual fashion, while a series of smaller plots seems to have been created along what became Bell (or North) Street, leading up past the manor house (Figures 10 and 23).

On the north, this early layout probably extended as far as the manor house's southern perimeter on the line of modern New Street, which may have followed the remains of an ancient earthwork called Grim's Ditch. On the south it most likely extended to the town ditch or brook, just north of modern Friday Street; the brook was mentioned frequently in medieval documents, and gave its name to Brook (or South) Street, the medieval names for Duke Street. Westwards the town adjoined the rural estate of Badgemore, whose boundary (mentioned in medieval property deeds) ran across West Street and Gravel Hill. 'Walls' mentioned in that area (see Figure 23) were probably low earthen banks or ditches designed to mark the town's edge, keep out stray animals, and help with toll collection: certainly there were never any town walls in the generally accepted sense.

These early plots along Market Place and Hart Street seem to have been 1½ perches (7.5m) wide, the perch being a standard medieval measurement of 16½ feet. By the 14th century the frontages were more varied – the result of 200 years of subdivision and amalgamation – but even so, most are still clearly recognisable as multiples or divisions of those original plots. Their length varied from around 19 to 32 perches (96–161m), providing space (as in other medieval towns) for outbuildings, livestock or crops. Dating them is difficult, but their size and shape are consistent with a town laid out around the 1170s, and they are unlikely to be much later. The Bell Street plots were very different: two perches wide but only 10–16 perches long. Nonetheless their relationship with the Hart Street plots suggests that they were contemporary, and they seem far too regular to be later impositions. Bell Street was bound to be a major thoroughfare, linking the market place with Northfield End and the manor house, and it was in the lord's interests to develop it as fully as possible.[13]

Duke and Friday Streets, by contrast, seem to have been developed a little later and in a more piecemeal way. The small, narrow plots fronting Duke Street had no attached land at the rear, and seem to have been cut from the earlier burgage plots running back from the market place, whose holders probably hoped to sublet them. The street remained unusually narrow throughout the Middle Ages, scarcely sufficient for two carts to pass side by side, and was widened to its present extent only in the 1870s when the entire west side was rebuilt. House plots along Friday Street show no sign of planning, and may have developed as an area of squatter settlement along the town's southern fringe. But by the early 14th century the street was extensively built up, and by the 15th it contained some relatively large high-status houses, parts of which survive. The northern side was taken into the town before *c.*1300, presumably following an agreement between the lords of Henley and Rotherfield Greys, though its southern side remained in Rotherfield Greys' parish until modern times. The street's name was probably derived from medieval fishponds at its eastern end, Friday being a fasting day when fish traditionally replaced meat.[14]

Near the river the planners may have incorporated a pre-existing church or chapel, since the medieval churchyard (51.5m wide before 19th-century enlargement) bore no obvious relation to the regular 1½-perch layout further west. Its odd position, jutting into and partly obstructing the way to the bridge, may have been seen as an advantage, helping to control access into the town and collection of tolls from market traders, much as gates and bars commonly did (see Figure 82). Nonetheless, the arrangement is unusual, and was even more pronounced before road-widening in 1782. The church began as a chapel subservient to Benson, but creation of the town lent it an entirely new urban status, and by the time it emerges into the written record around 1202 it was well

Figure 12 Unlike the streets in the main part of the planned town, Duke Street remained unusually narrow until 1872–3, when the jettied timber-framed houses along its west side were demolished for road widening. House plots here were apparently taken from the long burgage plots running south from the market place, and can only have accommodated small cottage holdings.

on its way to becoming a fully independent parish church with its own rector and endowment. The rector's house lay on the opposite side of Hart Street, occupying a large plot near the river. Unlike the churchyard this was apparently made up of four 1½-perch plots combined into a single unit, which had perhaps been given for this purpose by the king soon after the town's creation. The rectory house was certainly established there by the 1240s, and around 1305 the rector extended the grounds southwards to Friday Street through a series of piecemeal purchases.[15]

Development of the waterfront was presumably as central to the scheme as the creation of a market place. Lords of Henley manor had interests in London's Queenhithe (the main off-loading place for goods conveyed downstream) by the late 13th century, and in the early 14th century claimed wharfage dues from London boats landing at Henley. By then there were several granaries along the riverside, both north and south of the bridge. In 1354 one had a cellar built into the bridge arch, and in 1405 that or another granary adjoined the small freestanding chapel of St Anne by the bridge entrance, which was associated with collection of alms towards the bridge's upkeep (Panel 1). As in the 17th and 18th centuries some sections of the waterfront may have been reinforced with timber revetments.[16]

Yet not even a new town such as Henley was entirely urban. North of West Street around the modern King's Road was an area of agricultural land known by the 14th century as Hen or Hemp Field – a reminder that in medieval towns urban and agricultural activities often co-existed. Medieval property deeds show that most houses around modern West Street held long strips of land in Hen Field, running up to Grim's Ditch from the backs of their gardens. These look like burgage plots in all but name, but the terminology is unusual, and the field seems to have been viewed differently from the rest of the town: certainly the plots there would have been exceptionally long, up to 272m or 54 perches. Presumably the area was a pre-existing field taken into the town at its creation, and possibly it still included land outside it. In 1424, for instance, the town paid for a common gate and style into Hen Field, which therefore cannot have been entirely divided up into private burgage plots. The field was still mentioned in the 1490s, and was perhaps only finally absorbed during the town's expansion in the 16th or 17th century.[17]

MEDIEVAL EXPANSION

Like many successful medieval towns, Henley was gradually extended as its trade and population grew. Piecemeal development

Figure 13 Above: property conveyance of 1307, granting a plot of land in 'La Nywestrete': the earliest firmly dated reference to New Street's existence. References to property on either side suggest that it was already well developed, though the north side may not have been fully built up until after the adjoining manor house was abandoned during the 14th century.

Below: New Street's south side today, still with several low-eaved 15th-century buildings.

along Duke Street and Friday Street has already been mentioned, but other extensions were clearly planned – if not by the Crown, then by some of the powerful and wealthy lords who held Henley manor for much of the 13th century. The first addition was probably the south side of New Street. The name alone shows that it was a later creation, and property deeds confirm that it existed by 1307 and possibly by the 1260s. Here the plots were much wider (three perches or 15m), reflecting their distance from the town's commercial heart where pressure on space was greatest; they were, however, quite short (only 12 perches or 60m), since they had to be carved from the back gardens of existing houses on Hart Street. The street's north side, where the plot sizes are different, may not have been developed until later, since it backed onto the manor house perimeter.[18]

Other changes arose from the division and partial abandonment of the manor house site after 1300. Henley's 13th-century lords included such national figures as Richard, Earl of Cornwall (d. 1272) and his son Edmund (d. 1300), whose numerous residences included nearby Wallingford Castle. Even so the manor house at Henley was still being kept up in the 1290s, when the hall and lord's chamber were re-tiled and a new hedge was laid around the perimeter. From the early 14th century, however, the Henley estate was split in two. A royal grant to the earl's widow in 1301 seems to have included the whole of the town up to modern Bell Lane, together with a small amount of land including Henley park. But a large block of land to the north remained associated with Benson manor until *c.*1340, when the Black Prince granted it as a separate estate called Fillets (from an Old English word for hay). As a result, the manor house site itself was apparently sliced in two. The northern part went with Fillets manor, which from the mid-14th century was centred on what became Phyllis (or Fillets) Court. The southern part, known later as Countess Garden, went presumably to Cornwall's widow, Countess Margaret, whose successors, with vast estates elsewhere, allowed the buildings to fall derelict. By 1381 the site was 'spoiled and dilapidated', leaving only a garden and pasture.[19]

This partial abandonment of part of the old manorial centre left the way open for a final expansion of the town. On New Street's north side, four-perch plots were laid out probably in the earlier 14th century, running back to the edge of the vacant manorial garden. Bell Street's northern end may have been redeveloped then or soon after. Both sides include some high-status 15th-century houses, of which one (dated to 1405) occupies an unusually wide plot backing onto Countess Garden. Possibly it was the first house on the site, reflecting renewed expansion around the former manor house area. Long before then, the borough boundary was extended northwards to take in this part of Bell Street, much as it had earlier

Figure 14 Two concealed, early 15th-century open halls on the south side of Gravel Hill (left) show continuing late medieval development on the town's western fringe. The buildings were just outside the urban boundary, but perhaps began as small 'renters' built for craftsmen processing rural produce here in the upper market place. The tall added cross wing (right) has been dendro-dated to 1454.

been extended to take in Friday Street. Henceforth the boundary ran along Bell Lane (the dividing line between Henley and Fillets manors), crossing the road to include plots laid out on Bell Street's west side (Figure 23).[20]

These changes marked the last major expansion of Henley until the 19th century, though piecemeal growth continued along its fringes – in the area between the town brook and Greys Road, for instance, which remained outside the town. Expansion up West Street and Gravel Hill was also a piecemeal process, captured in 14th-century property deeds which show houses spilling over the town boundary into Badgemore, and in a run of small 15th-century houses along Gravel Hill, built possibly for craftsmen processing rural produce. The houses' date suggests that fringe development revived within a century of the Black Death, and from the late 15th century to the early 19th, as population grew, the process continued, with piecemeal building along West Street and south of Friday Street. Even so, it was the 1880s before wholesale suburban growth finally swamped the historic core created by Henley's medieval planners.[21]

Henley and the River

Like most planned medieval towns, Henley was not created at a single stroke. Traces of its complex early origins lie buried in the modern town plan as they do in those of most small towns – from the evidence for early roads and droveways to the regular plot boundaries of the planned town. Taken together, these hints shed valuable light on Henley's origins, though it remains the case that only future archaeology can answer these questions entirely satisfactorily.

At the same time, planned towns like Henley represented hard-headed entrepreneurial ventures involving high degrees of risk. As the king and his advisors assessed these risks and opportunities, the town's riverside location must surely have been one of the factors in their minds, weighed alongside its promising road communications, the volume of local trade, and perhaps the success of informal markets near the river crossing or at the gates of the manor house. Even so, they can scarcely have appreciated the extent to which the new town's fortunes were to become so completely enmeshed with the Thames river trade, not only over the next century, but to the end of the Middle Ages and beyond. It is to that trade, and to the significance which Henley came to assume within it, that we now turn.

Chapter 3 The Medieval River Trade

Like all rivers, the Thames has met innumerable human needs, serving variously as frontier, food resource, and power source. For millennia it has also provided a crucial and much used transport corridor from the coast. By the late Anglo-Saxon period this corridor linked south midland England with London and the Continent, and with some interruptions it remained one of the country's chief arteries for trade and communication until the arrival of the railway in the 19th century. Not for nothing do two of the best-known books about the river describe it as the Thames highway.[22]

Henley's success rested above all on its key position on the river, most particularly in relation to London (68 miles downstream) and the surrounding road network. By the 14th century it had emerged as one of the key inland ports in the country, funnelling foodstuffs into the capital, and other goods in the opposite direction. But its relationship with the river was not a static one. How did use of the river develop, and what, combined with London's inexorable expansion, did this mean for Henley?

RIVER VERSUS ROAD

Contrary to popular conception, medieval people were frequently on the move. Medieval Europe was a dynamic and heavily commercialised society, which from the 11th or 12th century had a sophisticated network of large urban centres, smaller towns such as Henley, and widespread rural markets, and which until the plagues of the mid-14th century supported a sharply growing population. As in the modern world, such a society relied for its continued prosperity on cheap, regular and efficient transport. Even for peasant producers the journey to the local market town was a familiar experience by the 13th century, while merchants, lords and officials frequently travelled long distances as a matter of course.

Much of this movement was by road. The so-called Gough map, created for unknown purposes in the mid-14th century, shows an extensive national road network radiating from London across the kingdom, linking the principal towns and ports (Figure 16). Much of this network was probably in place by the late 11th century, and written evidence fills in many of the smaller, more local routes which linked towns, villages, farmsteads, and fields. Henley, as we have seen, was well served by at least two major roads: the (partly diverted) Roman road from Oxford and Dorchester through to Cookham and London, and the north–south road from Reading to Great Marlow, High Wycombe and beyond. Both connected with more distant routes to Wales and the west and to southern ports such as Southampton (where Henley merchants traded in the 15th century), while the building of a new bridge in the 12th century was typical of the investment in road transport which characterised the period. A network of smaller roads linked Henley with surrounding towns and villages, as the routine carting of large quantities of grain clearly shows.[23]

But for movement of bulk goods, coastal and inland water transport was crucial and could be massively cheaper than road transport, which was commonly at least double the cost by water. Accounts from the 1290s suggest that the cost of importing grain to London by cart could, in fact, be up to 12 or 18 times that of bringing it along the coast or lower Thames. These differentials underpinned the medieval river trade. Yet the balance was a delicate one, reliant on the availability of safe, regular, and

Figure 15 The bustling waterfront at the Tower of London around 1500, with London bridge in the background. The river trade with London was vital to Henley, which became a major inland port funnelling grain into the city.

Figure 16 Part of the 14th-century Gough map (with east at the top), showing towns, roads and waterways around the lower and middle Thames. Reading and Wallingford are near the middle, Oxford at the bottom, and London (depicted as a large castle) at the top. Henley is not marked, though by then it was well established as an important inland port on major routes.

relatively trouble-free navigation along a reasonably direct route. This the Thames generally provided – though not always equally along its whole length, and not without significant changes over the medieval period.[24]

THE THAMES HIGHWAY

The Early River Trade

Long before Henley's creation as a planned riverside town, the Thames was a major transport artery. Perhaps the most striking evidence is the recent discovery of artificial canals dating mostly from the 10th or 11th century, cut to bypass particularly tortuous stretches, or to link important land-locked estates with the main channel. One was at Abingdon just below Oxford (Figure 17), while a channel closer to Henley seems to have linked Wallingford with nearby Blewbury, where Wallingford tenants were required to transport goods by horse or water in the 1060s. Place-names incorporating the word *hythe* (meaning landing place) suggest a network of loading and unloading points by the late Anglo-Saxon period, and several recorded salt ways – part of an important medieval distribution network – seem to have also intersected the Thames, implying that salt was transferred from wagon to boat for its journey to London and places in between. As in the later Middle Ages this was probably part of a much wider trade, with bulk goods such as grain, wool, cloth and minerals being conveyed downstream to the Thames estuary, and goods such as pottery or herrings making the more difficult return journey. London certainly had commercial landing facilities by 898–9, when the

Figure 17 The Swift Ditch near Abingdon, one of several artificial canals identified on the middle and upper Thames. It was created by Abbot Orderic of Abingdon abbey between 1052 and 1066, to help shipping from Oxford avoid a difficult stretch between Thrupp and Barton (the present main course).

bishop of Worcester and archbishop of Canterbury were each given permission to moor their ships at Aethelredshithe. By the 13th century this was known as Queenhithe, and was the quay most frequently used by boats passing down the Thames.[25]

Possibly the pre-urban settlement at Henley participated in this early river trade. Bolney ('Bull hythe') lay only a mile or so to the south, its name (like many other hythe names) suggesting a significant trade in domestic livestock. Rotherfield ('open grazing for cattle') lay only a short distance to the west, and was probably linked by droveways to the river. A further clue may lie in Henley's later right to salt tolls, a hint, perhaps, of earlier involvement in the distribution of salt from Droitwich. Whatever the case, by the 13th century the newly founded town was clearly established as an inland port. In 1205 King John had his plate carted to Oxford from Henley where it had presumably gone by river, and in 1256 wine sent from London for the royal palace at Woodstock was similarly shipped to Henley and transferred to carts. In 1292 the bishop of Lincoln had provisions sent to Henley, from where they were shipped to his town house in London.[26]

In all these cases Henley's role was as a trans-shipment point, with goods to or from London sent by boat, and goods destined for further upstream sent by road. The implication is that this was sometimes the cheapest option, and for traffic to Oxford this may well have been the case. A large southward loop in the Thames meant that the road distance was considerably shorter, and

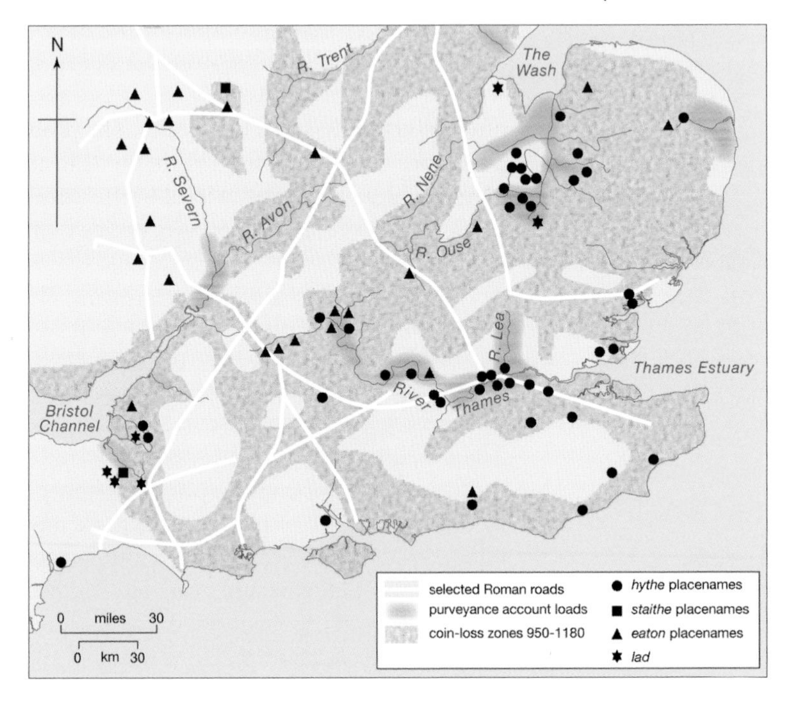

Figure 18 Some evidence for inland water transport between the 10th and 13th centuries. Place-names incorporating *hythe* and *staithe* imply early landing places; those incorporating *eaton* (river settlement) may refer to places which had special responsibility for keeping the river navigable; and the name *lād* implies an artificial watercourse. The grey stippling shows areas where coins lost between 950 and 1180 have been found, suggesting commercial activity: these include the area around the Thames. Orange areas along rivers mark documented cargo journeys, drawn from medieval purveyance accounts. Redrawn (with permission) from J. Blair (ed.), *Waterways and Canal Building in Medieval England* (2007).

presumably this affected the relative costs. Even so, the river was still sometimes used for entire journeys. In 1205 the monks of Beaulieu abbey were granted free passage for their 'ships' carrying corn to London from Faringdon on the upper Thames, while in 1234 timber for building work in Oxford was taken upriver from Reading. In these circumstances Henley may not have benefited at all.[27]

But from around 1300, changes on the river led to a decrease in its use for large-scale commercial traffic upstream from Henley, cementing the town's crucial role as an inland port and entrepot. What were they, and how did they affect the town?

Head of the River?

From the 12th and 13th centuries some stretches of the Thames became harder to navigate. The chief cause was an increase in the number of mills, weirs and fishtraps (Figures 19–20). These had existed since Anglo-Saxon times, though from the late 11th to the early 14th centuries they seem to have proliferated in unprecedented numbers. Up to a point this probably helped navigation by penning back the river, increasing its depth, and (like a modern lock system) helping to regulate its descent in a series of gradated steps. But all these structures created physical barriers across the stream, which could only be negotiated through the relatively crude mechanism of the flashlock (see Panel 2). As a result they added considerably to the journey time, the risk of accident, and the overall cost, quite apart from the sometimes exorbitant tolls charged to boats passing through, or the delays caused by millers wanting to keep their millponds as high as possible, who were often reluctant to open their gates. The problem was recognised in a series of royal injunctions from the 12th century on, including Magna Carta, which demanded (quite unrealistically) that fish-weirs be removed from the Thames and Medway. The building of new bridges and causeways probably further impeded navigation, by limiting the size of boats and creating silty stagnant pools.

It used to be thought that by the mid-14th century such difficulties had made the Thames above Henley all but impassable, leaving the town as the highest navigable point on the river, and so explaining its emergence as the pre-eminent trans-shipment point for goods passing to and from London. There is an element of truth in this, though the picture which has emerged in recent years is more nuanced. Sizeable boats did occasionally penetrate up to Culham (and possibly even Oxford) as late as the mid-15th century, though for regular commercial traffic such journeys were clearly becoming less and less cost-effective, and consequently less and less frequent. The reasons are now fairly clear. First, though

Flashlocks

Figure A *A punt shooting a flashlock on the upper Thames (near Northmoor) in the 1850s, from SC Hall,* The Book of the Thames *(1859). The paddles to the left of the opening have been removed to control the water level. On the lower stretches near Henley the process was less dramatic, but still time-consuming and with a risk of grounding in low water.*

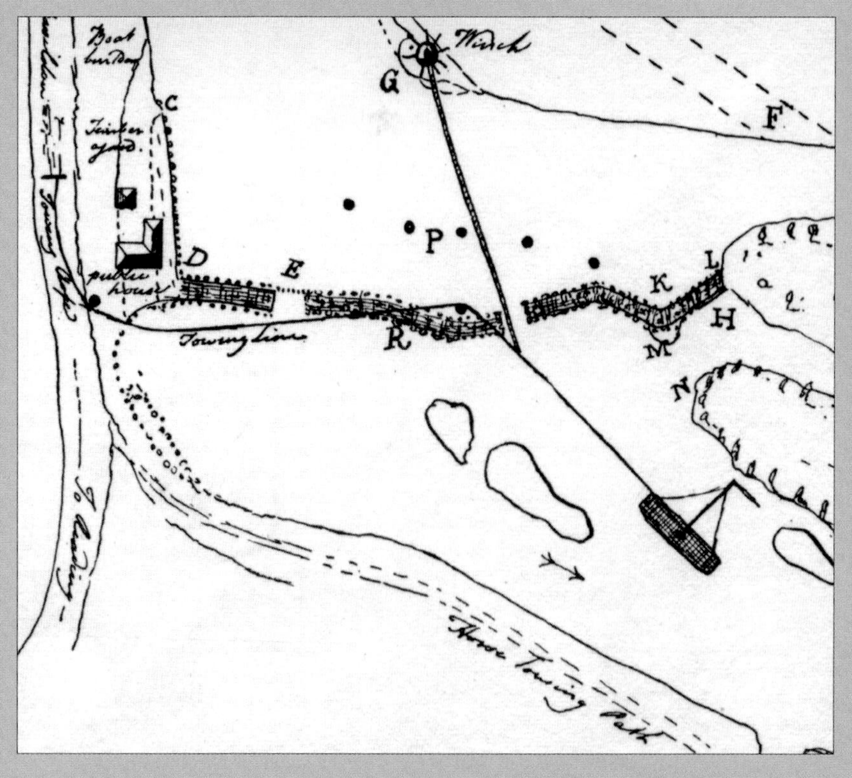

Figure B *Copy of a Thames Conservancy plan of Whitchurch mill-dam and flashlock in 1786, showing a barge being pulled upstream. A towing line runs round a post by the lock-opening to another post on the left bank. A second line, apparently attached to the first, runs to a land-winch on the right-hand bank, which is hauling the boat through. The first line was presumably attached to an onboard winch to take up slack, similar to the 'shout winch' mentioned in 1383.*

Figure C *Eynsham weir and flashlock (upstream from Oxford) in 1883, showing the open passageway next to the weir. The boat-slide (on the right) was a modern innovation, over which light punts could be dragged.*

In a modern poundlock, gates at each end allow water to be pumped in or out to equalise the water level before the boat enters or leaves. But the earliest Thames poundlocks were built in the 17th century, and most of them much later. Until then, fish- or mill-weirs could be passed only through a flashlock.

In these, part of the weir was made up of removable wooden paddles set between vertical baulks or 'rimers', which in turn were secured to a wooden sill on the river bed, and to a horizontal swinging beam above water level. To open the lock, the miller or keeper removed the paddles and rimers individually, then swung the beam on its pivot to open the gap. Boats going downstream were carried through on the resulting cascade or 'flash' of water (Figure A) – a risky exercise for heavily laden barges, although on the river's lower stretches the flash was less extreme than higher up (see Figure 41).

Boats going upstream had to be physically dragged up through the lock after the main 'flash' had subsided and before the paddles were replaced. By the 14th century this was usually with the help of cables attached to a fixed onshore winch, used sometimes in conjunction with a second winch aboard the vessel (Figure B). Cables could break with disastrous consequences. At Hambleden lock (a little downstream from Henley) in 1383:

> John Willus and Robert Asshele together with many others hauled up a shout [or boat] ... with two cables and two devices, one called the land winch and the other the shout winch; and when the shout was in the lock the cable fixed to the shout winch broke ... and then the other cable pulled back the land winch in such a way that it struck each of them on the left side of the head such that their heads were totally shattered.

More routinely, boats had to wait for the weir to be closed and the river above to rise high enough for them to continue, which in dry seasons might take several days. Similarly those travelling downstream had to wait for the miller or owner to release the flash, which millers were often reluctant to do as they wanted to keep the water level as high as possible to power the mill. As late as 1793 a bargemaster complained that mills either side of Goring lock sometimes drew off so much water as to hinder entrance into the lock.

Despite these disadvantages, cost, self-interest, and the absence (until the 18th century) of a single body with overall responsibility for the river left most flashlocks in place until modern times (Figure C). On the Thames, poundlocks were built at Iffley, Sandford, and Culham (Swift Ditch) between 1624 and 1632, but only after the establishment of the Thames Commissioners in 1751 did the vast majority of flashlocks begin, very slowly, to be replaced by modern gated locks (see Chapter 7). At Eynsham, upstream from Oxford, a new flashlock was constructed as late as 1913, and the last on the Thames (at Eaton weir) was removed only in 1937.

Further reading: Lewis, MJT, Slatcher, WN and Jarvis, PN, 'Flashlocks on English Waterways: A Survey', *Industrial Archaeol.* 6 (1969), 209–53; Peberdy, RB, 'Navigation on the River Thames between London and Oxford in the Late Middle Ages: a Reconsideration', *Oxoniensia* 61 (1996), 311–40 (including winches and Hambleden).

Figure 19 This 19th-century fishtrap near Caversham shows clearly how such structures impeded navigation, unless circumvented by flashlocks. Medieval fishtraps followed a broadly similar construction, with nets or elongated wicker baskets attached to a weir flung across the channel.

weirs and flashlocks affected the whole river they were by no means evenly spread. Between London and Henley there were probably only five locks in the Middle Ages (all upstream of Maidenhead), whereas from there to Oxford there were at least another 20, within a broadly similar distance (Figure 20). Falling demand from upstream towns such as Oxford and Wallingford (both of which experienced economic difficulties during the later Middle Ages) probably further reduced profit margins, while the size of boats (and therefore cargoes) on these higher stretches was in any case considerably smaller. In turn, less regular traffic led to neglect of the river and its infrastructure – lock-side winches for hauling boats upstream, for instance – prompting a spiral of decay which was not fully reversed until the 16th and early 17th centuries.[28]

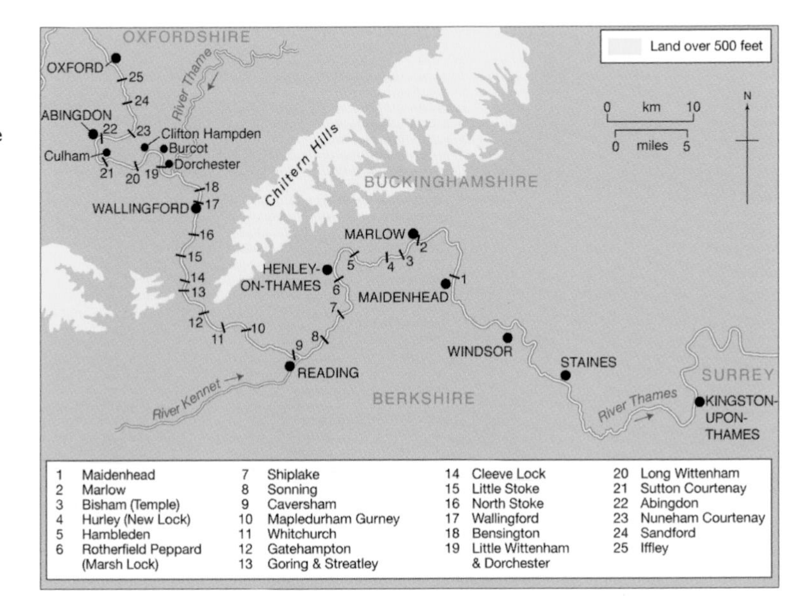

Figure 20 Mill-dams and flashlocks in the mid-Thames valley around 1350. Between London and Henley there were only five, but from there to Oxford another 20, adding greatly to journey times, cost and risk. (Redrawn from RB Peberdy, 'Navigation on the River Thames', *Oxoniensia* 61 (1996), 318.)

Whatever the root cause, the effects on Henley were entirely beneficial, placing it in an enviable position compared with its upstream rivals. In 1295, the cost of shipping a quarter of grain the 68 miles from Henley to London worked out at under 2d. But shipping it just an extra 10 miles from Reading almost doubled the cost to over 3d., making it more economical to cart grain or other goods to Henley and load them onto boats there. A well-documented example is Merton College's manor of Cuxham just over the Chilterns, which habitually sold its grain through Henley despite having closer access to the river at Wallingford, a few miles upstream.[29]

By around 1300, therefore, Henley was set to emerge as one of the chief entrepôts and inland ports on the river. But what drove the river trade was demand, and by the 14th century that demand came overwhelmingly from London.

FEEDING LONDON

Already an important port and trading centre under the Romans, London was re-established during the 7th century, when *Lundenwic* was developed in the modern Covent Garden area. Rapid expansion followed, and by 1300 London had reached its medieval peak, with a population (second only to Paris) of probably between 80,000 and 100,000. By contrast even major regional centres such as Norwich, York or Bristol scarcely exceeded 25,000 people, and only a small handful of towns had more than five thousand.

Such an enormous population needed feeding, which in an agricultural society could be achieved only by importing grain and other essentials from a sizeable hinterland. It has been estimated that the city required some 165,000 quarters of grain a year, roughly equivalent to nearly 29,000 metric tonnes. Almost equally important was the import of firewood, needed not only for domestic heating and cooking but for commercial food preparation (particularly baking and brewing) and industrial use.

The patterns of London's grain and firewood supplies were reconstructed in some detail during the 1980s and 1990s as part of a large-scale project entitled 'Feeding the City'. This drew not only on records of the port and corporation of London, but on manorial accounts for rural estates within London's hinterland, showing the destination of the grain produced, the transport methods used and the costs involved. The project clearly demonstrated the extent of London's supply zone, which stretched across ten or more counties from Kent and Essex on the east, Bedfordshire and Northamptonshire on the north, Surrey on the south, and parts of Oxfordshire, Berkshire and Buckinghamshire on the west – an area of some 4,000 square miles. Within that area, crop production and estate management were significantly geared to the London market, both in terms of crops grown and of the proportion sold. Wheat, for instance, which fetched a high enough price to bear significant transport costs, came mostly from the outer limits of the supply area, while cheaper grains such as rye or oats tended to come from nearer the capital, with estates specialising accordingly.

The shape and extent of the supply area were governed above all by transport costs, in which access to navigable water figured large. The most important of London's grain-supply centres were those near good-quality waterways, which could collect grain from a wide local hinterland and convey it cheaply to London by boat – and of these, as we have seen, Henley was fast becoming pre-eminent, at

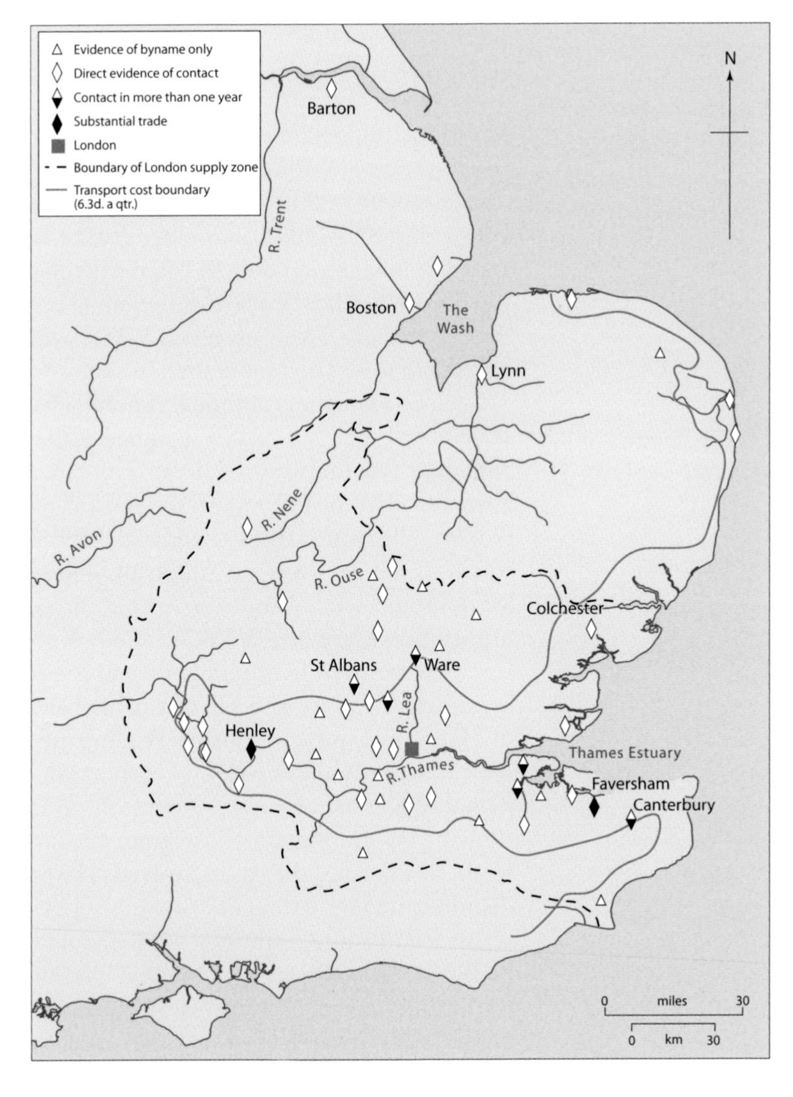

Figure 21 London's supply zone around 1300. The diamonds mark places where London cornmongers were active 1270–1365: Henley and Faversham stand out. The red line contains the area within which the cost of transporting wheat to London was no more than 6.3d. a quarter, and shows the crucial importance of water transport both along the Thames and along the coast. (Adapted from Campbell *et al.*, *A Medieval Capital and its Grain Supply* (1993), Figs 5 and 7).

least within the crucial Thames valley supply corridor. By 1300 only Faversham, east of London on the Thames estuary, had such close associations with London cornmongers, reflecting the fact that transport costs from both places were virtually identical. Within Oxfordshire, Merton College's estate of Cuxham (mentioned above) provides a good example of the way in which grain was regularly shipped through Henley for London. In the 14th century the reeve (or college agent) visited the town up to 40 times a year to sell grain in bulk at the weekly market, and perhaps for that reason the estate maintained an above-average number of cart horses. The costs were clearly worth it, since London demand kept corn prices artificially high. On the rare occasions that Cuxham grain was sold at Oxford, prices were markedly lower.

Similar patterns are found in the supply of firewood, for which Henley was well placed through its proximity to the extensive Chilterns woodlands. Merchants specialising in wood imports (often called bushers, woodmongers or timbermongers) were recorded in London from the early 13th century, and like the cornmongers had connections up the Thames valley to Henley and beyond. In 1341 London woodmongers brought talwood, halfwood and firewood from Filletts manor in Henley, although firewood may have been loaded at smaller landing points as well.

Grain and firewood was a one-way traffic, but despite the cost and difficulty of hauling boats against the current there was an important upstream trade as well. As the Cuxham records show, boats frequently returned with heavy or perishable goods such as herrings, fruit and millstones, or with wine, iron, and possibly coal – all unloaded at Henley for trans-shipment to Oxford, Woodstock, and further afield. Similar patterns appear in the correspondence of the local Stonor family (based a few miles north of Henley at Stonor Park), who in the late 15th century imported dried and salted fish, hogsheads of wine, spices, glassware, and a silk gown, conveyed upriver by their 'bargeman' William Somer (of Queenhithe), then carted overland from Henley.[30]

By then the town was firmly established as a lynchpin in the London supply network, a position which it retained until the 16th or 17th century. What did this mean for the townspeople, and what was their involvement in this expanding long-distance trade?

THE RIVER TRADE IN HENLEY

Up to the mid-14th century, the Henley grain trade seems to have been dominated by wealthy London-based cornmongers operating on a very large scale. Quite a few owned property (and particularly granaries) in the town, from which they shipped downriver the

Medieval River Barges

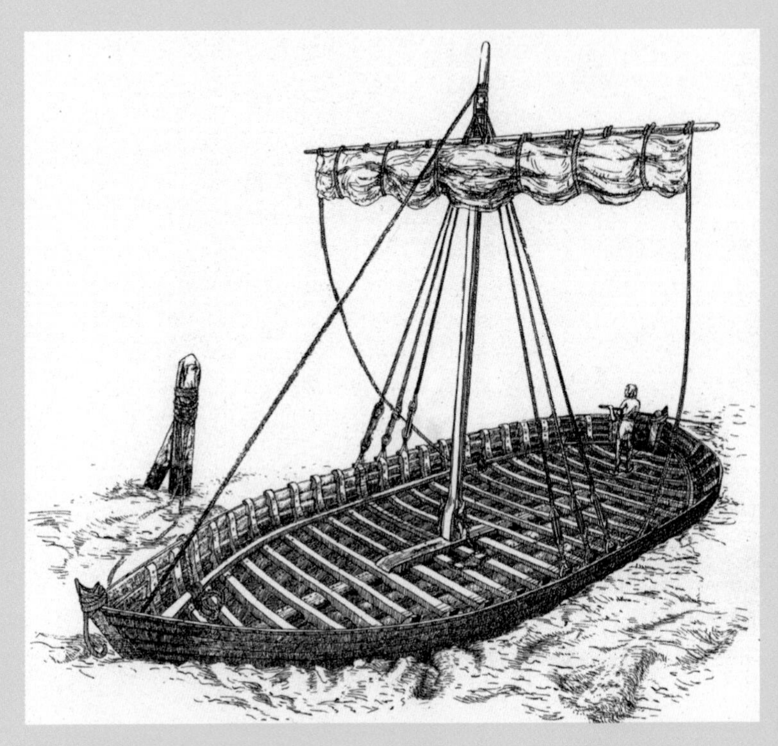

Figure A *Artist's reconstruction of 'Blackfriars 3', a 15th-century flat-bottomed shout recovered in 1970. Barrels or other cargo would have been laid flat in the bottom of the boat, which showed no trace of the internal planks used to support cargoes such as stone. The mast could be lowered by lifting it from its socket and sliding it aft. (From P Marsden,* Ships of the Port of London: 12th to 17th Centuries AD *(English Heritage, 1996))*

The vessels used on the Thames and other inland waterways in the Middle Ages have to be reconstructed from documentary references and illustrations, from information about the size and depth of medieval flashlocks, and above all from a small handful of excavated medieval wrecks. Of those, the most important for the Thames region is an almost complete 15th-century river barge known to specialists as 'Blackfriars 3' (Figs A and B). This sank in London around 1480–1500 probably in a collision, and was discovered on the riverbed in 1970.

The Blackfriars wreck is of a type particularly associated with the Thames, and known throughout the Middle Ages as a 'shout' (from the Dutch *schuit* or *schuyt*, meaning a flat-bottomed river-boat). Its general shape and size (*c.*14.64m long x 4.4m wide), broad flat bottom, and overall stability made it eminently suited to negotiating river shallows and flashlocks, and to carrying considerable loads. Like most such boats it had a mast which could be lowered when passing under low bridges, and which probably carried a single square sail: a similar arrangement continued on Thames barges in

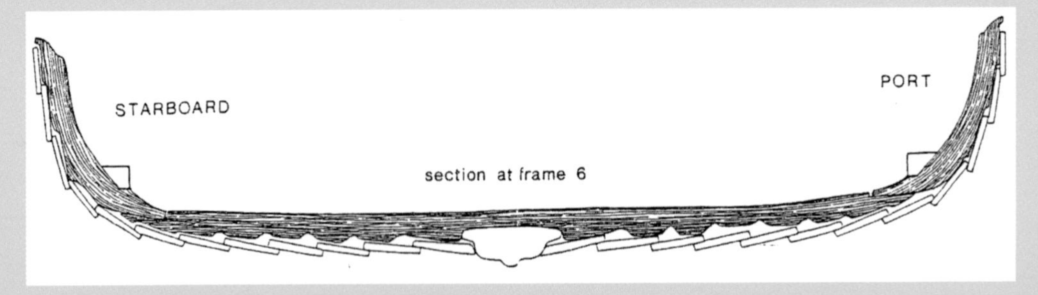

Figure B *Blackfriars 3: cross-section, showing the wide flat bottom which made such boats so well suited to shallow inland waters.*

the 17th century (Figure 41). Steering was probably by means of a steering oar as shown in the reconstruction, since no evidence was found for a sternpost rudder. All the timbers were of oak, secured with wrought-iron rivets, and the vessel was clinker-built (i.e. with its planks overlapping); the caulking between the planks (to give a watertight seal) was matted goat hair. The boat had seen considerable repairs, and seems to have originally been built around 1380–1415. In other words it enjoyed an operational life of at least 65–70 years, which seems to have been fairly common.

The boat's size implies a standard crew of two, presumably the bare minimum for negotiating flashlocks. In good conditions sail and current may have provided sufficient power downstream, but for the upstream journey rowing, poling and hauling from the bank must have been essential (see Figure C). Journey times between London and Henley must have varied considerably according to river conditions and delays at flashlocks, which could amount to several days. An upstream trip in May 1476, however, was expected to take four to five days, remarkably similar to the average reported in the 1790s.

Analysis of the boat's structure concluded that it could carry a weight of 7.4 metric tonnes, though recent work has suggested that this may be an underestimate. Whatever the case, documentary references to shouts carrying over 200 qrs of wheat (around 35 tonnes) from Henley to London in 1345 show that Blackfriars 3 was not the largest of its type. Some shouts must have been considerably longer, possibly over 20 metres, though any great increase in width would have made it too difficult to negotiate the flashlocks and higher stretches. As it was, the boat's width of 4.4m would have easily fitted through the standard 5.5m flashlocks recorded on the Severn in the 1380s, or through a 7.6m weir on the Cherwell mentioned in 1260, though not through a 10ft (3.9m) weir on the upper Thames beyond Oxford recorded in 1261. That far upriver, only the smallest logboats, punts and flat-bottomed shouts can have penetrated.

Sources: Marsden, P, *Ships of the Port of London: 12th to 17th Centuries AD* (1996), 55–104; Blair, J (ed.), *Waterways and Canal-Building in Medieval England* (2007), 112–26, 284–5; Kingsford, CL (ed.), *The Stonor Letters and Papers 1290–1483* (Camden 3rd ser. 29–30, 1919), II, 5.

Figure C *A 14th-century illustration of a boat being towed upstream. An account of 1351–2 describes a vessel being hauled up the Severn in similar fashion, for which additional men were hired. (British Library Add. MS 41230, f.169)*

grain stockpiled from surrounding agricultural estates. In the words of one historian, Henley must 'have seemed like an up-river London colony', a place 'where Londoners met merchants from other Thames-side towns'.[31]

Their presence and activities can be demonstrated from a variety of medieval records, in particular London wills and corporation records, Henley property deeds, and (for the 1330s) Henley manorial court rolls. At least 24 such people have been identified for the period *c.*1280–1350, of whom perhaps 12 were active together around 1320, when the evidence is fullest. Many were expressly called cornmongers, and included the merchants John Husbond, Walter Neel, Roger and William (le) Palmer, and Adam Wade. Wade (d. 1310) owned property at Queenhithe (where he lived) and in other London parishes, but also had two granaries in Henley (one of them north of Friday Street near the river), and a stone house near the bridge. Other London merchants held shops and stalls there. Robert Adrian, for instance, bequeathed stalls, houses, and agricultural land in Henley in 1327.

But not all these large-scale London merchants were exclusively cornmongers. A few of the largest were fishmongers, who had close connections with the grain trade and who possibly traded salted fish in both directions. Particularly prominent in Henley were three members of the de Chigwell family, of whom Alan (d. *c.*1345) had property at Kingston upon Thames and in Henley fronting the river. Another merchant had property in Henley and at 'the salt hythe' in Queenhithe, suggesting that the long-established salt trade down the river also continued. Other goods, as we have seen, included firewood downstream and bulk or luxury items upstream, the trade almost certainly controlled by similar types of people. Some (like Alan de Chigwell or the cornmonger Walter Neel) owned their own boats, although given the scale of the river trade there may well have been a small fleet of vessels run by professional operators, from whom merchants and consumers like the Stonors might commission transport as required.[32]

That is not to say that Henley did not have its own trading classes (see Chapter 4), although at first very few seem to have been able to compete with the large-scale London merchants, or to have been actively involved in the Thames grain trade. Possible exceptions are Robert of Shiplake, a wealthy townsman who rented two granaries and served as warden of the town guild, and Thurstan de Ewelme, who in 1317 owed a Londoner the large sum of £60. Over all, however, the scale of the London merchants' business operations and the capital they commanded seems to have prevented Henley's inhabitants from securing a foothold. Like so much else this changed after the Black Death, which devastated Henley and London as most other places. In the short term this must have seriously undermined the river trade, although recovery was fairly swift, and in the later Middle Ages higher living standards and increased purchasing power kept demand from London high despite the dramatic fall in population. What the disruption also seems to have done is to break the London cornmongers' stranglehold of the Henley grain trade. In the capital itself their numbers and influence waned markedly by the later 14th century, and in Henley, for the first time, local men started to take over the town's granaries and the trade they represented. Richard Jory, a prominent townsman since the 1320s, acquired two granaries in 1354, while another prominent inhabitant (William Wakeman) obtained a granary in New Street in 1357. Thenceforth references to London merchants in Henley all but cease.[33]

The Later Middle Ages

For the rest of the Middle Ages the river trade through Henley remained largely in the hands of local men. Among the most prominent were the Henley merchants John Deven (active 1422–70), John Logge (active 1433–70s), and particularly John Elmes (active 1417–60), who may still have occasionally traded upriver to Oxford. As well as granaries in Henley Elmes owned property in Wallingford and Abingdon, and in 1449 he disposed of an Oxford property adjoining a wharf on the Thames, which was converted soon after into a garden. This, it has been suggested, may reflect the final abandonment of sporadic upstream navigation to Oxford, spurred by the mounting difficulties described above and by Oxford's mid-15th-century stagnation. Other Henley tradesmen used the river to obtain goods and raw materials from London, as reflected in debts owed to London fishmongers, ironmongers and grocers. The town's riverside granaries were still occupied by local people in the late 15th and early 16th centuries.

Despite these continuities, trade through Henley experienced changes. For several decades from the 1430s the grain trade seems to have been briefly eclipsed by an expanding trade in wool, in which Deven, Logge and especially Elmes became heavily involved alongside their other activities. The national increase in raw wool exports during the period prompted several landowners within Henley's hinterland to invest in sheep-farming, and the acquisition of property in the town by sheep-farming gentry such as the Fettiplace and Danvers families, combined with the arrival of immigrants from Berkshire towns such as Reading, all point to a new role as a wool-exporting centre, supplying the Berkshire cloth industry and overseas markets. Some of this trade was apparently based on traditional road and river routes through Henley to London: in 1443, for instance, John Elmes and a London fishmonger were owed money by a London woolpacker. Some of it was overland to Southampton, however, through which Elmes and others exported wool and imported wine, fruit, millstones, and dyestuffs.

But the phase was relatively short-lived. From the 1490s new rules by the town guild to regulate the local grain trade show that Henley's traditional role of funnelling foodstuffs downriver to London was regaining its ascendancy, fuelled by renewed demand as the capital began once again to expand. By 1493 there was sufficient trade for townsmen to demand tolls from outsiders taking grain to granaries for sale to Londoners, while in 1517 the borough assembly compiled a list of 'all the corn buyers of this town', naming 15 or 16 prominent townsmen who together made up around half of Henley's burgesses or governing body. Trade with Southampton ended around the same time, so that as Henley emerged from the Middle Ages into the Elizabethan period, its traditional role as an entrepôt supplying London along the river continued unabated. During the 16th and early 17th centuries that role was set to continue, until the reopening of the Thames to Oxford and beyond changed the dynamics of the river trade yet again.[34]

The Wider Town

Like all planned towns, Henley represented an entrepreneurial investment involving a fair degree of risk. Some towns failed, while others, like Henley, went on to establish themselves within the national market network. In Henley's case the overriding factor was its position within the local road and river transport system in relation to London – a position which by *c.*1300, following changes in the state of the river, was probably even more advantageous than it had been at the town's creation. From then until the 17th century Henley stood at the gateway to the Thames supply corridor to London.

How this affected those most directly involved in the river trade – the grain merchants and fishmongers, or the wood traders and woolmen – we have already seen. But on the basis of this trade, medieval Henley developed into a complex and vibrant small town with its own organs of government, a rich social and religious life, and a variety of trades and crafts by which the bulk of the townspeople earned their living. It is time to turn to the medieval town in more detail.

Chapter 4 A Medieval Trading Town

Henley's medieval development was conditioned above all by its proximity to London, and by its key position within the road and river network. But alongside the grain merchants, fishmongers and (briefly) wool merchants mentioned above, what sort of people lived in the town and how did they earn their living? How was the town run, and what impact did its economy have on its buildings and physical growth? What can we learn of its social and religious life? The range of evidence available to answer these questions varies greatly across the medieval period, from the earliest fragmentary sources for the 13th century through to the fuller (though still incomplete) town records of the 14th, 15th and early 16th centuries. Buildings, too, survive in larger numbers from the later Middle Ages, casting additional light on the development of the town and the lives of its people.

THE SHAPE OF THE TOWN

Henley's basic layout resulted from medieval planning, as we have seen. But from around 1300, the survival of property conveyances and other documents allows us to paint a more detailed picture of the town, amplified from the later Middle Ages by the earliest surviving buildings. What form did the mid-14th-century town take?

As with most medieval towns, the countryside encroached on all sides. North of the Dorchester road (the modern Fair Mile) was the lord's deer park, created before 1272 probably by Richard, Earl of Cornwall. South of the road were small fields, closes and woodland belonging to the lord of Badgemore, while nearby, on the town's northern edge, was Fillets manor house, on the site of modern Phyllis Court. Continuing down Northfield End, a greater density of buildings (including, by the 14th century, a horse-powered grist mill) announced the outskirts of the town. Entrance into the town itself, however, near Bell Lane, was probably marked by timber 'bars' similar to those recorded at the western end of the market place on Gravel Hill. Beyond the bars buildings became yet denser, laid out (particularly on the west) on regular burgage plots. Most would have been timber-framed and probably thatched, with a central open hearth (see below).[35]

Continuing south along Bell Street (then called North Street), some houses may have had arched shop windows closed by

Figure 22 Shops and stalls in a late medieval town. By the 14th century many of Henley's craftsmen, retailers, and victuallers had shops or stalls in front of their houses, complementing the trade in grain and other goods at the weekly market and annual fair. Some trade looked westwards across the Chilterns, though the all-important river trade with London remained the key to Henley's success.

shutters, similar to those which survive in some other towns. Certainly there were shops around the main crossroads and along Hart (or High) Street, one of them at the crossroads' north-east corner, and most of them with domestic accommodation above or behind. At the crossroads itself was a market cross mentioned from 1308, which by the 15th century had a roof under which trading took place.

East and west of the cross, rows of shops and other buildings occupied the middle of the street by the early 14th century, a feature found in many medieval towns. A tavern there with an upper room and associated shops was mentioned in 1357, while in the 1480s a new guild hall was built in the Middle Row west of the crossroads. Buildings there were known later as Fisher Row (on the north side) and Butcher Row (on the south), reflecting the trades carried out. Butchers here were occasionally fined for slaughtering in the street, suggesting (as we might expect) that the area was probably not always very salubrious. Beyond the market place, according to later documents, was a 'common dunghill', perhaps associated with the town's agricultural western fringe near Hen Field, where a barn was mentioned in 1404–5. Further up Gravel Hill, by the mid-15th century, was a row of small timber-framed houses, perhaps occupied by semi-rural craftsmen. Here, town and country came very close.

Further east, along Hart Street, the urban character intensified, with more shops, some major inns by the mid-15th century, and at the far end the parish church. By the 1350s this was already a building of considerable size and status, though still lacking some of its side chapels. Possibly it had a central tower incorporating some 12th-century Norman work, swept away when the present bell tower was added in the late 15th or early 16th century. Further on, beyond the rectory house gateway, the road continued to the medieval bridge (Panel 1), branching north and south along the all important waterfront with its granaries and storehouses. Here, in the earlier 14th century, London-based boatmen and merchants supervised the loading of grain consignments onto wide flat-bottomed shouts.[36]

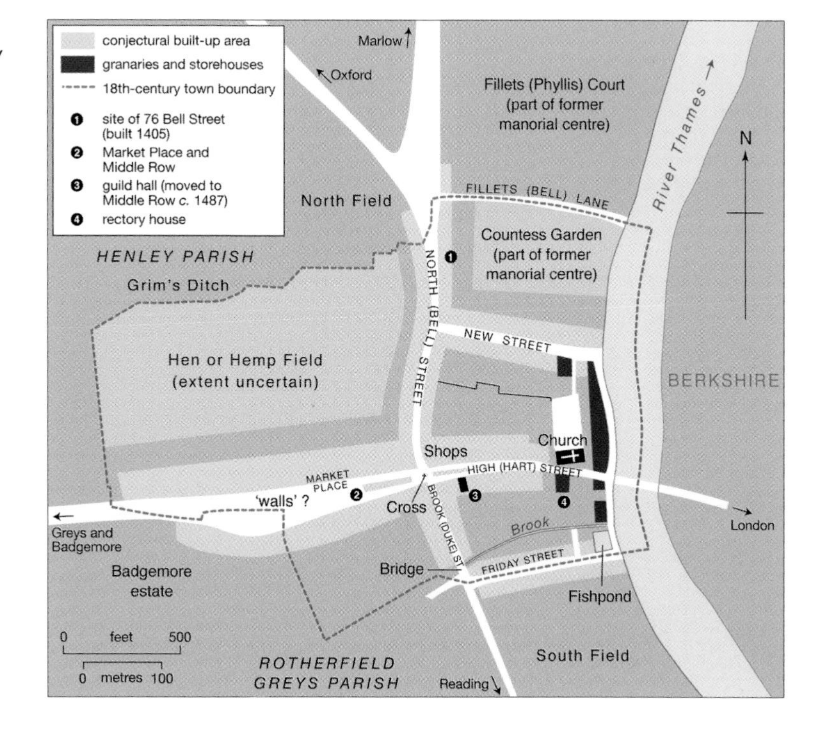

Figure 23 Conjectural reconstruction of Henley c.1350, showing the main streets and areas of houses, shops and other commercial or public buildings. The reconstruction draws on property deeds and other town and manorial documents, as well as on physical remains. (Adapted, with permission, from Peberdy, 'Henley', Map 2.5; original © R.B. Peberdy 1994)

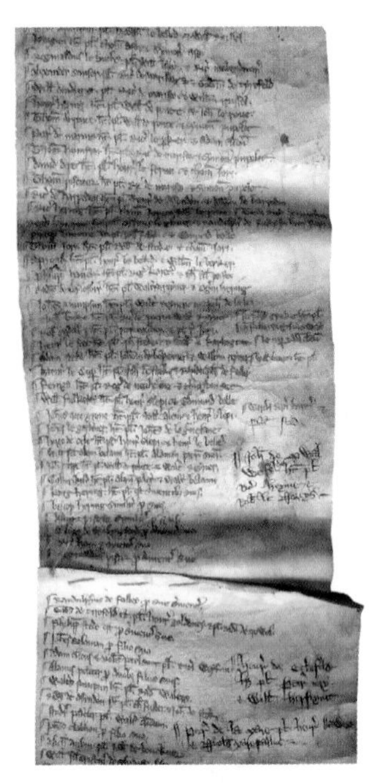

Figure 24 Part of a list of Henley townspeople compiled *c.*1296, probably by the town guild. Combined with taxation lists and manor court rolls, it helps give some idea of the size of Henley's population. The list names residents who stood surety for the good behaviour of fellow townsmen: a heading in Old French calls it 'Les nuns de gent de la vile de Henle ... et les nuns de pleges' (names of the people of the town of Henley ... and of their pledges).

How big was the medieval town? Estimating medieval populations is notoriously difficult, since figures must be teased from a variety of sources including taxation lists, manorial records, and (in Henley's case) guild and property records. By 1300 Henley seems to have contained at least 200–250 households, a total population of between 1,000 and 1,500: since most early 14th-century 'small towns' had populations of only 500-1,000, this places it towards the larger end of the scale. Numbers probably continued at this level until the catastrophic plagues of the mid-14th century, which killed at least a third of Europe's population but whose impact on particular towns and villages varied considerably. In Henley, the evidence of property deeds and guild membership suggests that the town suffered above average losses, inflated, perhaps, by its close connections with London and the wider world. Up to two thirds of the population may have died in 1348-9, followed by mortality of nearly 30 per cent in the plague of 1361–2. If so, the number of Henley people paying poll tax in 1377 suggests that, like many towns, it made a remarkably quick recovery. By then there may again have been between 225 and 275 households, and records show no general signs of long-term dilapidation or of vacant property.

Such a recovery presumably reflected Henley's attractiveness to incomers, who could exploit the opportunities which the Black Death had created. A possible example is the merchant William Woodhall, who appears in Henley records from 1350, was town warden by 1352, and at his death in 1358 had widespread trading connections in Oxfordshire, Middlesex, Surrey and London. Possibly he was a Londoner who had settled in Henley to escape the Black Death, and the appearance of new names in the town's guild records suggests that newcomers continued to replenish the town into the 1420s. During the mid-15th century there is some indication that the process may have slowed, with the population remaining static or even falling; nonetheless, there were some exceptionally prosperous merchants such as John Elmes (see Chapter 3), while the significant number of 15th-century buildings in Henley points to continued wealth and confidence among some townspeople at least. High-quality 15th-century houses survive throughout the town, while a cross wing added to houses on Gravel Hill in 1454 shows that building also continued on the town's edges. From around 1500, with a marked revival of the grain trade, the population rose again, and by the 1520s had probably reached 1,000: around 210–220 households, slightly fewer than its early 14th-century peak. The building of large lodging ranges behind the *Old White Hart* inn in the 1530s (Panel 6) is further proof of a substantial upswing in the economy.[37]

MARKET, TRADES AND CRAFTS

As we have seen, Henley's medieval economy was dominated by the London grain trade and by the town's crucial role as a trans-shipment point. But like all small towns, Henley fulfilled a more general marketing role within its immediate area, and required an infrastructure of trades, crafts and services to support both its own population and that of the surrounding countryside.

As suggested in Chapter 2, the creation of a weekly market at Henley may have predated the planned town. By the 13th century, as in modern times, it was held on a Thursday, thus avoiding direct competition from neighbouring markets (which were held on different weekdays). The main commodity was undoubtedly grain, but the market must have also sold goods shipped upriver from London, and the leather, metal and textile goods produced by the town's own craftsmen. In 1306–7, for instance, the reeve of Cuxham (presumably in Henley negotiating grain sales) bought 'diverse articles' there for the warden of Merton College in Oxford, most likely purchased at the weekly market. Livestock was probably also traded, particularly during the 15th century when sheep farming and wool figured larger in the local economy.[38]

Regulation of the market, by the 15th century at least, was through the town guild, which sporadically appointed a clerk of the market to oversee its administration and to check weights and measures, and porters who may have overseen the transfer of goods between waterfront storehouses and the market area. New rules implemented in the late 15th and early 16th centuries were concerned primarily with grain sales. After the sub-bailiff rang the market bell at 11 a.m. inhabitants had an hour to make their purchases before the large corn buyers and others were admitted at midday, while in 1516 the corn buyers were required not to buy wheat except at the agreed price, not to bribe suppliers or get them drunk, and not to buy in wheat direct from the countryside. That last ruling suggests a good deal of informal trading outside the market, and probably this was the case for all goods.[39]

The area served by the market can be partly reconstructed from surnames in manorial and town records, in taxation lists, and (from the later Middle Ages) in wills, which together give some indication of the trading and social links between town and countryside. These suggest an unusually large hinterland extending into south Oxfordshire, south-west Buckinghamshire, and Berkshire (Figure 25). Westwards it stretched across the Chilterns to include such places as Benson, Ewelme and even Chinnor, although eastwards it seems to have extended only a little way beyond the river; probably this reflected competition from Marlow, and possibly it perpetuated older trading patterns

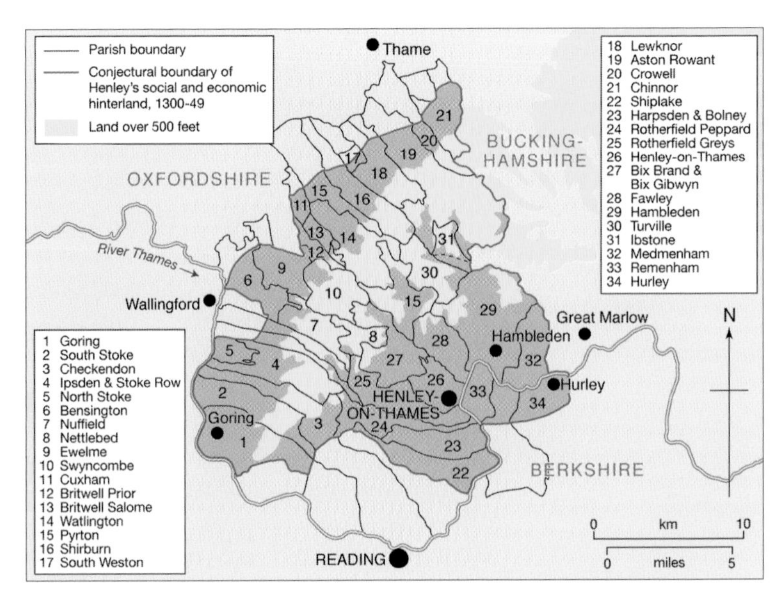

Figure 25 Henley's early 14th-century hinterland, based on evidence from manor court rolls, town charters, and taxation lists. The area encompasses some 34 parishes in three counties. Despite some variations in the 15th century, the core area remained relatively stable throughout the Middle Ages. (Redrawn, with permission, from Peberdy, 'Henley', Maps 4.4–4.6; originals © RB Peberdy 1994)

predating the building of Henley bridge. The hinterland was overwhelmingly agricultural, dominated in the 13th and early 14th centuries by grain production, though with a smattering of resident gentry such as the nearby Stonors and Harpsdens, whose consumer needs may have helped fuel Henley's economy. Nevertheless the majority of those trading at the market, large-scale corn merchants aside, were most likely ordinary tenants and peasant farmers. Late medieval links with the Thame area may have been forged during the 15th-century expansion of the wool trade, representing places which sent stock to Henley market, or from which Henley men bought wool.[40]

Medieval fairs fulfilled different functions, and often attracted traders from far beyond the market hinterland. At Henley, the right to hold an annual fair on 29 August was granted by King John between 1199 and 1204. Probably it traded in all sorts of goods and livestock, though as the date fell just after the annual harvest the fair, too, may have been geared to the all-important grain trade along the river. In 1440 a later lord and lady of Henley (acting in harness with the town guild) exchanged it for two new fairs on 24–6 February, and for three days in May or June, depending on the date of Easter. That second fair, which would sometimes have followed the summer shearing, may have specialised in sheep or wool, reflecting the temporary shift towards the wool trade noted in the previous chapter. As with the market, all tolls collected from traders belonged to the lord and were itemised in annual accounts. In 1296–7 they were worth around 4s. a year, just under a quarter of the tolls from the weekly market.[41]

What of the trades and crafts practised within the town? Once again no medieval source gives a clear overview, and the picture has to be teased from scattered references in town and manorial records and (later) from wills. As in most towns there were significant numbers of service trades, including provision of food and drink. Bakers and butchers were mentioned throughout, and from the 15th century there is increasing evidence of innkeeping and victualling. In part this may simply reflect better documentation, though the development of the wool and cloth trade in 15th-century Henley may have created new needs, with wool merchants travelling into the town from greater distances. The (*Old*) *White Hart*, after which Hart Street is named, existed by the 1420s (Panel 6), and other inns or hospices were mentioned in the 1430s–40s, when the town's hostelers formed a recognised trading group. The surviving *Catherine Wheel*, also on Hart Street, was mentioned in 1499.

Other services included building trades. Carpenters were recorded in large numbers in the 15th century, unsurprising in an area in which timber-framing predominated. Tilers were mentioned from the 1390s, and from the late 13th century a few potters, who like their counterparts at Nettlebed used local clay and supplied neighbouring parishes. One, William the Potter, became steward (or warden) of the guild, and around the 1280s seems to have had a furnace or kiln on New Street. The town's ironmongers, blacksmiths and coopers must similarly have provided goods and services not only within the town but outside it. Leather workers included skinners and tanners as well as shoemakers, while textile workers included weavers, dyers, fullers, tailors and mercers, particularly from the 15th century. Their numbers were never sufficient to suggest really large-scale manufacture at Henley as part of the Berkshire cloth industry, although in 1498 Henley's weavers, mercers and tailors were each formally constituted into separate craft guilds.[42]

Some of the raw materials for such crafts, particularly skins and wool, came probably from the market hinterland described

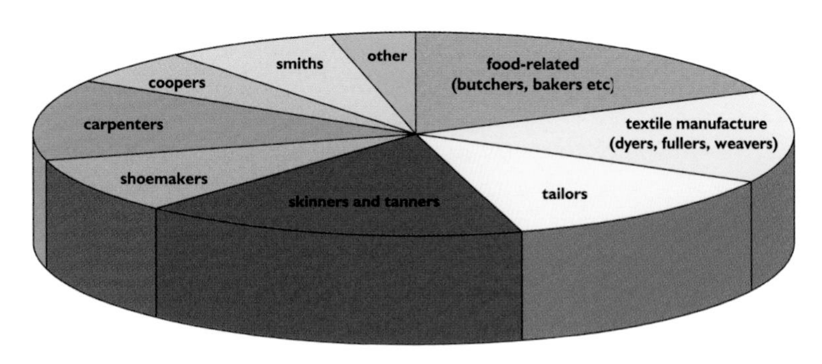

Figure 26 Trades and crafts mentioned in Henley *c.*1420–90, based chiefly on manor court rolls and the guild's Assembly Books. Leather working seems to have fallen off by the early 16th century, though the number of weavers increased. Food-related trades (including butchering, baking and victualling) remained important throughout. (Source: Peberdy, 184)

above, but for this too the supply corridor along the Thames was important. Several Henley craftsmen and traders used London suppliers, who presumably transported their goods upstream in the same boats used for downstream grain consignments. The smith William Ayleward owed money to a London ironmonger in 1464, while the dyer Hugh Barrey had dealings with a London grocer, and William Bodyngton with a London haberdasher. The upstream trade in wine, fish and luxuries also fed Henley's market and economy. Bodyngton and Thomas Spyre, a Henley chapman or general dealer, owed debts to London fishmongers in the mid-15th century, while a century earlier a Henley tavern owner left timber to a London vintner.[43]

WEALTH AND STATUS: THE TOWN ELITE

How wealthy was medieval Henley, and how was that wealth distributed? Only at certain points do we catch an overall glimpse, based on such records as the late 13th-century *Nuns de Gens* list (see Figure 24), manor court rolls, or taxation lists.

Before the Black Death, the wealthiest and most influential people in Henley were the large-scale London-based merchants described in Chapter 3. Probably this explains why Henley ranked so surprisingly low in terms of its taxable wealth, which was based usually on movable goods (see Figure 27). The volume of trade through the town was considerable, but those benefiting the most were outsiders with property and commercial interests in Henley, rather than prosperous Henley-based entrepreneurs. Thus in 1327 only 11 per cent of Henley's townspeople were wealthy enough to pay substantial amounts in tax (3s. or more), compared with 21 per cent in Reading and Wallingford and 30 per cent in Abingdon.[44]

Yet throughout the Middle Ages Henley did have a few wealthier and more influential inhabitants, particularly from the 1350s as control of the grain trade passed from Londoners to Henley-based merchants. The most notable included Robert of Shiplake and (to a lesser degree) John of Harwell (early 14th century), Thomas Clobber (1380s–1430s), and in the mid-15th century merchants like John Elmes (d. 1460). All rose to serve as town warden, and all enjoyed above-average wealth based probably on trade. Shiplake may have been involved in the grain trade, while Clobber (whose surname suggests family origins as traders or chapmen) had business connections as far as Devon. Elmes, as we have seen, had widespread trading interests through London and Southampton.

Beneath such men was the bulk of the town's population. Surnames and other evidence suggest a large and substantial

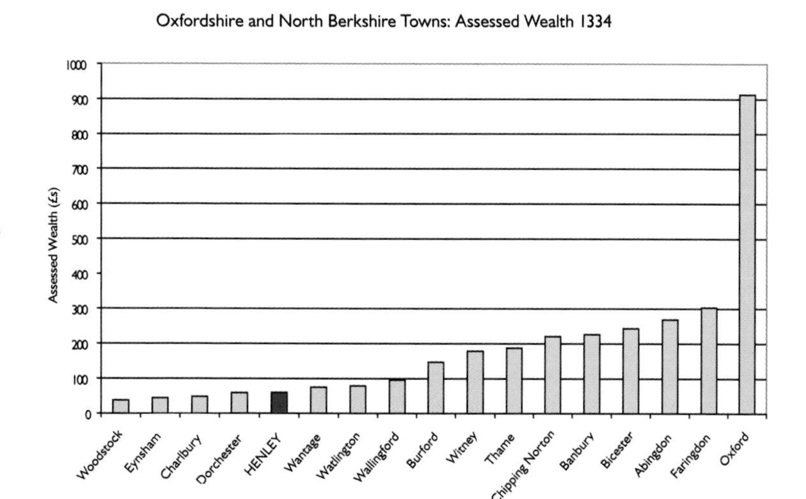

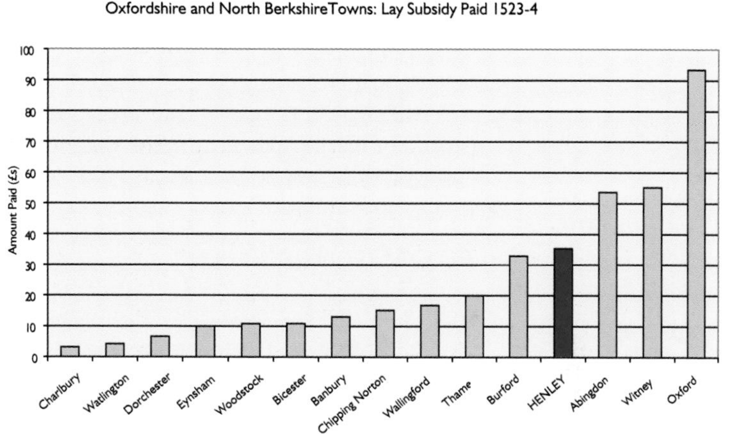

Figure 27 Comparative wealth of Oxfordshire and north Berkshire towns, based on taxation lists for 1334 (top) and 1523–4 (bottom). Henley's surprisingly low ranking in the early 14th century probably reflects the dominance of London merchants. After Henley-based merchants seized the initiative from the 1350s the town's taxable wealth increased, as seen in the 1524 lists.

body of moderately prosperous craftsmen and small traders or shopkeepers, which together may have comprised some 55–70 per cent of adult householders. Below them was the barely visible mass of labourers and poor, who rarely appear in the records but who may have made up another 30–35 per cent. The broad picture was similar in the early 16th century, when the wealthiest few included the trader and town warden Richard Brockham, the fuller and innkeeper Robert Kenton, the glover John Hogge, and the butcher John Jessop.

Status was based not solely on wealth, however, but on involvement in town affairs. From the 13th century the Henley merchant guild gradually assumed responsibility for running the town, but membership was strictly controlled. A fundamental division, therefore, was between guild members or burgesses and the rest of the populace. In the 1290s the guild had around 47 members, perhaps a fifth of the adult male population, and in the late 15th and early 16th centuries around thirty. Among those was a smaller elite which regularly witnessed town charters and dominated town offices. In the 14th century it included (alongside the likes of Robert of Shiplake) townsmen such as Thomas Folyot, Richard and Thomas Jory, or Thomas of Shirburn, all of whom seem to have been large traders or merchants. Craftsmen, by contrast, seem at first to have been excluded, a prejudice which has also been noted in York. From the 15th century craftsmen appeared in larger numbers, presumably in response to the general fall in town population and guild membership: town officers *c.*1400 included tanners, tailors and a hosteler, and by mid-century there were nearly equal numbers of craftsmen and traders or shopkeepers. By the end of the century there were further signs of change, with less evidence of government by an inner clique, and greater reliance on the entire burgess body, which seems to have attended increasing numbers of meetings. Possibly this was associated with increasing challenges to the guild's authority around the same time, particularly in connection with market regulation.[45]

Status within the urban hierarchy, therefore, derived above all from wealth, occupation, and involvement in the town government. How did this operate?

TOWN GOVERNMENT

Figure 28 The medieval seal of the town guild, as preserved on some early 14th-century property charters. The Latin legend translates as 'seal of the community of Henley'. The guild's increasing responsibility for the church, the bridge and for large amounts of town property enhanced its corporate identity, and made possession of a common seal essential.

Until a self-governing corporation was created by the royal charter of 1568, Henley remained a seignorial town. In theory this meant that authority remained with the manorial lord (or 'seignor') on whose land the town had been founded, and that town government was enacted through the lord's court. In the early 15th century the court still met every three weeks, and the lord's steward held an annual view of frankpledge; but in reality the business of both became increasingly subservient to government by the merchant guild. Between the 1330s and 1420s court business fell by two thirds, much of it duplicating guild legislation, while the same townsmen seem often to have served as both manorial and town officers. The court's most valuable function seems, in fact, to have been the hearing of debt cases. This was, in other words, a forum used by townspeople for their own convenience rather than as an instrument of lordly control. By then the court may even have met in the guild hall (see below), since the manor house was abandoned in the 14th century.[46]

The guild itself began as a subordinate merchant body tolerated by the lord, to whom members each owed a 5d. annual fee in the 1260s–70s. Gradually it acquired virtual autonomy. By 1300 it was responsible for the bridge and church, for the support of which townspeople gave significant amounts of property: by 1349 the guild or its officers probably already received the rents from around 35 houses in the town, and by the 1380s (following the Black Death) the number was 115, producing larger rents from Henley for the guild than for the lord. To discharge its functions the guild had its own seal, and the terminology of contemporary documents makes clear that it claimed to represent the whole 'community of the town': indeed it clearly exercised authority not only over the burgesses but over the whole populace. Its functions are seen most clearly in its medieval Assembly Books, which survive in a virtually unbroken sequence from 1395. These detail the regular meetings of the burgess body or 'congregation', which could fine burgesses for non-attendance. Elected officers included the town warden at the head (originally called steward or seneschal), two bailiffs, two constables and two bridgemen, who administered property given for the church and bridge. Others included a bellman or town crier and tasters of victuals. The guild's remit was wide, focusing (alongside care of the church and bridge) on law and order, street sanitation, removal of nuisances, price enforcement, and market administration. Almost certainly there were subsidiary meetings whose records do not survive, such as the common councils and warden's courts mentioned in the 15th century.[47]

The guild had its own hall by the early 15th century, situated apparently on the south side of Hart Street just east of the cross-roads. New benches were provided for the council chamber in 1419, and in 1487–92 the guild built a new hall in the Middle Row, a conscious symbol of its authority, resources, and self-esteem. The building seems to have been timber-framed, with a jettied upper storey providing a large first-floor council chamber. Seventeenth-century paintings show it surmounted by a large lantern or cupola, though that was presumably a later addition. Some medieval guild halls had an open area below for market trading, though in the 18th century the ground floor here was occupied by a hall and kitchen. Possibly that was always the case, and an 18th-century ground-floor gaol a little further along the row may have also reflected medieval arrangements. Certainly the hall must have been solidly built, since it continued to serve the town authorities until the Middle Row's demolition in the 1790s.[48]

Despite the potential clash of interests, relations between lords and townspeople seem to have generally been amicable – a situation no doubt helped by the fact that most 14th- and 15th-century lords of Henley were wealthy landowners with extensive estates elsewhere, and took little direct interest in the town. An exception may have been the notorious robber baron John Moleyns (d. 1360), who in

The Chantry House: An Architectural Conundrum

The Chantry House is a late medieval timber-framed building north-east of the church. Its two main floors open onto the churchyard; below is another floor which, because of a drop in ground level, faces only eastwards to the river, and is reached through the yard of the *Red Lion* inn. The name associates it with medieval chantry priests (see main text), but originated only in the 20th century. More likely the building had commercial uses associated with the river. Certainly it is the finest timber-framed building in Henley, and on the churchyard side was clearly designed for show.

Written Evidence

Title deeds survive from 1445, when the Henley merchants John Elmes and John Deven bought 'a building and vacant plot' east of the churchyard. Probably this included the site of the Chantry House, which was almost certainly not yet built. The deeds are largely silent until 1552, when Deven's successors sold a building called the School House, and four tenements or chambers called the priests' chambers. This could have been a single building in dual use, but more likely refers to two separate buildings. Either way the Chantry House's two upper floors were used as schools until the 1770s, while the ground floor was let to the *Red Lion*, which later acquired the whole building. In 1923 it was sold for use as a parish room.

Figure A *The Chantry House from the north-west. The lowest floor (see Figs B and E) is only exposed on the east because of the drop in ground level, and so is not shown here. The quality of the framing, with its large curved wall- and wind-braces, can clearly be seen. (Drawing by John Steane)*

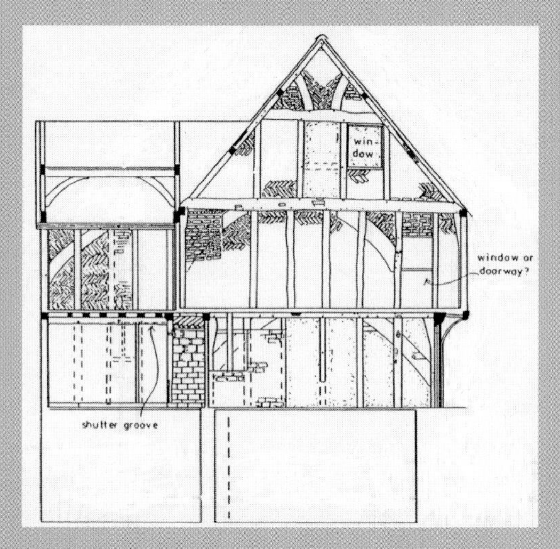

Figure B *The timber frame of the south gable, where it adjoins the* Red Lion. *One of the curved braces was positioned to allow for a connecting doorway to the* Red Lion *or its predecessor. (Drawing by Linda Hall)*

The Building

Dendro-dating of the building's fast-grown timber proved inconclusive, so only stylistic dating is possible. Some investigators have suggested it was built as early as 1400, but more likely it is mid- or late 15th-century (Figs C and D). Investigation in 2004 concluded that the five-bay top floor was originally divided into four separate chambers and a landing (with stairs from the middle floor), with a well-lit corridor on the river side: an arrangement found in many medieval inns, including the *Old White Hart* at Henley. The top floor had a storage loft above, destroyed when the large school room was created. The main entrance to the middle floor was through an impressive doorway towards the churchyard (Figs C and D); a separate stair or hoist-opening connected it to the open-fronted ground floor at wharf level. The building's southern end connected with the *Red Lion* or its predecessor, since the timber framing allowed for a connecting doorway (Fig. B).

Origins and Use

What can we surmise about the building's use? Nothing unequivocally links it with the four priests' chambers, which may have stood elsewhere in the churchyard. Until 1923 it does not seem to have been church property: on the contrary it lay outside the churchyard

Figures C and D *The Chantry House from the west (churchyard) side, showing the projecting first-floor jetty with its elaborately moulded primary timbers: jetty plate, bressumer and braces (all supporting timbers), and a Tudor-type arched door head. All these mouldings are typical of the 15th and early 16th centuries. The large doorway gave access to the main floor, which consists of a large room and may have been used as a trading floor.*

among a complex of granaries, woolhouses and malthouses. Elmes and Deven were leading merchants with commercial premises nearby (Elmes's granary was mentioned in 1470), and most likely this was a speculative development, intended to give visiting merchants a meeting place and accommodation for their goods, pack animals and themselves. A north-south lane between the building and the churchyard formerly linked Hart Street with New Street, which helps explain the imposing west façade: the middle floor, entered from this side, would have been the most important room, perhaps the trading floor. The relationship with the *Red Lion* buildings further suggests large-scale commercial development, involving adjoining riverside properties.

Whatever its origins, the building's only proven use is as a school house from the 16th century, and it was still known as the Old Grammar School in the 1920s. The modern name reflects 19th-century speculations about its use – speculations which on closer scrutiny seem to be supported neither by the documents nor by the building.

Figure E *The three-storeyed riverside elevation, originally double-jettied, and with a long row of windows to the top floor. The projecting wing was a near contemporary addition. The ground floor was originally an open-fronted storage space or shelter, with a substantial flint retaining wall at the back, and posts supporting the front jetty of the first floor. The porch and most windows are modern.*

Further Reading: Hall, L, and Moir, J, 'The Chantry House, Henley-on-Thames: Report and Survey' (TS Report for PCC, 2004); Steane, J, Gibson, R and Cottingham, A, *The Chantry House and the Oldest Part of the Red Lion* (Henley Hist. & Archaeol. Group 1994); Dunn, M, *The Chantry House at Henley-on-Thames: Archaeological Analysis of a Late Medieval Timber-Framed Building* (BEAMS Ltd 1999).

Figure 29 Henley church's importance by the late 12th century was reflected in its emergence as the centre of a rural deanery: an administrative grouping of parish churches presided over by a rural dean. This early 13th-century rural dean's seal from Henley shows an angel, probably a reference to the Annunciation since Henley church was dedicated to the Virgin Mary.

1337–40 acquired both Henley and Fillets manors. Moleyns secured additional manorial rights including the right to a private gallows, and his unenviable reputation may explain why the town warden was briefly called 'mayor', as part of a show of strength and defiance on the part of the guild. By contrast, there were some striking examples of co-operation between lord and townsmen, who both stood to gain from a prosperous urban economy. In 1328–9 Hugh d'Audley unequivocally backed the town's claim to tolls from London merchants trading there, while the new fair grant in 1440 seems to have been jointly secured by the lord, warden and guild.[49]

THE LIFE OF THE COMMUNITY

As with many towns, much of the evidence for Henley's medieval communal life revolves around religion. Henley church was relatively wealthy, its land and tithes worth over £13 a year in 1291, and for the most part it was served by high-status rectors who did not always live in the town. There seems, however, to have been a fairly large church establishment. Assistants were mentioned frequently, and in the early 16th century there were at least five chaplains besides the rector, alongside additional clergy in lower orders.[50]

Some priests were employed in the various chantries and religious fraternities recorded in the town. Chantry priests were normally engaged under the terms of a parishioner's will to say masses for their soul, but in Henley chantries in Henley church associated with the chapels of the Blessed Virgin and St Catherine assumed wider communal significance, and from the 14th century were administered directly by the guild. The chapel of the Virgin became effectively a guild chapel, and it may be significant that it was built shortly before 1311, just around the time that the guild was establishing

Figure 30 St Leonard's chapel on the north side of Henley church, built by the wealthy merchant John Elmes shortly before his death in 1460. Elmes requested burial there, and left money for a priest to say daily masses for his soul. Much of the town's communal life revolved around the church and religious festivals, though secular festivities are also recorded.

its autonomy. St Catherine's chapel acquired additional communal functions in the late 15th century, when the town's weavers (reflecting St Catherine's association with spinners and other craftsmen) kept a taper burning before the altar there. Around the same time a group of townspeople established a Fraternity of the Altar of Jesus, similar in purpose to the religious associations found in many late medieval towns. Members, who included women as well as men, paid a small fee, and the Fraternity acquired its own vestments, plate, and altar images: probably it was housed in the church's south-east chapel, which was rebuilt around that time. Individual townspeople also enriched particular side-altars or endowed chantries, among them the prominent merchant John Elmes (d. 1460), who built the chapel of St Leonard on the church's north side. Four 'priests' chambers' in the churchyard were mentioned in 1553, though their association with the so-called Chantry House on the churchyard's east side may be spurious (see Panel 4).[51]

Henley's guild records hint at the popular religious festivals common to most towns by the later Middle Ages. In the early 16th century there was an Easter 'Resurrection Play' presumably dramatising the events around Christ's tomb, while 'gear' for a Corpus Christi pageant and procession was mentioned in the 1530s and 1540s. At this the consecrated host would be processed along the streets, probably accompanied (as in some larger towns) by banners, lighted tapers, images of saints, and possibly floats. Other diversions, though still tied to the religious calendar, were of a more secular nature. In 1498 the burgesses agreed that the warden should perambulate the town's main streets over Christmas 'to drink, make merry and visit his neighbours' houses', an attempt, perhaps, to promote social cohesion at a time when the guild's authority was under pressure. Games at Hocktide (the second Monday and Tuesday after Easter) included a version of the popular 'wife gathering', at which groups of local men 'captured' local women (and vice versa) and released them on payment of a fine for the church coffers. Whitsuntide games included a King Game or Play, probably involving election of a mock king or queen for the day, and from the 1490s to 1520s there was a Robin Hood game, found also at nearby Thame. On such occasions the normal rules of social precedence and propriety were temporarily suspended or inverted, albeit in carefully controlled ways and with proceeds going usually to the church. By contrast, everyday gambling, dicing and cards were frowned on by the town authorities, probably as much for the risk of violence as on moral grounds. Thus in 1510 Nicholas Wellington undertook to prevent 'dice, cards, and other illicit games' from being played on his premises, under pain of imprisonment and a 10s. fine.[52]

Building in Timber, Flint and Brick

In the Middle Ages most buildings were constructed from local materials. Timber is widely available in the Chilterns and was the most natural building material. Chalk and flint are also plentiful, though chalk is not generally suitable for exteriors, and flint needs square-cut stones or bricks to stabilise the angles of buildings. Flints were, however, used extensively for cellars and foundations, and the *Old White Hart* has a chalk-lined cellar. Good building stone had to be expensively imported, usually by river, and was confined to important buildings such as the church or the medieval bridge, where flints were used with regularly cut stone blocks or ashlar (Panel 1).

Only a small proportion of Henley's medieval buildings survive, so that caution is needed when generalising about their construction. The town's surviving timber-framed houses are in the box-frame tradition (Fig. A), in which cut and squared timbers were prepared, marked up, and assembled as roof trusses and wall panels. These were erected on site, and the framing forming the side and end walls was usually filled with wattle and daub. Many such houses were jettied, the joists of the upper floor carrying the upper storey (or storeys) out beyond the ground-floor rooms. This gave greater stability, and added space to the prestigious upper floors.

Medieval roof structures took various forms. Henley's roofs display an eclectic mix, which perhaps reflects the varying influences experienced in a trading town. The commonest is the side purlin roof (Fig. B), but there are examples of crown-post roofs (Fig. C) at 20 Bell Street (*Ye Olde Bell*, built 1325), at Baltic Cottage (built 1438) and the *Old Broad Gates*. Timber lends

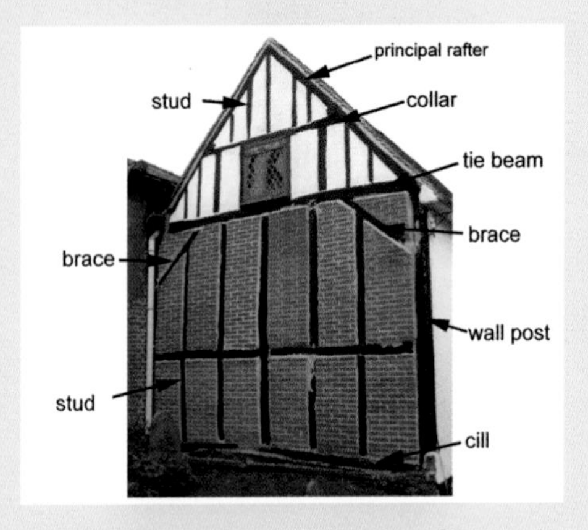

Figure A *The gable end of a box-framed building in Church Avenue. The tall rectangular panels have been infilled with bricks, which probably replaced earlier wattle-and-daub. The frame consists of tall corner posts; a horizontal cill beam at ground level, on which the posts and studs stand; a tie beam holding the posts together at eaves level; and principal rafters forming a triangular roof truss (one of several trusses along the length of the building). A collar runs between the principal rafters, bracing the truss.*

Figure B *Part of a traditional side-purlin roof, with a vertical crown strut and two raking struts supporting the collar. The purlins run horizontally along the length of the roof, supporting the common rafters. Added strength is given by the wide curved wind-braces, and by the arch-braces just visible below the long tie-beam. The high-quality framing shown here is hidden inside 44 Hart Street (Speaker's House) (Figure 34). The brick stack is a much later insertion.*

Figure C *(Above left) The trees for the crown-post roof of 20 Bell Street were felled in 1325, making it Henley's oldest known surviving house. The slender hexagonal shaft stands on a large central tie beam; its four curved braces spring from the richly carved capital and support the roof timbers. The unusually early date and the quality of the carpentry are strong indicators that it was a high-status building belonging to a wealthy owner, of which only this part survives.*

Figure D *(Above centre) The north entrance gate of the Ewelme Almshouses (c.1430–50) shows the virtuosity of 15th-century brickmakers and bricklayers, who used a variety of moulded and shaped bricks to decorative effect.*

Figure E *(Above right) Granary Cottage at Thameside: a unique example of the combined use of flint, stone, brick and timber. All except stone are materials easily found locally.*

itself to elaborate carved decoration, and examples can be seen both inside and outside Henley's higher-status medieval buildings (e.g. the Chantry House, Panel 4). At 76 Bell Street (Fig. 32), dated to 1405, mighty arched braces rise from posts carved to resemble stone pilasters with capitals, supporting a roof structure embellished with cusped wind braces.

Brick was available from the numerous kilns around Nettlebed, which drew on local resources – clay, sand, and wood (for fuel). Around 1430 the duke and duchess of Suffolk used brick for the almshouse and school which they founded at nearby Ewelme (Fig. D). In Henley, bricks were first used for chimney stacks in timber buildings, helping to safeguard against fire. By 1531 they were being used as walling material at the *Old White Hart* (Panel 6), in combination with timber framing. Even so, it was not until the late 17th and 18th centuries that brick became the dominant building material in and around Henley (see Chapters 6 and 8).

Figure F *Early handmade bricks at Ewelme School. Their size (only 1½–1¾ inches thick) and the wide lime-mortar joints are typical of the period, and can help us to date early brick buildings. Here the bricks are laid randomly, without any recognisable bond. (For 1530s brickwork laid in a regular English bond, see Panel 6,* Old White Hart*).*

Figure 31 This 12th-century stone doorway, with characteristic zig-zag moulding, was re-used in a later house in Hart Street, as shown in the drawing; probably it came from the nearby church during 17th- or 18th-century restoration work. It was later moved to Fawley Court. Stone is rare in Henley, and was only imported for high-status structures.

SECULAR BUILDINGS

Constant rebuilding has obscured much of the evidence for Henley's medieval buildings. Duke Street and the southern part of Bell Street were largely rebuilt in the late 19th and early 20th centuries, while many of the buildings along Hart Street and Market Place now have 18th- to 20th-century brick and stone façades or early 20th-century mock timber-framing. Even so, enough survives (much of it hidden behind later fronts) to construct a general picture, which can be amplified from written evidence and from drawings and photographs. Most of the town's buildings were certainly timber-framed, although flint, chalk, brick and (very occasionally) stone were also used (Panel 5).

The dating of medieval buildings has made great strides in recent decades thanks to dendrochronology, a technique based on scientific analysis of growth-rings in the building timbers. Several Henley houses have now been dated using these methods, though as not all timbers are suitable many still have to be dated on stylistic grounds. This can be difficult, since construction techniques varied from region to region and often remained in use for centuries. Many of Henley's surviving medieval houses appear to date from the 15th century, which was clearly a period of considerable building activity; nonetheless, some are earlier, and others substantially later.[53]

Medieval Houses

As we have already seen, trading and domestic premises were closely intermingled in a town like Henley. First, though, what sort of houses did Henley's medieval inhabitants live in, and how many of them survive?

Most medieval houses were grouped around a central hall, which was open to the rafters and heated by a central open hearth. Smoke escaped through an opening in the roof, often leaving tell-tale signs of sooting which can sometimes help us identify houses of medieval origin. Usually there were two-storeyed wings at either end, one containing service rooms and the other private chambers. The main entry was generally through a passage at the hall's lower (or service) end.

In Henley, a good example is the building on Bell Street (Figure 32), now concealed behind a later front and divided into Nos 74, 76 and 78. Here the hall's roof and (concealed) timber-framing have been dendro-dated to 1405, making this one of the oldest houses so far discovered in Henley, though the storeyed cross wings were rebuilt slightly later. The work includes high-quality decorative carving, indicating that it was probably built for a wealthy merchant.[54]

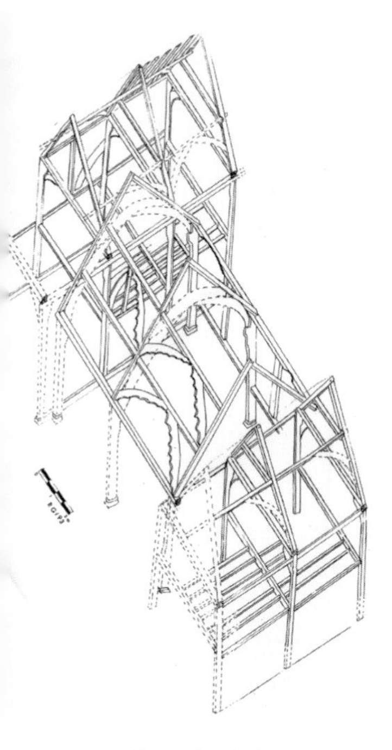

Figure 32 Like many of Henley's medieval timber houses, that at 74–78 Bell Street is hidden behind a later brick façade. The former hall (dated to 1405) is in the central part, now painted pink, and was originally open to the roof. The former cross wings to either side were always two-storeyed. Entry was through the passage on the hall's south (right) side. The drawing (by Ruth Gibson) shows the house's medieval construction; dotted lines show timbers which have disappeared, but whose presence can be inferred from standing remains.

Several other buildings show traces of similar origins. Near the market place, Nos 20/22 Hart Street probably also began as a hall and cross wing, though the roof has been replaced and the hall has had an upper floor inserted (Figure 33). Speaker's House nearby (Figure 34) was probably the cross wing for a hall at No. 46, and has an impressive medieval roof structure: possibly it contained the private chamber, with services (now gone) beyond No. 46. The site, by the church and bridge, was a prominent one, and in its original form this was probably a building of high status. Nearer the river, Baltic Cottage (on the south side of Friday Street) has been dendro-dated to 1438. The ground floor lies 1½ feet below the modern street – a further indication of the house's age – and here there is an impressive crown-post roof (see Panel 5), smoke-blackened from a former open hearth at ground-floor level. Before it received a new east wing around 1800 the house may have adjoined the river frontage, and this, too, was probably a merchant's dwelling. More humble medieval dwellings are less likely to have survived, though a terrace of small one-bay hall-houses on Gravel Hill, built probably in the early 15th century, may be an exception (Figure 14).[55]

In towns, pressure on space sometimes led to houses being built gable-end to the street, with the hall positioned behind and other rooms arranged in a variety of ways. One Henley example is the *Bear* on Bell Street, where a small hall dated to 1438 survives at the back. Overall, though, not enough survives to know how typical this was. Property deeds show that burgage plots were divided and combined from an early date, giving Henley's wealthier inhabitants the chance to assemble quite wide plots, and certainly the houses mentioned

Figure 33 Nos 20/22 Hart Street began probably as an open hall and two-storeyed cross wing. The hall (on the right of the picture) still has its medieval cross-passage entry, while the wing has its curved arch braces, and a projecting first-floor jetty which added space and stability. In its first-floor east wall is Henley's earliest known timber window (*c.*1400), now blocked by the adjoining building. The window is narrow, with only its cusped head showing; it was unglazed, but shows evidence of a vertical sliding shutter to keep out the cold.

above had fairly generous frontages. The hall and cross wing at 20/22 Hart Street measure 32 feet, while the Bell Street house – well away from the market area – occupied a frontage of 60 feet.[56]

All these houses had smoky open hearths, although in towns it was not uncommon for some houses to have fireplaces relatively early. No medieval fireplaces are known in Henley, though a 15th-century house at 93/95 Bell Street (again concealed behind a later front) probably had one. This, too, was most likely a wealthy merchant's house, its timbers moulded with double hollow chamfers on the posts and beams, and its southern part may originally have contained an open hall. But if so it had no central hearth, since the medieval roof-truss in the attic has no sooting. Possibly this end was built as a hall for reasons of tradition and prestige, its comfort improved by a fireplace with a flue, as in the new hall of the *Old White Hart*, built *c.*1530. Most of the town's surviving medieval houses acquired fireplaces only piecemeal, as part of a widespread process of rebuilding from the 16th century (Chapter 6). Baltic Cottage, for instance, was upgraded with the insertion of a large central chimney stack and the addition of a cross wing in 1538.[57]

Figure 34 Speaker's House in Hart Street, which probably began as a wing for an adjoining hall at No. 46 (on the left); possibly it contained the private chamber. Its roof structure has an impressive crown strut fan truss with wide wind braces. The gable beyond belongs to an early/mid-17th-century house, forming an impressive group opposite the church at the eastern entrance to the town.

Few of these buildings retain their original timber façades, which must once have been as imposing as some of the interiors. Elsewhere in the town, timber-framed structures survive behind front ranges which have been entirely rebuilt – an economical way of updating an old house with minimal upheaval for its inhabitants. Longlands in Hart Street, 20 Market Place, and Saragossa House in New Street all acquired 18th-century fronts, impressive reception rooms, grand staircases, and fireplaces on all floors, while the old timber-framed wings at the back continued as kitchens and service ranges. Another example is 35 Market Place, where the creation of the access to Greys Road car park exposed long timber ranges hidden from public view for centuries.

Commercial Buildings

The distinction between commercial and domestic buildings was never clear cut in medieval towns. Tradesmen and craftsmen worked mostly at home, either in the house itself or in outbuildings and workshops on the back plot, and many had shops or stalls at the front (see Figure 22). The structural evidence has usually been lost, but 14th-century property deeds describe several houses with ground-floor shops fronting the street, and domestic accommodation above or behind. In 1341 a building at the crossroads had an 'upper corner room' above a stall or shop occupied by William Remenham, while in 1346 a shop or stall in High Street had a solar or upper chamber above and another chamber behind.[58]

Upper floors in medieval towns were often used for storage. Barnaby Cottages on New Street (Figure 13), built as two houses *c.*1450–1500, have high-quality timber framing and very substantial floor joists, probably for heavy goods storage. Cellars, too, were used for goods, even in a town as low-lying as Henley. A shop or workshop in the Middle Row had a cellar in 1487, while a surviving example at the *Old White Hart* has a medieval chalk-block vault with chamfered ribs. Many others have substantial flint walls, some with quoins or relieving arches in narrow (therefore early) brick, while another at 40 Hart Street has some rare brick vaulting. At the *Angel on the Bridge*, a segmental flint-and-stone arch of the medieval bridge serves, with its adjoining abutments, both as part of the cellar and as foundations for the pub's north front wall (Panel 1).[59]

Figure 35 Tudor and Anne Boleyn Cottages on New Street: small remnants of a good-quality, 15th-century, jettied house with cross passage, of a type once commonplace in the town. Unlike so many Henley houses, it does not hide its age and craftsmanship behind a brick or stucco exterior. The passage now gives access to a further seven cottages, built on the burgage plot at the rear.

Nothing survives of the granaries which lined the waterfront by the early 14th century, though there are some later remains at 67–73 Friday Street and 10 Thameside. Built in at least two stages, these long jettied ranges (partly dendro-dated to 1549) appear to have been designed for storing heavy goods at first-floor level, as shown by their large flat and square-laid joists. By contrast, the ground-floor ceiling beams have decorative stops and chamfering, suggesting that these rooms were for residential or trading use rather than mere storage. The buildings were still used as granaries in 1790, when they were mentioned as the starting point for a perambulation of Henley's boundaries. Another possible survival is the so-called Chantry House near the church (*c.*1475–1500), which on its east side opened towards the river and may have been used for commercial purposes. Its date and function remain uncertain, however, and by the 1550s its upper floors were apparently used as a schoolhouse (see Panel 4).[60]

A particularly important class of commercial buildings was Henley's medieval inns, which from the 15th century were

The *Old White Hart*: A Medieval Henley Inn

Though many Henley inns are recorded from the 15th century, only the (*Old*) *White Hart* (mentioned from 1428–9) retains substantial medieval work and a traditional courtyard plan. The existing lodging ranges date from the 1530s, but as the plan is typical of many other medieval inns it may have been built in this form at the outset. Recent investigation (including dendrochronological dating) has increased our understanding of how the buildings evolved, shedding new light not only on the *White Hart* but on Henley's wider economic fortunes.

Courtyard and Front Range

Like most medieval inns, the *White Hart* is arranged around a courtyard entered through a gateway from the street (Fig. A). The front range is the oldest part, with a street frontage of some 75 feet (probably three medieval burgage plots). Below is a vaulted chalk-lined cellar with chamfered ribs, probably dating to *c.*1300; in the roof above the present carriage-arch area are remains of two medieval crown posts (see Panel 5), both of them once painted, and with sooting from a former open hearth below. The present large carriage arch was probably built with the lodging ranges in 1530–1, and most likely replaced a narrower passage.

The Tudor Lodging Ranges

New lodging ranges were built around three sides of the courtyard in 1530–1, running back around 290ft from the street. Together they contained some 22 guest chambers, built above stables and service rooms and reached from an external timber gallery, which may have run uninterrupted around the whole yard. The gallery probably also served for watching public entertainment, and projected over the yard by up to a metre – further at one point in the east range, where it accommodated a privy for guests. Despite this luxury the chambers seem to have had no fireplaces, although horses below would have generated warmth. The decay of the ceiling beams in the former stables may have resulted from the destructive ammonia vapours generated by the animals.

Most of these ranges are of narrow, hand-made 'Tudor' bricks (Fig. D). Presumably this represented a major investment, as bricks were still a luxury: this is the earliest known brickwork in Henley. The gallery walls, however, are timber framed.

Figure A *The courtyard of the* Old White Hart, *looking south to the carriageway and Hart Street. On the left is one of the 16th-century lodging ranges with its projecting first-floor gallery (now filled in), and the projecting former privy. On the right is the 16th-century hall, originally open to the roof but with a brick fireplace in its south wall.*

Figure B *Three carved balls on a corbel in the hall, perhaps associated with St Nicholas of Bari, patron saint of wayfarers – appropriate in an inn for travellers by road and river.*

Figure C *Reconstruction of the 1531 hall on the courtyard's west side, with its central arch-braced truss, first-floor outside gallery, and gable-end brick fireplace. The drawing is based on the surviving structure, though the brickwork, tiles and internal flooring are all conjectural. The brick front wall, windows, and later internal features have been omitted to give a clearer idea of how the building may have looked in its original form. (Drawing by kind permission of Hume & Son, © K.F. Hume)*

The Hall

Part of the new west range had no upper chambers. Instead there was a two-bay hall, open from floor to apex, with a central arch-braced truss with decorative mouldings (Figs B and C). The hall had two long windows high up in the brick west wall, and a wide brick arch for a fireplace in the south gable. Possibly it replaced the earlier smoke-filled hall in the front range, which was remodelled to provide the upper rooms and wider carriageway that modern travellers required.

The *White Hart* and the town

What prompted these improvements, which must have required a considerable financial outlay? The names of the owner, innkeeper and builder are unknown, but the investment fits with other evidence for an economic upturn in 16th-century Henley, as the grain trade revived and population increased. With merchants and other consumers drawn to the town's shops and market the *White Hart* occupied a prime location, and continued to serve the town and its visitors into modern times.

Figure D *1530s brickwork in the west wall, laid in English bond (alternate rows of headers and stretchers), and with a diaper pattern picked out by using over-fired 'blue' bricks. This became increasingly fashionable during the 16th century. Though brick later became ubiquitous, this is the earliest that has so far been discovered in Henley. (Photo Derek Toms)*

Survey work by Ruth Gibson and members of the Oxfordshire Buildings Record and Henley Archaeological & Historical Group; dating by the Oxford Dendro Laboratory (report 35/2008) mentioned in increasing numbers (above). Of those which can be identified, most, like the *Catherine Wheel* on Hart Street, have been altered beyond recognition, while others, despite containing medieval fragments, may not have become inns until much later. Neither the *Broad Gates* in Market Place nor the *Bear* in Bell Street are recorded as inns before the mid-17th century, though the former has a medieval crown-post roof (see Panel 5), and the latter a heavily smoke-blackened rear hall (with a smoke-bay) dated to 1438. The hall was enlarged in 1590, probably to serve as a kitchen when the building became an inn. The *Red Lion*, which may have been an inn by 1532, similarly has three timber-framed first-floor chambers attached to the south wall of the medieval Chantry House (Panel 4). By far the best preserved example is the *Old White Hart*, which although much altered still retains its 1530s courtyard plan (Panel 6).[61]

Moving On

Over the last three chapters we have gradually built up a portrait of medieval Henley, encompassing its planned origins, its emergence as an inland port, its inhabitants and buildings, and its daily life. Many of the themes explored in these pages continued well beyond the Middle Ages, in particular Henley's involvement with the Thames river trade. Nonetheless, the 16th and 17th centuries saw an important new phase, marked not only by the massive social and religious upheavals of the period, but by more local shifts in commerce and the river. It is to these – beginning with new developments in Thames navigation – that we now turn.

Figure 36 Timber-framed and jettied former granaries at the corner of Friday Street and Thameside, now private houses. Dating partly from the early/mid-16th century, they are the sole remnants of the granaries and warehouses which lined the waterfront throughout the Middle Ages. Baltic Cottage, built as a hall house in 1438, can be seen on the extreme left, with its later rendered façade and large central stack.

Chapter 5 Opening the River: Trade and Navigation 1540–1700

Throughout the Middle Ages, Henley benefited above all from its unique position in relation to London. As the effective head of Thames navigation, it became one of the conduits through which goods were funnelled in and out of the growing capital: the bedrock of the vibrant small town described in the preceding chapters.

But from the 16th and 17th centuries, with the reopening of commercial navigation to Oxford and beyond, that pre-eminence slipped away. For a town so intimately bound up with London and the river, the consequences could have been catastrophic. Disaster was averted first by increased metropolitan demand as London continued its inexorable expansion, and second by the development of a home-grown malting industry, which like much else in the Chilterns was also geared to the changing demands of the capital. As a result, Henley's long-established role in the river trade survived in modified form, while its close relations with London – not only in matters of trade, but socially and culturally too – continued unabated, as we shall see in the following chapter.

First though, how and why did the patterns of trade and navigation which had so benefited medieval Henley begin to shift, and how did this affect the trading life of the town? The story is an interesting one, encompassing pioneering bargemen, major feats of engineering, and far-reaching changes way beyond Henley itself.

OPENING THE RIVER

In the summer of 1635, the Oxford scholar Thomas Crosfield made the following entry in his diary: 'The last of August 1635 a barge was brought up the Thames to Oxford, which was the first ever came.' The statement was not literally true: river traffic made the journey frequently in the early Middle Ages, before the river's upper stretches became increasingly tortuous and obstructed. But this was certainly the first barge to complete the journey in living memory, and possibly for 180 years or more. How and why did this change come about?[62]

By the mid-15th century, if not before, serious commercial traffic to Oxford had probably ceased altogether. Yet in the 1560s the river was certainly passable as far as Culham, some 10 miles downstream from Oxford. We know this from an unusually

Figure 37 London and the Thames in 1647, by the Bohemian etcher Wenceslaus Hollar. Old St Paul's (burned down in the Great Fire) is in the background; Paul's wharf, Broken wharf and Queenhithe, all used by Henley traders, are shown along the waterfront. On the left are two square-sailed Western barges, of a type familiar on the middle Thames (see Figure 41). The city's inexorable expansion, which saw the population grow from around 60,000 in the 1550s to 200,000 by 1603 and 575,000 by 1700, ensured continuing demand for goods channelled through upstream ports such as Henley.

detailed source which casts an illuminating window on the mid-16th-century river trade: the accounts of Thomas West of Wallingford, an enterprising young trader, barge owner and shopkeeper who died in the winter of 1573–4. West's probate inventory contains not just the standard list of household items, but extensive details of his business dealings. Debts owed him show that he had an extensive trade network stretching from Deptford below London to way beyond Oxford, with stockpiles of wood and coal stored on riverside wharfs at Pangbourne, Wallingford, Burcot, and Culham. Goods for Oxford were generally transferred to wagon at Burcot, where West had his own agent. His area of activity included Henley, where we find him dealing in barley, malt, fish and tar.[63]

West has been presented as a pioneer, his ability to penetrate so far upstream attributed partly to a portable winch mentioned in his accounts. This, it has been suggested, allowed him to haul himself upstream through semi-derelict flashlocks or weirs, and certainly when it needed repair in 1567 he was unable to proceed without it. But in fact this was probably a standard item on all river barges, either an onboard winch similar to that described in the accident at Hambleden lock in 1383 (see Panel 2), or a standard barrel-windlass used mainly for raising and lowering the mast. In reality, the river may have always remained passable for some vessels as far as Burcot or Culham, and the changes taking place were perhaps not so much technological as economic. Oxford, like Wallingford itself, was only just emerging from a long period of stagnation, which had probably made it uneconomical to ship valuable cargoes up the tortuous and neglected stretches of river beyond Henley. That a hard-headed trader like West now found it worthwhile suggests that the balance was shifting, and he may not, in fact, have been unique. In 1585 a petitioner in a dispute over flashlocks claimed that the number of barges on the lower Thames was 'increased from ten or twelve to fourscore', while the upper river had probably always remained open for shallow-draught barges and punts carrying local produce and cereal for mills.[64]

Even so, West may have needed an adventurer's nerve to navigate what must, after a century of neglect, have been a difficult and dangerous passage. The problem was compounded by the fact that barges were becoming larger. West's accounts tell us little about his vessel or his volume of trade, but according to a contemporary barges 'were become of greater burthen, almost double what they used to be', while bargemasters often 'laded them beyond reason'. If true, this helps explain why the relatively narrow Culham–Oxford stretch remained so difficult. Quite apart from the lack of maintenance, the gradient there is steeper than on any other

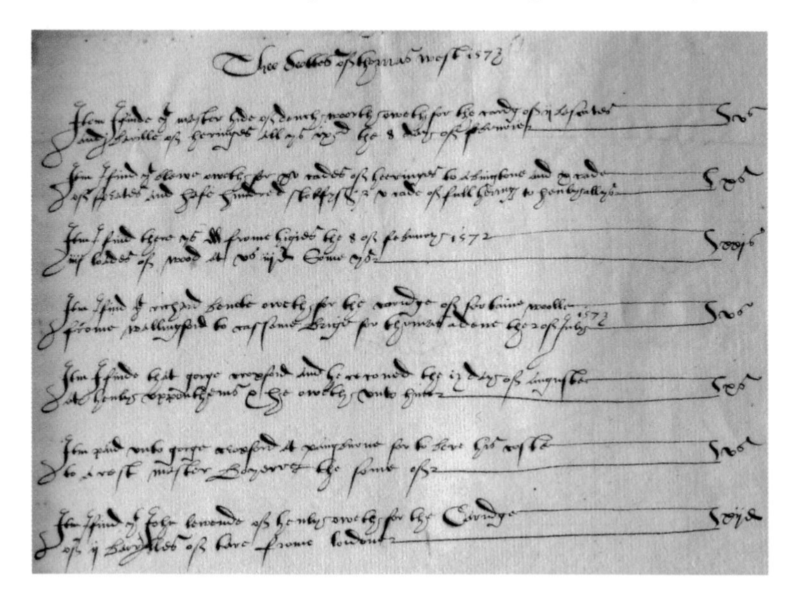

Figure 38 Part of the accounts copied into Thomas West's probate inventory, mentioning (final two lines) that John Lewende of Henley owed him 1s. for shipping two barrels of tar from London. The accounts reveal West's extensive trade network along the Thames, from Deptford below London to Culham near Oxford.

stretch of the river, making it hard to maintain an adequate head of water without especially large mill-dams.[65]

Whatever the case, West's activities are typical of a new-found interest in upstream navigation, which in the next century received the backing of state legislation. An Act of 1604 charged 18 commissioners (recruited from the counties of Oxfordshire, Berkshire, Wiltshire and Gloucestershire) to re-open the river from Burcot to Oxford, empowering them to raise taxes, engage labourers and engineers, and agree compensation. The work proved sporadic, but in 1623 a new Act set up a more efficient commission of eight (four each from the city and university of Oxford), and this time they were successful. The commissioners' most tangible achievement was the construction of the first three gated pound-locks on the Thames, at Culham, Iffley and Sandford, a technology which was still very new in England. Trans-shipment from Burcot (already cheaper than using roads alone) was still necessary in 1628, but a wharf was built at Oxford's Folly Bridge soon after, and the first barge, as we have seen, made its successful maiden voyage to Oxford just a few years later. The opening of the Burcot–Oxford section restored navigation not only from London to Oxford but much further. The 1623 Act expressly stated that the Thames westward from Oxford was for many miles 'already navigable and passable for boats of good burthens and contents', while in 1641 the water poet John Taylor succeeded in rowing as far as Cirencester, and dragging his boat across to the Severn – admittedly a far cry from navigating a river barge, but

Figure 39 Culham Lock in 1888, a modern-style poundlock with gates at each end. The original Culham lock, built by the Oxford-Burcot Commission between 1624 and 1636, stood three miles upstream towards Abingdon, and was one of the three earliest poundlocks on the Thames. Such locks, known originally as 'turnpikes', were still relatively new in England: the first was built on the Exeter Canal in the 1560s, and one on the River Lea in the 1570s. The lock shown here was built in 1809, after the stream passing through the original lock had been largely abandoned.

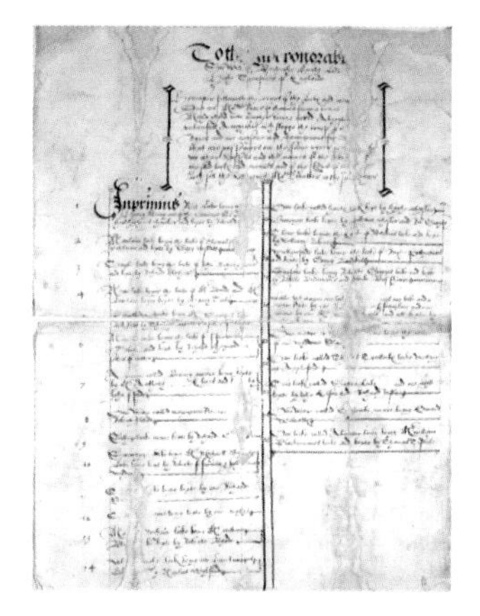

Figure 40 Part of John Bishop's survey of locks and weirs between Maidenhead and Abingdon, submitted to Elizabeth I's minister Lord Burghley in September 1580. Burghley seems to have taken a close interest in engineering works on the Exeter Canal and River Lea, which reflected the new expertise being developed in Italy and elsewhere in continental Europe.

symptomatic of the growing recognition of the potential for inland water transport.[66]

What factors drove these brave new initiatives? First must surely have been the regeneration and growing demands of Oxford, since the financial investment needed was considerable. Oxford City Council raised taxes and loans to meet its engineering costs, and once reopened the river and its new locks required constant attention, as the collapse of the Culham lock at Swift Ditch in 1650 clearly showed. What made it worthwhile were the anticipated benefits of a restored river trade with London. The 1623 Act expressly mentioned plans to export Headington building stone to the capital and Oxford's increasing need for cheap coal, fuel 'and other necessaries', while the 1604 Act looked forward more generally to the 'benefit and enrichment' of the city and county. A lesser reason, again symptomatic of the expanding economy, was to reduce increasing wear and tear on the medieval road system. Both Acts mentioned the problem, and in 1630 a Royal Proclamation forbad the use of four-wheeled carts on roads to London.[67]

That is not to say that the restoration of upstream navigation solved the familiar difficulties of medieval river transport. From Culham to London bargemen still relied on flashlocks (see Panel 2), and the old issue of lock-keepers charging excessive tolls or refusing passage persisted into the 18th century, despite government attempts to regulate it. So, too, did dependence on the weather, which could delay barges for weeks or months if water levels were too low or too deep. The real (and continuing) dangers associated with flashlocks were graphically illustrated in a series of petitions during the 1580s, some decades before the Oxford–Burcot Commission, but broadly contemporary with West's activities. Behind them was one John Bishop, who in an address to the queen's minister Lord Burghley alleged not only that locks on the Thames were increasing in number and size, causing more fatal accidents, but that many were illegal and run by unscrupulous owners. His slightly later and highly emotive attack in verse (addressed to the queen herself) did not go unchallenged, but demonstrates both the genuine risks faced by barge owners such as West and his successors, and the contemporary strength of feeling:

> One Farmer [the lock-keeper] hath a lock in store
> That hath made many a child to weep.
> Their mothers beg from door to door
> Their fathers drowned in the deep.
> At Farmer's lock four men be lost
> Of late I put you out of doubt.
> Three were drowned, the streams them tossed,
> The fourth he had his brains knocked out.[68]

HENLEY AND THE RIVER TRADE

During the mid- to late 16th century, as West plied his trade between London and Culham, Henley's medieval role as a major supplier of wood and grain to London continued unabated. Over a third of London's recorded grain imports were shipped from there during the 1560s–70s, and occasional complaints by the London authorities that grain or timber was being stockpiled at Henley show the importance still attached to the trade, despite occasional downturns. In 1559 the London mayor and aldermen were authorised to ship 6,000 loads of wood stored at Henley and Weybridge 'against the winter', and grumbled that water-carriage charges were being artificially inflated. In 1596 they demanded that corn held up at Henley should be released 'to the great relief of the City, which is at this time in great scarcity'.[69]

Even so the reopening of the river to Oxford and beyond fundamentally changed the position which Henley had enjoyed throughout the later Middle Ages. Now, for the first time in centuries, upstream towns could compete on more equal terms in conveying foodstuffs and fuel to the capital, while for goods going inland there was no longer any commercial imperative to transfer to road at Henley. Clearly the economic consequences could have been severe. What seems to have saved the town, as suggested above, were two related developments: first and most crucially the continuing expansion of London, which seems to have supplied enough demand to maintain Henley alongside the other riverside Chilterns ports; and second, the development at Henley (as at several other Thames-side towns) of malting, again geared to the demands of the capital. In addition, Henley and its neighbouring towns retained at least one natural advantage over their upstream rivals, despite the reopening. Even in the mid-18th century the river above Reading (where the River Kennet joins the Thames) seems to have been markedly shallower, and therefore more difficult for the largest barges to negotiate.[70]

Quantifying these assertions is difficult, since we have insufficient evidence to compare the volume of late medieval trade through Henley with that in the later 17th century. Only with the Parliamentary Reports of the 18th and 19th centuries does that sort of information become available. Judgements have therefore to be based on more general accounts of the river trade through Henley, and on evidence for the town's continuing economic vitality. Certainly Henley's population seems to have continued to rise during this period. In the 1520s, as we have seen, it was probably around a thousand, with perhaps 220 houses. By the 1640s the adult population alone seems to have numbered at least 1,500, and a century later (despite serious mortality from plague in the 1660s) there were thought to be 3,000 inhabitants and 500 houses. Even allowing for exaggeration, this hardly suggests a town in serious difficulty.[71]

The main strands of Henley's 17th-century economy were summarised in some well-known contemporary descriptions. Among the fullest is that of the London cartographer and bookseller Richard Blome, who in 1673 published a famous description of Henley in his book *Britannia*.

> Henley ... enjoyeth a considerable trade for malting; its inhabitants (which for the most part are bargemen or watermen) gain a good livelihood by transporting of malt, wood, and other goods to London, and in return bring such commodities as they and the inhabitants of the adjacent towns have need of, at easy rates; and its market, which is on Thursdays, is very considerable for corn, especially barley; which is brought them for their great malt-trade, there being oft-times in one day sold about 300 cart-load of barley.

Daniel Defoe, famous as the author of *Robinson Crusoe*, painted a similar picture a few decades later, describing Henley's 'great business ... by the trade of malt and meal and timber for London', which was shipped on 'great barges ... as the other towns do'. The reference to 'other towns' is significant: like Blome, Defoe emphasised that this was an economy in which riverside towns such as Reading, Maidenhead, Marlow, and even Abingdon all shared. In addition, the Chilterns towns benefited from the export of a 'vast quantity' of local beechwood, 'without which the city of London would be put to more difficulty than for anything of its kind in the nation'. Uses included cart wheels, turnery, chair-making, and (perhaps most important of all) fuel, both for private and industrial consumption and for the royal palaces – indeed Thomas West was supplying wood to the royal purveyors as far back as the 1570s, reflecting Elizabeth I's dislike of coal. Defoe's list of upstream cargoes traded through Reading and presumably Henley included coals, salts, grocery, tobacco, oils and heavy goods – again, not dissimilar from the goods traded earlier by West, save for the newly introduced tobacco.[72]

Unpublished documentary sources amplify the picture. Among the most useful are the probate documents (wills and associated inventories) which survive in increasing numbers from the late 16th and early 17th centuries. A rough count of the trades pursued by those making wills between 1530 and 1700 shows 30 of them (around 13 per cent of specified occupations) directly associated with the river, among them 26 bargemen and three fishmongers.

Figure 41 Jan Siberechts' view of Henley from the Wargrave Road (painted 1698) complements contemporary descriptions. The barge passing through Marsh Lock carries a cargo of logs and probably malt or barley, while a second barge is visible downstream. By the waterside near the town are stacks of wood awaiting loading. Smoke twisting from chimneys in the town may indicate the numerous malt kilns. The surrounding landscape features the resources singled out by contemporaries, with its small inclosed fields turned over to grain, livestock and hay, and plentiful woodland crowning the surrounding hills.

Another 29 (over 12 per cent) were maltsters, and three were timber merchants or woodmen (Figure 47). The real proportions were much higher, since people did not always accurately describe their own trade: many maltsters, for instance, simply called themselves yeomen in their wills. A more detailed survey of the period 1698 to 1706, based on data from the parish registers, has concluded that over a fifth of the working population were bargemen, and over a tenth were maltsters. Another 14 per cent were labourers, of whom some presumably loaded or unloaded barges at the Thames wharfs, helped haul vessels upstream, or worked in the maltings.[73]

Malting and Timber

By the 17th century, then, malt, grain and timber were the mainstays of Henley's economy and downstream river trade. How far back did this go, and how were these industries organised?

Unmalted barley had, in fact, been one of the high-quality brewing grains shipped through Henley to London throughout the Middle Ages. For medieval people ale was an important source not only of safe liquid intake but of nutrition, and in the later Middle

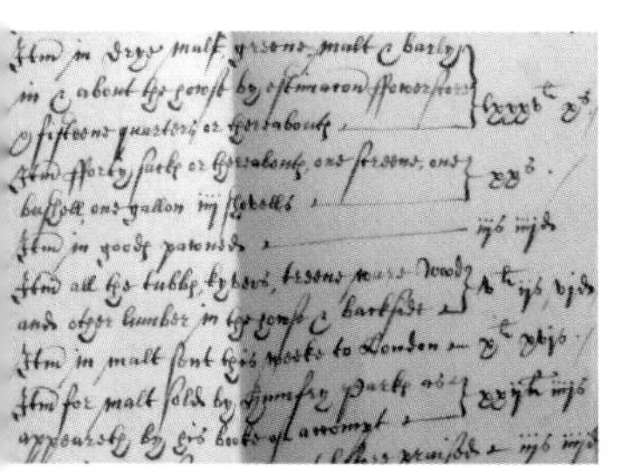

Figure 42 Part of the probate inventory of the Henley maltster John Morris (d. 1632), listing the moveable goods he owned at his death. The extract begins with 95 qrs of 'dry malt, green malt and barley in and about the house', valued at £85 10s. Further down is 'malt sent this week to London' (£10 16s.) and 'malt sold by Humfrey Parke' (£22 4s.). (Oxfordshire Record Office, MS Wills Oxon. 299/1/53)

Ages, as living standards rose, its consumption seems to have increased. By the late 14th century rural manors on the edge of London's supply zone were increasingly malting their own barley before sending it on to London, which (because malt is less bulky) reduced their transport costs. By the 16th century Hertfordshire, Bedfordshire, Cambridgeshire and Norfolk had become the most important malt-producing counties in England, playing a key role in supplying the capital's expanding brewing industry.[74]

Henley fits into this pattern, although here there is no clear evidence for large-scale commercial malting before the 1590s, when John Kenton was supplying malt to London and Windsor. This we know because the Windsor brewer John Alley alleged that Kenton had defrauded him, charges which Kenton vociferously denied. By the 1630s Henley had at least nine maltsters, some of whom had other interests as well, and in the late 17th and 18th centuries the number was even larger, possibly as high as 40 by around 1700. Wills and probate inventories not only help us to identify the maltsters, but give some indication of their wealth and business operations. John Grant, for instance, who died in 1662, left 60 quarters of malt in store worth £93, credits of £180 for 'maults at London', and £120 in ready money – a huge sum which had perhaps been recently paid him for a malt consignment, and which suggests a very substantial business. William Elton (d. 1674) left 110 quarters of malt and was owed over £100 from business contacts, many of them also in London. Other examples abound.[75]

Over all, the inventories suggest that Henley's 17th-century maltsters were among the town's most prosperous inhabitants, although much of their wealth (as in these examples) was usually bound up in their business, either in malt and grain, money owed, or in some instances as a part-share in a barge. Malthouses often adjoined their houses, which was normal for industrial premises in the period: indeed the Oxford antiquary Robert Plot reported that many malt kilns in Henley were ingeniously built up against kitchen chimneys, allowing the same fire to serve both. Nonetheless, the household furnishings recorded in some maltsters' inventories suggest both domestic comfort and a degree of social aspiration (see Chapter 6).[76]

The timber trade is well illustrated in the inventory of George Cranfield (d. 1667), a timber merchant whose estate of nearly £385 included stocks of ash, oak, beech and willow. Although based in Henley Cranfield operated on a large scale, buying in timber from Hambleden, Turville and Fawley (in Buckinghamshire), and leasing or owning wharfage at Sonning, Maidenhead, Hambleden and Medmenham, as well as at Henley and London. Timber shaped for shipbuilding was presumably destined for the London

Figure 43 Beechwood shipped through Henley in the 17th and 18th centuries came from throughout the Chilterns. Fawley woods, just north of the town, still covered an extensive area in the 1780s, as seen in this late 18th-century estate map. Neighbouring woods around Henley Park were cleared in the later 17th century, when the Whitelockes and others sold large quantities to London dealers.

naval dockyards. Cranfield cannot have been unique, though not all those involved in the trade expressly called themselves timber merchants. The prosperous trader Ralph Messenger, for instance, was called 'gentleman' at his death in 1668, though his will and inventory show him leasing woodland and stockpiling large quantities of timber and malt presumably for shipment. Back in the 1570s, Thomas West and his father were similarly involved in leasing a wood for felling, and sold timber and billet for over £400.

Yet not all wood sales required a local middle man. Ten thousand loads of firewood cut from Henley and Fawley woods in the 1630s seem to have been sold directly to a London woodmonger called Mr Brown, the carriage costs of £1,000 (presumably by river) met by the vendor, Sir Bulstrode Whitelocke. Even so, Whitelocke made a handsome profit of £3,000.[77]

Figure 44 Trade token (private coinage) issued in 1668 by the Henley fishmonger William Robinson (d. 1698), who had a house in Fisher Row in the market place, and went on to serve as town bailiff and mayor. The design includes a fish, possibly a dolphin. Several Henley tradesmen issued similar tokens, though this is the only one explicitly related to a river trade.

Henley's Bargemen

What, then, of Henley's bargemen? By the end of the 17th century this seems to have been the largest single source of employment, with numbers (based on births and burials in parish registers) probably rising. Yet this was not an entirely homogenous group. A few, as at Oxford or Reading, were part-owners of barges and presumably worked as contractors for local wood or grain merchants, drawing on hired labour or family members. Lawrence Green (1568), Thomas Doe (1592) and James Guille (1665) each owned a quarter share of a barge, while Nicholas Savage (1639) owned a set of barge poles. Some others had no equipment, and were perhaps hired barge-hands rather than bargemasters, although as a group they were not obviously poorer than those with their own barges. Possibly some of them worked with business partners or relatives, or even hired barges. The barges themselves were most likely built in London, where several Henley bargemen apprenticed their sons to shipwrights in the late 17th and early 18th centuries.

Taken as a whole, Henley's bargemen were not especially wealthy. This was, after all, a service trade reliant on the malting and timber industries, and much of the resulting profit seems to have been siphoned off elsewhere. The average value of their goods, as recorded in probate inventories, was around £26 before the Civil War, and around £15 later on – a fall which perhaps reflected increased competition on the newly opened river. Yet neither were the bargemen particularly poor. Most seem to have had houses of at least three to four rooms with adequate if basic furnishings, and at least two (like Thomas West in Wallingford) had shops. Nicholas Savage had £80 loaned out on bond, suggesting a tidy disposable income.[78]

In Oxford the barging community developed an increasingly separate identity, and by the 18th century was often viewed with suspicion. In Henley there is no particular evidence for this in the 17th century, although the nature of the work, with long periods spent away in often dangerous conditions, must have created a strong sense of cohesion. Presumably there was a distinction between the relatively prosperous bargemasters and the wider community of bargemen and river-workers, whose reputation for

Figure 45 The waterfront in Henley around 1690, a detail from a painting by Jan Siberechts (see Panel 7). Square-ended Western barges, their decks protected by canvas tarpaulins, lie tethered to the shore, which slopes to the water: the stretch shown here (from the bridge towards New Street) was not properly embanked until the 18th century. The buildings included storehouses and granaries, with most storage probably at first-floor level. Some goods and poles have been laid out on the shore, as described in later documents. (© Tate, London 2009)

roughness and violence, whether deserved or not, found its way into national legislation. A 1695 Act made barge owners liable for any damage caused by the 'rude and disorderly persons ... managing the said barges', whose activities were alleged to include illegal shooting and fishing, damage to locks and weirs, and stealing beer and cider from the cargoes. In Henley nothing in the corporation minutes suggests that disorderly behaviour was seen as a major problem, and what rulings it passed to regulate the barge trade were fairly routine. In 1585, for instance, the corporation instituted fines for the masters or owners of barges sailing on a Sunday, while in 1665 bargemen were forbidden to import goods from London during the plague. On the other hand the presence of such a large river community may well, as in some other towns, have contributed to the town's markedly Whiggish politics during the later 17th century, as we shall see in the next chapter.[79]

Change and Continuity

Despite the profound changes wrought on the river during the 16th and 17th centuries, Henley's traders found ways of continuing its long-established role as an inland port. Clearly there were modifications, in particular the development (not confined to Henley) of an important malting industry. But alongside the maltsters, the working community of bargemen, timber merchants and grain merchants continued their activities on the earlier pattern, against the changing background of increasing upstream water traffic.

But the upheavals of the 16th and 17th centuries were not confined to river navigation or London's growing economic demands. Throughout this period Henley, like the wider world to which it was so well connected, was changing in innumerable ways, reflecting radical shifts in religious and political outlook, in technology, art and architecture, and in the nature of society. All these developments were reflected in the 16th- and 17th-century town, whose role in many of the key national events of the period once again reflected its proximity to London and its location on a key transport artery. What other changes did the town see during this critical period, and what roles did it come to play (albeit fleetingly) on the national stage?

Chapter 6

Reformation and Revolution: Henley 1540–1700

Figure 46 The lawyer and Parliamentarian Sir Bulstrode Whitelocke (1605–75), whose family lived at Fawley and later at Phyllis Court. During the Civil War he commanded the Parliamentarian garrison at Henley, and despite his relatively moderate views achieved high office under Cromwell. He acquired Henley manor in the 1650s.

Between the early 16th century and the early 18th English government, society and religion experienced profound upheavals. Henley was affected by these changes like any other town, though here its position on a major transport artery and its close relations with London were additional factors, leaving it particularly open to new influences, and occasionally lending it political or military significance. Its place in the religious Reformation, the Civil War and the Glorious Revolution is outlined below, together with the development of its houses and buildings. First, though, what sort of people lived in Henley and the surrounding rural area during this critical period, over and above the maltsters, bargemen and timber merchants described in the previous chapter?

THE SOCIAL SCENE

Trades and Crafts

By the later 17th century perhaps a third of Henley's working population were bargemen or maltsters, reflecting the continuing centrality of London and the Thames in the town's commercial life. Over a tenth were labourers, of whom a large proportion were probably involved in the river trade or malting in one way or another. That leaves just over half (around 55 per cent) who earned their living in other ways.

Wills and probate inventories do not represent the whole population, but give some idea of the range of occupations (Figure 47). For the period 1531 to 1700, around 230 Henley wills describe the person's occupation explicitly. The largest single group (over a fifth) was involved in food and drink provision: butchers, bakers, brewers, and innkeepers or victuallers. In a town of probably over 2,000 inhabitants, with most of the working population engaged in full-time commercial activity, this is not surprising, and reflects a broad continuation of the medieval pattern. Commercial inns, as we have seen, were a feature of the town by the 15th century, and by the 1750s (when the town's licensed victuallers were first recorded systematically) there were at least 36 inns, pubs or alehouses in the town. Butchers were the next largest group, many of them still with stalls in Butcher Row. (A Quaker who unwisely preached near there in 1658 had butchers'

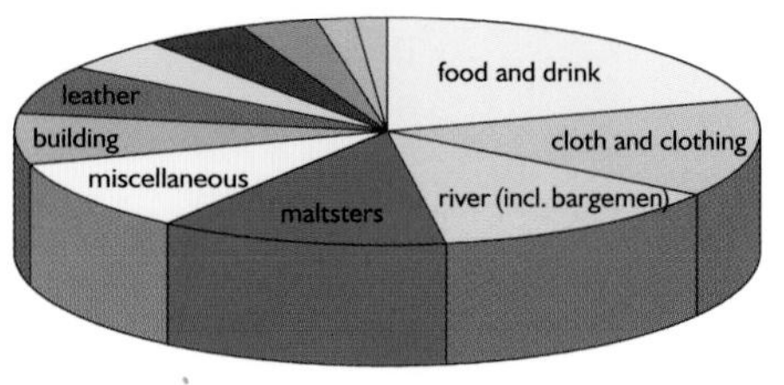

- food and drink (incl. butchers, bakers, innkeepers) (21%)
- cloth and clothing (incl. tailors, drapers, mercers) (14%)
- river trades (incl. bargemen) (13%)
- maltsters (13%)
- miscellaneous (10%)
- building (incl. carpenters, bricklayers) (7%)
- leather (incl. shoemakers) (7%)
- professionals (incl. clergy, surgeon) (5%)
- metal workers (incl. blacksmiths) (4%)
- labourers (3%)
- services (incl. barbers, apothecaries) (2%)
- timber trade (1%)

Figure 47 Henley wills proved between 1531 and 1700 give some indication of the range of occupations in the town. Figures exclude those for whom no trade was given, or who were described only as yeomen or gentlemen. Information in the parish registers suggests that the proportion of maltsters and especially bargemen may have been considerably higher, particularly by the later 17th century.

offal thrown at him by hostile passers-by.) Domestic baking and brewing still catered for some immediate needs, but buying in of bread and other essentials became increasingly common. Grocers started to be recorded soon after 1700, reflecting a widespread expansion of food retailing in provincial towns.

The next largest groups were those involved in textile or leather goods, building trades, and metalworking, again a pattern familiar from medieval Henley and small towns generally. Textile trades still included some small-scale manufacture, with a smattering of weavers, a shearman, and (in 1558) a dyer, but most were tailors or drapers, of whom 15 made wills between 1530 and 1700. Another seven were mercers, people who sometimes specialised in high-quality fabrics, but who often traded in a wide range of other goods as well. Ambrose Freeman, who died in 1662, had stock worth an astonishing £500, mostly fabrics, but including apothecary's wares, oilskins, Spanish leather skins, and groceries, much of it probably brought upriver. Most leather-workers were shoemakers or saddlers and horse-collar makers, who again produced everyday goods needed both by the townspeople and by those in the surrounding countryside. Three tanners recorded between 1599 and 1671 (including two members of the Osgood family) presumably helped supply these local craftsmen. Metalworkers, too, were dominated by traditional craftsmen such as blacksmiths, while a locksmith who died in 1639 no doubt served both the town and surrounding area. Building workers included not only the traditional carpenters and joiners but bricklayers and glaziers: a symptom of the new styles and materials which by the later 17th century were starting to transform Henley's physical appearance (see below).[80]

More exceptional was the wealthy merchant and glass manufacturer George Ravenscroft, who in 1674 was licensed to set up a glass manufactory at Henley in premises off Bell Street.

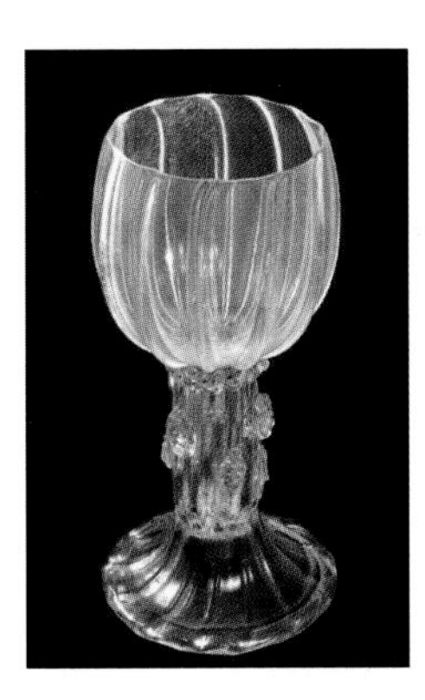

Figure 48 An example of Ravenscroft glass, manufactured by George Ravenscroft around 1675, possibly at the Henley glassworks. The hollow stem is decorated with six raspberry fruits, and bears Ravenscroft's seal (a raven's head).

Ravenscroft's role in the development of lead crystal is rightly celebrated, but his main production centre was in London and his association with Henley fleeting. As a Catholic he had links with the Catholic Stonor family of nearby Stonor Park, but was probably also attracted by the area's plentiful wood supplies and by easy transport along the Thames, which was far better suited than roads to delicate products such as glass. Some fine examples produced at Henley still survive and may have found a ready market in surrounding country houses, though Ravenscroft's business horizons extended far beyond the middle Thames.[81]

Another 72 of those making wills called themselves yeomen, which by the 16th century usually meant a farmer of moderate (and sometimes substantial) means. Some *were* farmers and may have lived in the parish's outlying rural part, but another was an innkeeper, and a significant number, to judge from their wills and inventories, were primarily maltsters. Such wills bring home the close continuing relationship between town and countryside in 16th- and 17th-century Henley. The bulk goods which flowed through its weekly market were predominantly agricultural – grain, malt and timber – and the same was probably true of the annual fairs. New September and November fairs granted in 1525–6 coincided, probably intentionally, with the barley harvest and the beginnings of the malting and brewing seasons, while another annual fair came to specialise in horses, and another in cheese.[82]

Finally, at the top end of Henley's urban hierarchy was a smattering of educated and professional people, whose numbers and social significance increased as the period wore on. Most were clergymen, though the surgeon Edward Stevens (d. 1663) presaged a trend which increased from the 18th century, and a 'musician', John Michell, died in 1639. Many more called themselves 'gentlemen', although the term (as with yeomen) can be misleading, since most were apparently merchants, traders or craftsmen made good. Nonetheless, they point to a veneer of prosperous inhabitants with social pretensions, reflected in well-furnished houses with probably at least one servant.[83]

But the social hierarchy did not stop there. On the fringe of the town and in country seats scattered around the area was a network of landowning gentry and aristocracy who, during the 17th century in particular, had a marked impact on local affairs. Who were these people, and how did they fit in?

Henley's Country Gentry

During the Middle Ages Henley manor was owned for the most part by large-scale landowners who lived elsewhere, and had little direct association with the town. Some owners of Phyllis Court lived locally, but otherwise the pattern of absentee lords continued into the early 17th century. Sir James Whitelocke, an eminent London-born judge and lawyer, bought the neighbouring Fawley Court estate in 1616–18, followed in 1622 by a part share in the Phyllis Court lands. His son Sir Bulstrode Whitelocke, another lawyer, went onto acquire Henley manor and park and nearby estates at Greenlands and Yewden, living first at Fawley Court and later at Phyllis Court itself, on the town's northern edge. Despite increasingly straitened circumstances (a legacy largely of the Civil War), the family continued there as Henley's most significant gentry family well into the 18th century.[84]

Figure 49 Part of the elaborate monument to the lawyer James Whitelocke (d. 1632) and his wife Elizabeth (d. 1631) in Fawley church, not far from Henley. Their house at Fawley Court, bought by Whitelocke in 1616–18, was ransacked during the Civil War, though their son Sir Bulstrode Whitelocke moved back there in the 1650s. The merchant and plantation owner William Freeman rebuilt it in classical style in 1684.

As a prominent lawyer and Parliamentarian who became (under Cromwell) Keeper of the Great Seal, Bulstrode was a national figure. But that did not prevent his continuing involvement with the area. His first legal work was for Henley townsmen, and around 1631 the corporation appointed him as counsel. An unsuccessful bid for parliament in 1640 was warmly supported by 'the town of Henley and the freeholders thereabouts', and he subsequently served as MP for nearby Marlow, as well as commanding the Parliamentary garrison at Henley during the Civil War. His earlier influence was reflected in an attempt in the 1630s to involve him in marketing a new and recently patented type of malt kiln in Henley, an apparently dubious scheme which Whitelocke rejected as 'illegal and dishonourable'.[85]

But the Whitelockes were not the only country gentry to play a role in local life. A little way south on the Berkshire bank, within easy view of Henley, was Perkes (later Park) Place, a country house owned (and subsequently rebuilt) by the local Draper family. Though clearly aspirational (and connected through marriage to the diarist John Evelyn), the Drapers were merchants involved in the Henley-based malt and brewing trade, with a wharf and a brewhouse in London – a good example of how new commercial money was increasingly displacing older wealth in the landed estates along the middle Thames. A little further south at Harpsden Court were the long-established Forsters, replaced in the 1640s by Whitelocke's friend and fellow lawyer Bartholomew Hall, while a little further east at Hurley were the aristocratic Lovelaces, also part of the Whitelocke circle. Among older families, the Catholic Stonors had long owned property in the town, and continued to ship timber from its wharfs. The owners of many of these estates formed part of a close social network, connected not only through class and lifestyle but through financial and business dealings. Their relations are evident in Bulstrode Whitelocke's diaries, a rich and entertaining source for national and local life.

Figure 50 The well-known diarist John Evelyn (1620–1706), whose daughter Susannah married one of the Draper family. Visiting Park Place in 1693, Susannah declared it her favourite of all the houses she had visited, 'upon the top of a very high hill, and ... before it at the bottom the prospect of the river Thames'. The Drapers were typical of the mercantile families moving into the Henley countryside during the 17th century.

Visits to 'Mr Hall's' were frequent, and in July 1648 we find the Halls and Whitelockes enjoying (with their servants) a family boat trip from Henley to Windsor – an early example of recreational use of the river. For light journeys road was both quicker and cheaper, though as Bulstrode himself noted 'this way by water is the most easy and pleasant'.[86]

Yet by the 1660s the financial position of many of these prominent landowning families was far from secure. Whitelocke himself suffered severely from the Civil War, which saw his houses at Fawley, Greenlands and Henley sacked or plundered, his estates damaged, and his legal business suspended. Many local landowners suffered similar problems, compounded in some instances by profligacy or incompetence, and in the Stonors' case by crippling recusancy fines. As a result, the later 17th century saw the increasing influence around Henley of a new breed of London-based bankers, money lenders and land agents, who through skilful manoeuvering extended their financial and landed interests along the river. The classic example is Sir Robert Clayton (1629–1707), who with his business partner John Morris amassed a fortune through offering credit to impecunious landowners, underpinned by mortgaging and interventionist estate management. Their dealings around Henley, spread over decades, won them estates at Hambleden and Hurley, and the Whitelockes, too, seem to have fallen within their orbit. Their Fawley estate was lost in 1678–9, sold to the merchant and West Indies plantation owner William Freeman.

This burgeoning commercial influence over the Henley countryside was not new. The wealthy London merchant (and sometime lord mayor) Sir John Spencer briefly owned Henley manor from 1599, while the Whitelockes themselves were descended from London merchants. Nonetheless, Clayton's activities illustrate the extent to which mercantile interests based on the Thames were increasingly infiltrating the social and cultural life of the area. The phenomenon was obliquely reflected in an enigmatic series of Henley landscapes by the Flemish painter Jan Siberechts, the background and significance of which have only recently started to be unravelled (Panel 7).[87]

RUNNING THE TOWN

During the Middle Ages Henley was run for the most part by its merchant guild, as we saw in Chapter 4. In 1525–6 the town obtained a confirmation of its rights from Henry VIII, which allowed the warden to be called mayor, but if the charter was ever implemented it seems to have made little difference in practice.

Jan Siberechts and Henley

During the 1690s the Flemish landscape painter Jan Siberechts (1627–*c.*1700) produced several enigmatic views of Henley and the River Thames. Unlike most such paintings, which celebrated the wealth and prestige of a particular landowner, the Henley series focuses on no single estate or country house and encompasses various viewpoints, subjects and moods. Most display a finely observed emphasis on the commercial and agricultural life of the area: Henley with its wharves, market and malt houses, the surrounding countryside with its fields, pastures and woodland, and above all the Thames as a working waterway, with its flashlocks, barges and cargoes. This suggests that the patrons were people with a commercial interest in the area, rather than the aristocrats and landowners who most commonly commissioned such landscapes.

Since 2001, research into the ownership of the various lands shown, combined with careful examination of the paintings themselves, has gone some way to unravelling the mystery, revealing a complex mesh of political, financial and family ties among local landowners, Thames merchants, City lawyers and financiers. Siberechts clearly moved in similar circles, cultivating not only aristocrats but merchants and lesser landowners to win his commissions.

One of the most famous paintings (Figure 41, dated 1698) is now thought to be associated with the Drapers, a well-connected mercantile family which acquired the Park Place estate (south-east of Henley) in the 1630s. Family members certainly commissioned work from fashionable artists and craftsmen including Dutch painters, and this view from Marsh Lock up the river to Henley is taken from their lands, celebrating

Figure A *'Landscape with Rainbow' (c.1690s), from a viewpoint north-east of Henley. Like the Wargrave Road view (Figure 41) this celebrates the commercial life of town and river, with its moorings, cargoes and Western barges. The double rainbow may be an allegorical reference to the Glorious Revolution of 1688, in which local families including the Whitelockes played a part. The Whitelockes may have commissioned this or an earlier version, while the Drapers commissioned a copy to go with their Wargrave Road painting. The odd perspective, which slightly distorts the geography, may be the result of combining different viewpoints, at least one of which was probably on the Whitelockes' land above Phyllis Court. (© Tate, London 2009)*

Figure B *Siberechts' 'View of a House and its Estate at Belsize in Middlesex' (dated 1696). Commissioned by the London goldsmith John Coggs, this is another example of Siberechts' work for upcoming wealthy merchants, and reflects their growing social aspirations. Compared with the Henley series, its depiction of a single country house and estate is more typical of what was by then a very popular genre. (© Tate, London 2009)*

Figure C *Jan Siberechts, painted by the French artist Nicolas de Largillière. (By permission of Nottingham City Museums and Galleries: the Castle Museum and Art Gallery)*

the commercial life of town and countryside. The elaborate draperies and textiles visible on figures in the foreground may be a pun on the family name. Probably it formed part of a pair with a companion view from the north-east (Figure A), and there may originally have been a lost central painting showing Park Place.

Another in the series (*A Prospect of the Thames near Henley*) was probably commissioned in 1697 by the wealthy London banker Sir Robert Clayton, and depicts the Thames-side estates in which he obtained an interest through skilful mortgaging and financial manoeuvering. Siberechts' minute detail parallels the rigorous land-surveying which made people like Clayton so successful, and probably appealed to these commercially-minded merchants, bankers and estate-managers. By contrast, the more lyrical and poetic of the Henley views may have been commissioned by local aristocracy such as the Lovelaces at Hurley, or the duke of Buckingham at Cliveden.

Sources: Wortley, L, 'Jan Siberechts in Henley-on-Thames', *Burlington Mag*. 149 (March 2007), 148–57; Wortley, L, 'City Merchants' Landownership around Henley-on-Thames and the Paintings of Jan Siberechts', in Galinou, M (ed.), *City Merchants and The Arts 1670–1720* (2004), 93–102; Hearn, K, 'Merchant Clients for the Painter Jan Siberechts', in *ibid*. 83–92.

Figure 51 The town's copy of the royal charter of 1568, which established a town corporation to replace the medieval guild. The initial E of the name Elizabeth contains a full-length portrait of the queen in full regalia. The new system of town government continued until 1722, when it was further revised under a charter granted by George I.

The system was finally overhauled in 1568, when for the first time the warden and burgesses were reconstituted as a town corporation with powers backed by royal charter.

The town's motives in seeking the charter may have arisen from the mid-16th-century Reformation. This was, of course, primarily a religious upheaval (see below), but much of the guild's accumulated property had been given by pious townsmen for purposes associated with the old religion, while the guild had also become enmeshed in running chantries and other pre-Reformation religious institutions. From the 1550s, with the brief exception of Mary's reign, all such practices were banned, and property given for their support was seized by the Crown. This made secular bodies such as Henley's town guild potentially vulnerable: the guild in Burford suffered similar problems, and had to repurchase many of its ancient properties during the later 16th century. Putting Henley's town government on a more secure footing was therefore very much in the town's interests, and the charter essentially rationalised the old system without fundamentally altering it. The elected warden and bridgemen remained, assisted by a new town council of 12 leading inhabitants. Crucially the town's property was confirmed, with the

Figure 52 The town seal adopted after 1568, showing a letter H below a ducal crown, and clouds above. The Latin legend reads 'Seal of the Warden of the town of Henley'. This seems to have replaced the medieval guild seal, which featured a lion rampant (Fig. 28).

new corporation given power to oversee the town, market, bridge, town gaol, and other affairs.[88]

Other changes were equally typical of the period. Throughout the Middle Ages care of the poor had remained primarily the responsibility of the Church; but with the dissolution of the monasteries, in a time of rising population and increased migration and vagrancy, new solutions became necessary, culminating in the Elizabethan poor law. Thereafter Henley, like any other town or village, was required to raise rates to support its poor, and by the 1570s appointed collectors or overseers on the standard pattern. Private charity from philanthropic townspeople continued through bequests in wills. At least 15 such charities were established between 1539 and 1700, many of them endowed with property administered by the corporation. In addition the town administered three sets of almshouses, replacing a late medieval predecessor. One, originally for eight people, was on the south side of Hart Street opposite the church, and was endowed by John Longland, bishop of Lincoln (d. 1547), a native of Henley. The others, in the churchyard, were endowed by the maltster Humphrey Newbury (d. 1665) and by Anne Messenger (d. 1670), the widow of a former warden.[89]

Education, too, benefited from local philanthropy. A school associated with the church was mentioned intermittently throughout the 15th and 16th centuries, and in 1604 the town obtained a royal charter to re-establish it as a grammar school, helped by a bequest from a prosperous Rotherfield Peppard farmer. But like most 17th-century grammar schools its curriculum was geared to a classical education, and only five years later a school better suited to the town's commercial needs – focusing on reading, writing and accounts – was founded by Dame Elizabeth Periam

Figure 53 The almshouses endowed by John Longland, bishop of Lincoln, shown here on their original site on the south side of Hart Street. They were rebuilt on the west side of the churchyard in 1830, three years after this drawing was made.

Figure 54 The imposing classical monument to Dame Elizabeth Periam (d. 1621) in Henley church. A daughter of Sir Nicholas Bacon, lord keeper of the Great Seal, Elizabeth came from an important legal, political and commercial family well known for its interest in learning. In 1609 she founded the Periam School in Henley, having settled at nearby Greenlands House after her husband's death. In 1620 she endowed a fellowship and two scholarships at Balliol College, Oxford.

(d. 1621), a recent incomer to the area (Figure 54). Both schools shared the so-called Chantry House in Henley churchyard, the grammar school occupying the top floor and the Periam school the middle one. Their governing bodies, typically for the period, were overwhelmingly secular, with members including the town warden, and gentry such as Bulstrode Whitelocke.[90]

REFORMATION AND RELIGION

Many of these social and institutional changes flowed in one way or another from the 16th-century Reformation – the great religious upheaval which in England replaced the late medieval Catholic Church with a new Protestant state religion. Henceforth Catholicism, still dominant through much of continental Europe, was officially viewed as both a political and an ideological threat, prompting the sort of paranoia associated in more recent times with the Cold War. In Henley there seems little doubt that some townspeople must have welcomed the changes. Lollard heretics (whose opposition to orthodox practices prefigured the Reformation) were established in the Chilterns and middle Thames by the mid-15th century, particularly around Amersham in Buckinghamshire, but also in Henley. These people formed a tight-knit network with connections far beyond the immediate area, fostered in part by itinerant preachers, but also by trade links along the river, which then as later acted as a conduit not only for grain and consumer goods but for ideas and books. The Henley smith William Ayleward (prosecuted in 1464) was one of several local Lollards with London trade connections, and in the early 16th century several later townspeople were still being punished for their beliefs, their names preserved by John Foxe in his famous 'Book of Martyrs'.[91]

Even so it would be misleading to depict Henley as necessarily a hotbed of heresy, and other Henley townspeople clearly felt differently. In 1539 (partway through Henry VIII's Reformation) the Henley corn dealer Thomas Wolley expressed his 'evil will for ... men of the new learning', and refused to allow his neighbours to hold a gospel-reading in his house. The reformer Miles Coverdale complained that 'beams, irons, and candlesticks' had still not been removed from the church, 'whereby the simple people believe that they will again be allowed to set up candles to images, and that the old fashion will return'. A stained-glass image of St Thomas Becket was still in the Lady chapel, and in the early 1540s the town guild still held its traditional Corpus Christi processions. Possibly the town was genuinely divided, although the majority most likely followed the line of least resistance, outwardly towing the current government line, and in their daily lives simply ignoring all but the most extreme differences over religion. Certainly most of Henley's rectors from the 1560s followed a cautious and middling course, at least in public. The chief exception was William Brice, a Presbyterian who served the church during the Cromwellian Commonwealth and was deprived after Charles II's Restoration. Thereafter, the Anglican Church in Henley settled for the most part into a period of quiet stability.[92]

Figure 55 John Fell, bishop of Oxford from 1676 to 1686, initiated rigorous enquiries into religious dissent in his diocese. Investigations by his predecessor Bishop Blandford in 1669 had already revealed a substantial Presbyterian meeting at Henley, allegedly frequented by soldiers and officers from Cromwell's disbanded New Model Army. (By permission of the Governing Body of Christ Church, Oxford)

That said, from the mid-17th century there were further signs of religious radicalism in the south-west Chilterns. Enquiries by the bishop of Oxford in the 1660s pinpointed this as one of three main areas of organised dissent, marked by a concentration of separatist groups dissatisfied with the Anglican establishment. Also noted were significant numbers of disaffected Presbyterian and Independent ministers, of whom many (like Brice) had lost their churches at the Restoration. The area's location on the fringe of the diocese and county may have been a contributory factor, attracting people keen to avoid the attention of the authorities. In Henley itself a short-lived Baptist group was mentioned in the early 1650s, and a more numerous Quaker group (including craftsmen and maltsters with London connections) met at a cottage in Northfield End by the early 1660s. Most important of all was a Presbyterian or Independent group, which met in the house of a London vintner and was said to have 300 members. Clearly it provided a focus for

Figure 56 The Friends' (or Quaker) meeting house at Northfield End. The main red-brick part on the right was rebuilt in 1894, but the timber-framed building survives from the group of cottages acquired in 1672, a decade or so after Quakers became established at Henley.

dissenters from far beyond the town itself, and formed the basis of a Congregationalist church which played an important role in Henley into modern times.

By the mid-18th century this group was eminently respectable, but in the 1660s–80s its suspected political as well as religious radicalism was sometimes too much for the authorities. The radical preacher Jeremiah Marsden (alias Ralphson), appointed minister in 1674, was imprisoned for sedition the following year, and his successor John Gyles (d. 1683) is said to have narrowly escaped arrest while preaching in Harpsden Wood nearby. In 1669 the bishop suspected that the leading promoters of the Henley meeting were disaffected ex-soldiers or officers from Cromwell's disbanded New Model Army, a claim extended to several other places in the Chilterns area. Such suspicions underline the extent to which religion and politics were inextricably linked in the 17th century, an explosive mix which twice burst onto the national scene: first in the Civil Wars of the 1640s, and second in the 'Glorious Revolution' which ousted James II in 1688. Henley was closely involved in both episodes, once again as a consequence not only of its social and political character, but of its proximity to London and its strategic position on the Thames. What role did it play?[93]

WAR AND REVOLUTION

The Civil War

Given its riverside location between London and Oxford, Henley could scarcely escape a prominent role in the Civil War. This was particularly true from the summer of 1642, when Oxford became the Royalist capital while London remained with Parliament. Towns such as Reading proved equally crucial, along with fortifiable riverside houses such as Greenlands a little way downstream; both became Royalist outposts until seized by Parliament during 1644. Henley's significance was summed up soon after by the Parliamentary commander Sir James Harrington, who recommended strengthening it 'in order to hinder the great [river] trade ... between Oxford and London, as also for the well-being of Reading and Abingdon, the great supplies of corn and wood for London, and ... [Henley's] nearness to the enemy'. Phyllis Court had already been fortified 'to watch the garrison of Greenland', and Henley remained a Parliamentarian stronghold until hostilities ended in 1646. Long before then the town experienced comings and goings by both sides. Prince Rupert had forces there in 1642 and 1643, when he had a man hanged from a tree at Northfield End, and in January 1643 there was a skirmish when Royalists trying to enter the town up Duke Street were met with Parliamentarian cannon fire. Victims of the carnage were buried in Henley churchyard soon after.[94]

The corporation minute books suggest that routine business continued much as usual, and Henley undoubtedly suffered less than places such as Reading. But even so the disruption and uncertainty must have been serious. As early as August 1642 the warden and corporation complained of the 'great peril' caused by the 'passing to and through our county of ... disorderly trains

Figure 57 This extraordinary drawing of the Civil War defences at Phyllis Court was made in 1786, copied, according to an inscription on the back, from a lost original discovered behind panelling during demolition work. If the story is true the artist exercised some licence, since the soldiers are wearing 18th- rather than 17th-century dress. Nonetheless, some details may be accurate, since Phyllis Court was certainly fortified, moated and equipped with a drawbridge during 1644. The house (seen from the north) would fit what is known of its history, but may be fanciful.

of armed men', and before Henley became a Parliamentary stronghold the townspeople must have been in a constant state of anxiety as to which side would visit next, what damage they would inflict and what goods they would carry off. Garrisoning Phyllis Court brought different woes, including frequent pillaging and increasingly mutinous behaviour from the underpaid soldiers. Bulstrode Whitelocke, placed in charge of the garrison for part of this time, did what he could, but with limited success: in one particularly gruesome episode a woman who had complained of mounting taxation was condemned to have her tongue nailed to a roadside signpost on market day, with a paper describing her 'crime' fixed to her back. The general economic dislocation was presumably longer lasting. Damage to Whitelocke's houses, lands and income caused him long-term problems, and though the river remained in constant use normal trade was virtually suspended. Henley bridge (like others in the area) suffered serious damage, but seems to have been fairly quickly repaired.[95]

The town's political allegiance, if any, is unclear, although we might expect tradesmen and merchants with London connections and possibly Puritan tendencies to be broadly sympathetic to Parliament. Even so, such sympathies may not have been universal. In the aftermath a handful of Henley people were fined for having helped the Royalists, and in 1655 there were attempts to oust one John Tyler (apparently a Presbyterian) from the corporation, and replace him with a man claimed to be a 'cavalier'. But the circumstances are unclear, and of the Royalist collaborators some at least may acted under duress. Whitelocke himself was a committed but moderate Parliamentarian who abhorred the war, and spent much of the 1640s and 1650s pressing for compromise; by contrast his near neighbour Lord Lovelace (d. 1670) was a staunch Royalist, which did not prevent the two of them maintaining cordial relations in the 1650s. Many other townspeople probably avoided extremes, keeping their heads down as best they could – which is not to deny that the town may have contained partisans for both sides.[96]

The Glorious Revolution

With the Commonwealth of the 1650s and Charles II's Restoration in 1660, a degree of peace and normality returned to Henley as to other towns. But the 17th century was to see one final convulsion: the overthrow (in 1688) of Charles's Catholic brother James II, and the near-peaceful installation of the Dutch (and Protestant) William of Orange as William III. Once again Henley found itself thrust briefly onto the national stage.

Unlike the Civil War, the English revolution of 1688–9 was predominantly a political coup effected by a relatively small elite, and in this London and its hinterland played a significant part. William's most natural supporters included the commercial classes and those of staunchly Protestant (if not necessarily nonconformist) religion, whose opposition to James's accession during the so-called Exclusion Crisis had earned them the nickname of whigs (or whiggamores). That support for the coup was especially marked not only in London but in trading communities such as Henley is therefore not surprising. Invited to invade in June 1688, William landed at Torbay on 5 November, and proceeded cautiously and in stages towards the capital; by 13 December he was at Henley, where Sir William Whitelocke welcomed him to Phyllis Court – a gesture which William's Parliamentarian father Sir Bulstrode would no doubt have condoned. There he was greeted by a deputation of peers, bishops and London aldermen headed by another familiar figure: Sir Robert Clayton, the London banker and former lord mayor whose business dealings with Henley's landed gentry were described above. A final local player was the 3rd Lord Lovelace (of Ladye Place in Hurley), who unlike his Royalist father emerged in the 1670s as a leading whig partisan. Soon after William's landing Lovelace led a party to meet the prince at Cirencester, where in one of the few violent skirmishes of the revolution he himself was captured and Whitelocke's son was tragically killed. For the elder Whitelocke, therefore, his reception of the prince at Phyllis Court must have been a poignant affair. The events seem to have been recalled in symbolic form a few years later in yet another of Jan Siberechts' enigmatic Henley paintings (Panel 7) – a symptom of the close political as well as business ties between these prominent Henley landowning families and the London commercial classes.[97]

Figure 58 John Lovelace, 3rd Baron Lovelace, painted by Marcellus Laroon the elder in 1689 (detail). Though the son of a Royalist, from the 1670s Lovelace emerged as a leading Whig violently hostile to the future James II, and played a prominent part in the Glorious Revolution. A close friend of the Whitelockes, he was at Cirencester when William Whitelocke's son Bulstrode was killed in a skirmish. (By permission of the Warden and Fellows of Wadham College, Oxford)

But if the 1688 revolution was engineered at the highest political levels, the town, too, was caught up in the political passions behind it. During the national crises of 1683, when government paranoia was at its height, Henley was a suspect place: 'too full of men of [whiggish] principles', and too 'convenient [a] hiding place as lying on the edge of the county'. Searches for arms unearthed a case of pistols and two swords hidden in a bag of meal. Among those singled out for 'whiggism' (and apparently associated with Lovelace) was Adam Springall, one of a prominent Henley family who went on to serve several terms as town warden. How far such claims were exaggerated by a nervous government is unclear, but the presence of a large barging community may have been connected: at Marlow, Abingdon and Oxford, bargemen were certainly associated both with whiggism and with other forms of political radicalism. Their role (if any) in Henley is unrecorded, but barging communities were clearly politically aware, and could occasionally exercise mass influence.[98]

REMODELLING AND REBUILDING

Politics and religion were not the only aspects of Henley's life to see radical change between 1540 and 1700. Siberechts' paintings of Henley in the 1690s show a town still made up almost entirely of timber houses, much as the medieval town had been. But the similarities are deceptive. Not only were brick and new classical fashions starting to creep in (see below), but across England standards of domestic comfort were changing. By Siberechts' time the town's surviving medieval houses had mostly been remodelled to meet these new aspirations, and many others had been rebuilt, resembling their medieval predecessors only superficially.[99]

The reasons for these changes and the pace at which they occurred, particularly in towns, are still being debated by historians. But the main factors were rising standards of living and a widespread desire for greater domestic comfort, both among the rich and among the 'middling sort' of people who were strongly represented in towns like Henley. Two new developments became especially important after the mid-16th century: the replacement of open hearths (see Chapter 4)

Figure 59 Siberechts' Henley paintings contain important information about the town's buildings. This detail from the Wargrave Road painting of 1698 (Figure 41) shows houses and granaries along the waterfront south of Hart Street, most of them timber-framed and two-storeyed, some with gables to the street. The multitude of chimneys shows that most had fireplaces. In the distance (left of the church) is the domed cupola of the guildhall.

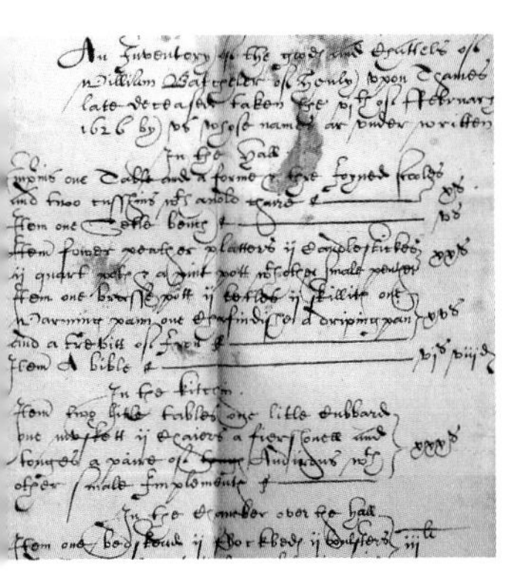

Figure 60 Part of the probate inventory of William Batchelor (d. 1626), maltster, describing furnishings in his hall, kitchen, and chamber over the hall. Such inventories were needed to establish the value of a person's goods before their will could be proved, and were a legal requirement. Since the appraisers generally proceeded room by room, the documents paint an invaluable picture of how houses were furnished and arranged. (Oxfordshire Record Office, MS Wills Oxon. 5/2/24)

with fireplaces and chimneys, usually of brick or stone, and the growing use of glazed windows. William Harrison, rector of Radwinter in Essex, noted in the 1570s that among the three things the old men of his village had found to be 'marvellously altered' in their lifetimes was 'the multitude of chimneys lately erected', and he also pointed out that glass had become both plentiful and cheap. Upper floors could now be inserted into existing open halls, and new two- or three-storeyed houses constructed with well-heated, well-lit rooms throughout. This process had transformed Henley's houses by the end of the 17th century.

Other factors were an increase in personal possessions and a trend towards greater privacy. This was naturally more evident at the upper than the lower end of the social spectrum. Harrison may have been exaggerating when he claimed that 'inferior artificers and many farmers ... [now] garnish their cupboards with plate, their joined beds with tapestry and silk hangings, and their tables with carpets and fine napery': there is little sign of this kind of wealth in the probate inventories of late 16th-century Henley tradesmen. But by the middle of the 17th century John Grant, a maltster who died in 1662 with goods worth £526, could entertain his friends in a 'wainscot [i.e. panelled] chamber' containing good joined furniture, two cupboards, a carpet and six cushions: an environment framed for polite living.

Most town houses in the 16th and 17th centuries were workplaces as well as homes. Thomas Barretes, who died in 1583, had only two rooms which we would now recognise as living rooms: a hall, which was virtually unfurnished, and a chamber above it, which he used as his bedroom. In addition, he had a kitchen with two tables, a settle and cooking implements; a shop or workshop with (among other things) bottles, barrels, boxes, glasses filled with rose water, and 'a piece of plate for the printmaker'; a 'vergys [or verjuice] house' with six gallons of vinegar; a 'boulting howse' for malt; and a stable with a loft over it. Most other inventories down to the end of the 17th century paint a similar picture. Henley's citizens may have aspired to gentility, but their aspirations had to be contained within a workaday domestic framework.[100]

Rooms and Layout

Despite such improvements, many people in late 17th-century Henley still lived in fairly small houses. This is clearly shown by the hearth tax returns of 1662, drawn up for a government tax based on the number of fireplaces each householder had

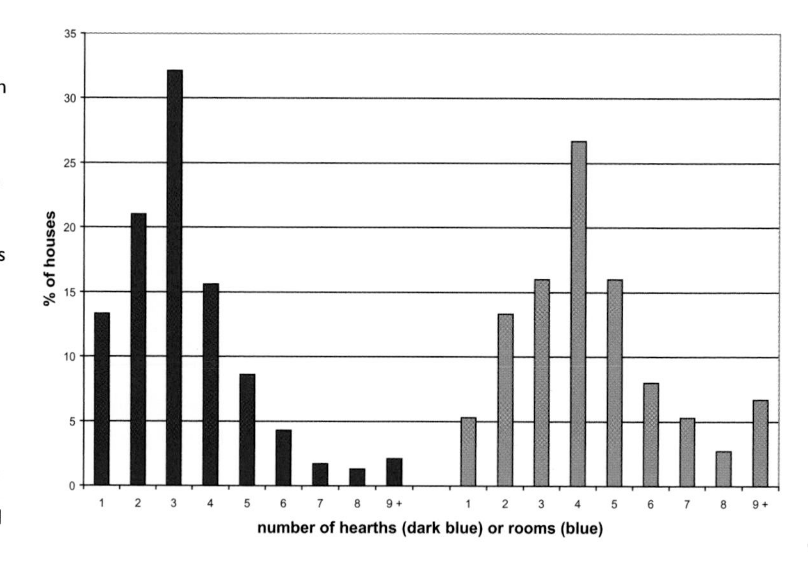

Figure 61 House sizes in 17th-century Henley, based on the 1662 hearth tax (dark blue columns), and a random sample of probate inventories (light blue columns). The hearth tax counted only rooms with a fireplace, while probate inventories listed rooms containing goods or furniture, including outbuildings. Both imply a significant number of houses with only one or two rooms, though most had three to six, and a few wealthy inhabitants had far more. Bulstrode Whitelocke's house (Phyllis Court) had 17 hearths, while the rectory house had six.

(Figure 61). The main differences from today were at the top and bottom ends of the social scale, and the proportion of those living in houses with just one or two hearths would probably be increased if we knew more about those too poor to pay, or who somehow evaded payment.[101]

Hearths did not equate to rooms, since many were unheated. Nonetheless, an analysis of 75 late 16th- and 17th-century probate inventories paints a broadly similar picture (Figure 61). The poorest inhabitants, who did not leave wills, are under-represented here, as are the richest. But the craftsmen, maltsters, traders and bargemen who formed the backbone of the town's economic life are strongly represented, and their inventories bring their domestic arrangements vividly to life. Outside the smallest houses, there was a tendency in the late 16th and 17th centuries towards a segregation of living space. This meant downgrading the hall (formerly a communal room for cooking, dining, recreation and even sleeping), and increasing the number of chambers or bedrooms. Cooking was generally transferred to a kitchen, leaving the hall as an (often largely empty) living or dining room. In larger houses, a parlour was sometimes introduced as a sitting or withdrawing room – that of Martha Barnes (d. 1662) was comfortably furnished, with hangings, stools, chairs, curtains, tables, carpets, cushions and fire irons. Such extra rooms already existed in some late medieval merchants' and craftsmen's houses, but they proliferated in the 16th and 17th centuries.[102]

To learn more about how houses developed, we must turn to the buildings themselves. Most can be dated only from stylistic details such as carpentry joints, carved decoration or window types, and in Henley this is trickier than in some other places. Henley's carpenters, for instance, generally avoided the decorative flights of fancy found in larger towns such as Stratford-upon-Avon (which would help with dating), while very few owners obliged us by carving dates or initials on their houses. Nonetheless, many houses confirm the widespread flooring over of medieval halls which is implicit in the inventories. One is 20 Hart Street, originally a hall with a cross passage and a cross wing at No. 22 (Figure 33). At some stage after *c.*1550 an upper floor was built over the hall and chimneys were inserted, while the street front was later plastered over (like many of Henley's timber houses) and given new casement windows. The roof is tiled, something that had occurred in most of the town by 1690, judging from Siberechts' paintings.

Most of the houses shown by Siberechts were two-storeyed, and some had rooms in the roof. Alongside these, the hearth tax and inventories show that there were still some single-storeyed houses with only one or two rooms, although apart from the Newbury and Messenger almshouses (which have been rebuilt) these have all now gone. Of Henley's surviving 16th- or 17th-century houses, the smallest originally had two or more floors behind a narrow street frontage, and contained three to five rooms in all. One room on each floor faced the street, and sometimes there was additional accommodation behind. An example is 7 Market Place (now Gabriel Machin's butcher's shop), where unusually for Henley the timber framing has remained exposed. Its narrow timbers forming square panels are quite different from the heavy timbers of medieval houses, and have decorative quatrefoils in the squares. The decoration recalls that of a much larger house in Oxford dated to 1622–8, providing a clue to the date of the Henley building.[103]

Figure 62 The timber framing of the large gable at 7 Market Place is probably early 17th-century, as indicated by its decoration and its relatively narrow timbers, but it fronts an older building. Its narrow front looks similar to some of the houses shown by Siberechts (Figure 59), though it could once have formed part of a larger structure.

Houses on wider plots could be double-fronted, with a room on either side of the entrance, two rooms above, and (sometimes) extra accommodation in a rear extension, giving a characteristic L-plan. No. 50 Market Place falls into this category. The house has two heated rooms on each floor, a back extension (perhaps originally a buttery) with a room over, and a cellar; the main entrance leads straight into the larger of the two ground-floor rooms, which probably began as a hall. This explains the off-centre placing of the front door, which became anathema to the classically influenced builders of the 18th century. Some other houses have a 'lobby entrance' arrangement, which was popular in south-east England during the late 16th and early 17th centuries. In these houses the chimneystack was placed in the middle of the building, with a lobby entrance in front of the stack, and hearths heating the main rooms to either side of it. Examples include 16 West Street

Figure 63 Ancastle Cottage, at the top of Gravel Hill, stood outside the town above the upper market place, and originally faced westwards away from the town. Probably it was built as a farmhouse rather than a town house, and its larger site allowed a more generous room layout. Here the chimneystack was placed in the middle, with a 'lobby entrance' in front of it and hearths heating all the main rooms.

and Ancastle Cottage, which stands at the top of Gravel Hill on the town's western edge and was probably built as a farmhouse. Here the plain square framing is exposed, with (probably later) brick infill. Originally it faced westwards away from the town, its jettied west front now concealed inside a 19th-century extension.[104]

Few of Henley's larger houses survive in anything like their original form. No. 14 Friday Street, on the town's southern edge, is a fragment of a much bigger house, built possibly by a maltster

Figure 64 Though 14 Friday Street is now only a fragment, enough survives to show that it was a very high-status house, with its moulded jetty joists, its row of first-floor windows flanking a larger one, and its use of close studding. Its style suggests it was built *c.*1580–1650, perhaps by a timber merchant or maltster. (Maltings of unknown date existed here in 1844.)

Figure 65 This fine 17th-century house near the bridge and church (48–50 Hart Street) must have been built for a prosperous inhabitant, with its impressive double jetty (or overhang) and elegantly moulded bressumers. The drawing shows it before 19th-century alterations.

or timber merchant and truncated when Queen Street was built in the 1880s. The mouldings of its window mullions suggest a date of *c.*1580–1650, and its detailing and construction are signs of its owner's wealth. But the most impressive timber-framed house of this period is 48–50 Hart Street, on a prime site opposite the church. Three storeys high, two bays wide and of double depth, it has four rooms on each floor and additional space in the attic, expressed externally by twin gables. Similar houses had been built in the larger towns of south-east England and the Midlands since the 14th and 15th centuries, but the early 17th-century date of this one is betrayed by the placing of chimneystacks between the main pairs of rooms, and by the use of ovolo (or convex) mouldings for the window mullions. The staircase, with its chunky turned balusters and hefty newels, is in a turret at the back, lit by a window clearly of mid-17th-century type.

Inns and Commercial Buildings

Some of the largest houses in Henley were inns, and here too probate inventories and surviving examples point to substantial rebuilding and remodelling. At the *Bear* in Bell Street a two-gabled extension was built next to the existing medieval building, extending over the carriage archway (Figure 67), while the 15th-century hall behind it apparently became the inn's kitchen. The new part had mullioned and transomed oriel windows and fireplaces in all four rooms, one of which must have been the 'new chamber' mentioned in the inventory of the innkeeper John Dolton in 1683. The extension was no doubt intended to provide comfortable accommodation for travellers along the Oxford road, who could have been entertained during their stay by the five musical instruments mentioned in the inventory. A similar rebuilding took place at the *Bull*, another medieval inn further south in Bell Street, where the first-floor front was probably also rebuilt in the mid- to late 17th century. Its three oriel windows are of the so-called 'Ipswich' type fashionable from *c.*1650, with arches in the central lights (see Figure 85).[105]

Probate inventories show that most 17th-century Henley houses had buildings on the burgage plots behind them. In larger towns such as Oxford population pressure led to these plots being filled with houses, some of them quite large, others small and often poorly built. In Henley, the buildings usually served some sort of industrial or service function. Names such as 'boulting house' (for flour), work house, wood house, malthouse, brewhouse and meal house appear regularly, although most of the buildings themselves have been rebuilt beyond recognition. An exception

Figure 66 A former malthouse or hop-drying kiln behind 57/59 Market Place, in which barley or hops were processed. The inserted frame of a ventilator for the kiln has a circular opening at the top. Possibly the building was adapted for hops (which are lighter than barley and require a smaller furnace) after new larger maltings were built nearby. Probate inventories show that such outbuildings were common in the 17th century, though few survive.

is a stable behind the former *King's Arms* in the market place, dendro-dated to 1603, and similar outbuildings survive behind many of the other older inns. Two other possible early survivors are an outbuilding behind 57/59 Market Place (used for a time as a malthouse or hop kiln), and a timber building with brick infill next to the churchyard, on one of the plots on the south side of New Street which later became part of Brakspears' Brewery. Along the waterfront, granaries, storehouses and malthouses continued in constant use and were shown in Siberechts' paintings, among them the 16th-century buildings which survive as Barn and Granary Cottages (Figure 36). Shops, too, were mentioned in tradesmen's inventories, but have left no structural trace.[106]

Brick and the Classical Tradition

The buildings discussed so far are timber-framed, but by 1700 brick was becoming established as a building material. Widely used for chimneys and infill panels throughout the period, it appears to have first been used on a large scale in Henley at the (*Old*) *White Hart* in 1530–1 (Panel 6), and featured prominently at nearby Greys Court and Lower Hernes Farm in the 1560s–70s. But brick was still expensive, and did not become common as a walling material until well after the Restoration: even then it was sometimes used only to refront older buildings in a more fashionable style. In the late 17th century bricks were made locally at Watlington, Russells Water and Nettlebed, and in 1665 brick was used for Watlington town hall. Three years later Ralph Messenger (apparently a timber merchant and maltster) had a stock of bricks at Henley worth £35, and brick was evidently used to remodel Henley's Longland almshouses in the later 17th century (Figure 53).[107]

Further encouragement came from the London Rebuilding Act of 1667, following the Great Fire of the previous year. Timber building was now not only revealed as potentially dangerous, which people already knew; it also became unfashionable, as the capital was transformed almost overnight into a city of brick houses. Of the earlier brick houses in Henley, 43 New Street may date from *c.*1670–1700, and so too may 82–84 Bell Street, a rebuilding of an older timber-framed house. Both have classically influenced elevations with tall, narrowish windows and wooden cornices: a plainly moulded one at 43 New Street, and with dentil decoration at 82-84 Bell Street. The first-floor windows have characteristic wooden mullions and transoms enclosing casements, which was usual before sash windows became widespread. Brick houses of this type were to proliferate during the 18th century, as Henley embarked on a period of intensive rebuilding which entirely transformed its character (Chapter 8). Meanwhile even timber

Figure 67 The former *Bear Inn* on Bell Street, showing the twin-gabled extension (with its projecting oriel windows) added in the 17th century. The *Bear* was first recorded as an inn in 1666, but at the back is a medieval hall dated to 1438, probably used as the inn's kitchen.

houses could be embellished with classical detailing in plaster, like one on the west side of Duke Street (now demolished) which, on stylistic grounds, may have been built around 1670.[108]

In the surrounding countryside new fashions penetrated even earlier, setting the tone for aspiring townsmen. The old manor house at Fawley Court, overlooking Henley, was replaced in 1684 with a sophisticated brick-built country house in the latest style, while at Park Place the Drapers, too, created a fashionable country seat which won praise from London sophisticates. In Henley the old gabled manor house at Phyllis Court (Figure 57) escaped the mania for rebuilding, a reflection, perhaps, of the Whitelockes' straitened circumstances – though even here there was cosmetic updating, since fittings sold off in the 1780s included classical fan lights and cornices as well as doors and timber floorings. Even so, it must have come to seem a hopelessly outdated anachronism among the fashionably refronted buildings of the town, a factor, no doubt, in its eventual demolition.[109]

Figure 68 From the late 17th century new classical styles began to permeate Henley, together with the more extensive use of brick as a fashionable building material. The front part of 82/84 Bell Street may date from around 1670–1700, ushering in a new phase which found its full expression in Henley over the next hundred years or so.

Towards the 18th Century

The changes which characterised the period from 1500 to 1700 were far-reaching, encompassing revolutions in political and religious outlook, in art and architecture, and in social life. Economically, too, this was for the most part a period of sustained growth, accompanied by steady population increase, and by rising standards of living for many if not for all. All these changes were reflected in 16th- and 17th-century Henley.

Yet through all the changes, there remained the crucial thread of Henley's close relationship with London and the Thames. For another 130 years that relationship continued to dominate the town, conditioning not only its commercial life but its social milieu, its buildings, and its physical development, as we shall see in Chapter 8. First, though, how did river and road transport in the Chilterns change during the age of turnpikes, river improvements, and canals, and how did this affect Henley and its neighbours on the middle Thames?

Chapter 7

The Age of Improvement: Road and River 1700–1830

Asked to characterise the 18th century, many historians would point to the improvements in transport, technology and agriculture which underpinned the industrial revolution. As usual, the picture is less straightforward than once thought. Transport improvements and the 'agricultural revolution' both had their origins much earlier, while the full impact of new turnpike roads was not really felt until the 1760s, and the effects of canal-building even later. But the changes were real and profound and, for a town as reliant as Henley on its place in the road and river network, bound to have important consequences. Like many Chilterns towns Henley benefited from the development of coaching, and while belated improvements in Thames navigation had more ambiguous results – arguably helping Henley's rivals as much as the town itself – its long-established relationship with London and the river continued unabated into the 19th century. Related improvements within the town affected not only trade and commerce but its general tone and appearance, encompassing broad new roads, the opening up of the market place, a new waterfront, and above all the graceful five-arched bridge which still marks Henley's eastern approach.[110]

Later on we shall look at Henley's social and cultural life during this critical period, and at how the remodelling of its buildings created the 'polite' brick and flint town which we see today. This chapter looks at the infrastructure which underpinned those changes, in particular at how improvements in road and river transport affected Henley in the final decades before the railway.

Figure 69 Henley around 1793, by the British landscape painter Joseph Farington. The new bridge was then less than ten years old, and associated improvements in the town were still underway. The *Red Lion*, one of the town's premier coaching inns, is just visible at its western end, and in the foreground is one of the wharfs, built up with timber revetments. Another wharf lay north of New Street, though in the 18th century river barges loaded and unloaded their cargoes along much of the waterfront.

Henley Stage-Coach.

Begins on *Monday December* 9. 1717.

AND ſets out from the *VVhite-Hart* Inn in *Henley*, every *Monday* and *Friday*, at Six a Clock; and comes to the *VVhite-Horſe* Inn in *Fleetſtreet* the ſame Nights: And ſets out again from the *VVhite-Horſe* every *Wedneſday* and *Saturday*, and comes into *Henley* the ſame Nights; with a good Coach and Six able Horſes.

Perform'd (if God permit) by

JOHN ALLEWAY.

NOTE, The Stage will begin to go three times a Week, from the 25th of *March* next enſuing, during the Summer-Seaſon. Likewiſe, That they do call at the *Black-Bear* in *Picadilly* every Journey

Figure 70 Handbill issued by John Alleway, advertising his winter service to London from the *White Hart*. Teams of six horses (with a rider at the front) were fairly common in winter, and on particularly steep stretches such as the ascent up White Hill; otherwise most stage coaches had teams of four, with no rider. The six-seater coach, slung from the frame on leather straps, is typical of the period.

TURNPIKES AND COACHING

From its creation Henley was dependent not only on the river but on good roads. From the 16th and 17th centuries England's medieval road system came under increasing pressure for several reasons, among them heavier use in an age of expanding economy and population, and the almost universal replacement of carts with heavy four-wheeled wagons. But as with the medieval period, we must be careful not to exaggerate the road network's shortcomings. One powerful indication that roads were by no means as poor as is sometimes claimed is the development of stage-coaching, which predated by several decades the 18th-century improvement of roads through turnpiking.

The first true stage-coaches were established in the 1650s, running timetabled public services and changing horses at specified inns. By the end of the decade, services linked London with towns as far afield as Plymouth, Shrewsbury and Edinburgh. Henley had its own service by 1668, when John Hathaway (d. 1700) issued a trade token, and by 1681 his coaches ran to London three times a week. By his retirement in 1694 he owned two coaches and nine horses, and his successor William Hall extended the service to Wallingford. Another Henley man, John Alleway, ran a London service from the *White Hart* by 1717 (Figure 70). None of these men are known to have been innkeepers, though like later operators they had close relations with particular inns in Henley and presumably *en route*. They were also substantial people. Quite apart from the actual coaches, the cost of maintaining and feeding large numbers of horses was considerable, and both Hathaway and Hall employed coachmen to drive their vehicles.

What sort of people used these early coaching services? For Henley there is no evidence, but diaries and correspondence suggest that the commonest passengers were gentry and professionals, clergy, scholars, military men, and (increasingly) women, who until now might not have been able to travel at all, and certainly not alone. This, in other words, was not just a transport but a social revolution. In addition, some of Henley's well-to-do already owned private coaches. As early as the 1640s Sir Bulstrode Whitelocke had a light 'chariot' that could get him to London in half a day, and in the 1660s he kept a more substantial family coach, which on one memorable occasion tipped over on a Henley street depositing his wife in 'a dirty hole at the brewhouse door'. These heavier coaches, whether private or public, were slower than Whitelocke's chariot, taking probably nearer a day to London in the earlier 18th century. Nonetheless, their relative comfort and (in the case of stage coaches) their regularity made them increasingly popular.[111]

Figure 71 Part of John Ogilby's famous route map published in 1675, showing the road through Henley to Nettlebed (at the top). Ogilby seems to have thought it reasonable, though the road from Maidenhead was 'unlevel and woody'.

Even so the inadequacy of many roads, particularly in winter, was increasingly recognised during the earlier 18th century, and was thrown into sharper relief by the fact that more people than ever were on the move. The solution was the development of toll or turnpike roads, so called from the gates or 'turnpikes' at which tolls were collected. These were individually established by Act of Parliament and run by local trusts, which oversaw their management and upkeep. The first was established in 1663, and from around 1700 they became increasingly common: by 1760 nearly 90 per cent of the main national coaching routes into London had been turnpiked. Henley's experience was typical. The road from Maidenhead to Henley bridge, dismissed as 'indirect, unlevel and woody' in the 1670s, was turnpiked in 1718, and the Oxford road through Dorchester and Abingdon, which had become rutted and dangerous because of the 'many heavy carriages' using it, followed in 1735–6. By the time the north–south road through the town was turnpiked in 1768 it formed part of an extensive network across the Chilterns and beyond (Figure 72). The importance attached to these improvements by local landowners and others was shown in the membership of the trusts: that for the Oxford road, for instance, included the mayors and corporations of Henley, Abingdon and Wallingford and the Vice-Chancellor of Oxford University, together with Gislingham Cooper of Fawley Court and several other landowners from the Henley area. Motives could be social as well as commercial. The Hatfield–Reading turnpike through Henley linked with roads to the fashionable spa resort of Bath, where two of its most prominent aristocratic sponsors are said to have made yearly excursions to relieve their gout.[112]

The earliest road improvements could be fairly cosmetic, but from the 1750s major engineering and rerouting became common. The steep ascent from Henley bridge up White Hill, still quite a haul today, was reduced in 1768, as described by Dr Johnson's biographer James Boswell:

> At Henley we came out and went and looked at the machine with which they are levelling a very steep hill on the London side, by digging it down and throwing the earth into the hollow at the bottom. This is done without horses, by two carts which are contrived to work as buckets in a well ... the weight of the loaded cart going down the hill pulls up the empty cart, which is filled, and then pulls up the other ... This method was invented lately by a Dissenting clergyman at Henley. It is exceedingly useful, by making that be done by two men which would require a great number of horses and oxen.

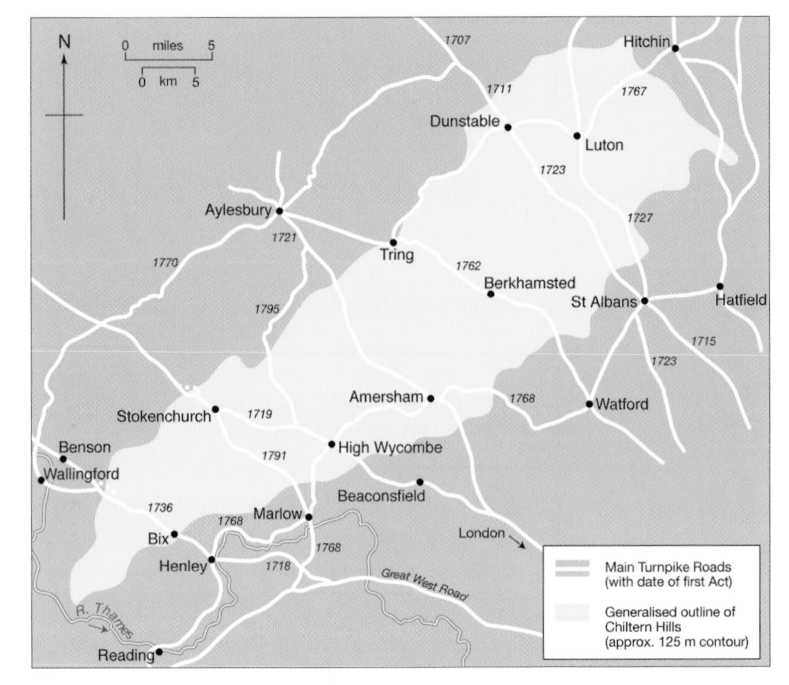

Figure 72 Turnpike roads through the Chilterns in the late 18th century, showing for each the date of the original Act. (Based on Hepple and Doggett, *Chilterns* (1994), 159).

The 'Dissenting clergyman' was the Congregationalist minister of Henley, Humphrey Gainsborough (brother of the painter Thomas), who besides being a respected member of the town community was an inventor and engineer. His wide scientific interests, shared with several surrounding landowners, were typical of the improving spirit of the period (see Chapter 8), and found a practical expression not only in road improvement, but in the construction of new poundlocks along the Thames and in hydraulic schemes for improving water supply to country estates.[113]

Figure 73 In the 18th century public and private improvement often went hand in hand. This picturesque 'rustic bridge', built around 1763 by General Henry Seymour Conway to adorn his Park Place estate, created a more direct route for the Henley–Wargrave road, which still crosses it. The design was by Thomas Pitt, but the engineer was probably Humphrey Gainsborough, Henley's scientifically minded Congregationalist minister.

Such road improvements prompted a further expansion of coaching, particularly after the introduction of steel-sprung suspension from 1752. Suddenly coaches could be both lighter and faster, heralding a golden age of stage-coaching from which Chilterns towns such as Henley all benefited. By the 1790s no fewer than eight long-distance coaches to London and several more from Oxford passed through the town every day, supplementing a daily service from the *White Hart* which left at 6 a.m. and returned in the evening. Coach-masters vied with each other for speed and comfort, as shown in their newspaper advertisements: in 1780, for instance, a 'neat and elegant post-coach' built 'upon an entire new construction' ran to London from the *Catherine Wheel*, while the following year the Henley coachmaster Richard Taylor advertised a new five-hour service to London from the *Bull* on Bell Street. The obsession with speed and competition was reflected in a warning by Henley corporation in 1787, threatening prosecution to coachmen and riders who passed through the town 'at a ... furious rate, thereby creating great danger both to themselves, the passengers ... and the foot passengers along the streets'. The well-to-do still ran private coaches as well, and commercial wagons added further to the volume of traffic. In the 1790s there were two locally run London stage-wagons a week, with wagons from a dozen other towns passing through regularly.[114]

The consequences for Henley, as for most coaching towns, were profound. Those who most obviously stood to gain were the town's innkeepers, who established close relations with coach-masters and expanded their premises accordingly. The *Red Lion*, virtually the first building travellers from London saw as they passed over the bridge, was rebuilt with a fashionable three-storeyed brick façade

Figure 74 The *Red Lion* inn by Henley bridge, virtually the first building travellers from London would see. Established before the mid-17th century, in the mid-18th it became one of Henley's most prestigious coaching inns, catering for private as well as stage coaches. Though the inn was heavily remodelled in the 19th century, parts of its distinctive brick façade probably date from a rebuilding around the 1720s. The porch replaced an earlier carriageway.

in the earlier 18th century, and around 1780 new stabling was built on the east side of its gradually enlarged courtyard, catering for private carriages as well as stage coaches. The *White Hart* (which became Henley's premier stage-coaching inn) and the *Bear* on Bell Street had stabling for over 70 horses by the 1820s, and the *Bell* (at Northfield End) for over fifty. Not surprisingly, some of the town's major innkeepers became substantial figures. Barrett March, who owned the *Red Lion* from the late 18th century, served four times as mayor, and at his death in 1816 left a fortune of £120,000. But not only innkeepers benefited. Coaching and travel brought incidental trade to the town, and presumably employment for large numbers of unnamed stable-hands, ostlers, servants and kitchen staff. Coach-building also developed. The coach-maker and ironmonger Henry Oakley had premises on Bell Street in the 1780s, while in 1805 Caroline Powys (off to visit her in-laws in Staffordshire) hired a post-chaise from a coach-maker on the Fair Mile, for a guinea a week.[115]

Coaching not only brought new prosperity to the town, it also helped establish it as a social centre. Suddenly Henley was on a transport route not only for bulk commercial goods but for the most fashionable elements of society, while quick and comfortable transport made it feasible for surrounding country gentry to slot it into the newly fashionable round of assemblies, balls and social seasons described in the next chapter. Celebrated visitors to the *Red Lion* included the lexicographer and wit Samuel Johnson (d. 1784), George III and his family, and possibly the 1st Duke of Marlborough (d. 1722), who is said to have kept a furnished room there. Consequently the remodelling of many of Henley's larger coaching inns reflected not just the increasing volume of traffic but their changing social role. The *Bell* was refurbished around 1794 with 'a spacious ballroom, comfortable sleeping rooms [and] four parlours', and was popular with local country gentry even before then. A grand supper and ball was hosted there by Lord Villiers in 1777, attended by guests from several neighbouring country houses; typically they arrived in a stream of private coaches, providing an unexpected talking point after highwaymen looking for diamonds robbed one of them on its way from Bolney Court.[116]

HENLEY AND THE RIVER

If coaching introduced a new, more fashionable phase in Henley's development, its relationship with the river remained the other main plank of its economy. From the early 17th century the Thames was open to Oxford and beyond (see Chapter 5), and in the 18th century it carried a large and regular traffic along the 138-mile stretch from London to Lechlade in Gloucestershire – further, in

Figure 75 The Sapperton canal tunnel on the Thames and Severn Canal gives some idea of the heroic engineering needed to create new waterways or improve existing ones. Opened in 1789, the canal created a continuous route from the Severn estuary to London. The tunnel was cut through an otherwise impassable stretch in Gloucestershire, and at 3,800 yards was then the longest tunnel in England. As it had no towpath, bargemen had to propel the barges by pressing their feet against the tunnel wall.

fact, following the opening of the Thames and Severn Canal in 1789, which created a continuous waterway from London to the Severn estuary. Government inquiries give some idea of the volume of trade. In 1767 over 56,000 tons of goods passed upstream above Marlow, of which nearly 9,000 (16 per cent) were landed at Henley. By 1788–9 the upstream total was over 70,000 tons, with downward traffic almost half as large again. These huge cargoes were carried in barges of ever increasing size (Panel 8), of which nearly 100 plied the stretches above London in the later 18th century, and nearly 200 in the early 19th.

Some of this trade continued earlier patterns. The Thames still supplied London with beech timber and fuel, and with flour, meal and malt, some of it manufactured in Henley. But by the 1780s trade in both directions was becoming more varied, particularly with the advent of new canals. Freight shipped downriver by the Oxford bargemaster Thomas Court included iron, copper, tin, manufactured metal goods, and bombshells, as well as large numbers of cheeses sent to London from Lechlade. Upstream cargoes included groceries, a wide range of foreign imports (including timber), ashes and rags used as manure, and hides bound for Gloucester or Tewkesbury. Another important freight was coal, shipped down the coast and through London. Underpinning this expanding traffic and the 'canal mania' of the 1780s–90s were the cost differentials outlined in previous chapters. Whatever the revolutions in road transport, for bulk movement of heavy goods a well-maintained waterway still offered massive savings in the pre-railway age, cutting costs per ton from London to Henley by over 70 per cent according to the agriculturalist William Mavor in 1809. With further improvement, thought Mavor, even those goods carried by wagon might be transferred to barge: fattened livestock, for instance, or perishables sent by road during the summer when waterways were most at risk of delay.[117]

How much of this expanding trade flowed through Henley? The only comprehensive figures are those appended to a parliamentary enquiry in 1793, which show that the volume of upstream goods landed there slipped from nearly 11,000 tons (over 18 per cent) in 1781 to a little over 6,000 (nine per cent) 10 years later. Probably that reflected increased competition from upstream towns such as Reading and Wallingford, as new poundlocks made access beyond Henley much cheaper. But this still represented considerable business, and statements made by Henley people in the 1780s, during a dispute over loading rights at the waterfront, show the extent to which the town remained enmeshed in the river trade. The landlady of the *Angel on the Bridge* described seeing bundles of flax and crates of earthenware and glass unloaded nearby, while others mentioned the regular landing of coal, rags and casks, pitch tar, and tallow. Some of this was loaded into wagons to finish its journey by road – some tallow, for instance, was for a Benson chandler, who had commissioned a Henley bargemaster to bring it from London. Others described the unloading of corn, which was no longer only exported through Henley but imported for resale. Barrett March, the wealthy owner of the *Red Lion* inn, built extensive new granaries along the waterfront for this purpose, and the bargemaster Bennett Gleed had a granary which he leased to a man from Kingston upon Thames. Alongside all this, the traditional export of malt downriver continued. One elderly bargeman recalled working 20 years earlier for a bargemaster from Wooburn (near Marlow), importing coal and groceries to Henley, then returning downstream with consignments of malt from the Henley maltster Mr Riggs.[118]

Improving the River

Despite the Thames's crucial importance, improvement during the 18th century was surprisingly slow in coming. Complaints about exorbitant charges remained common, and in the 1770s bargemasters were still negotiating the medieval-style flashlocks which John Bishop complained of in the 1580s – now in massively larger barges, which ran increased risk of running aground and blocking the river. One reason was the lack of a single co-ordinating body with the funds and authority to do what was necessary. A Parliamentary Act of 1751 tried to address the problem by creating a Thames Commission to regulate costs, locks and river traffic west of Staines. But as it lacked the power to build new locks or towpaths and had a ludicrously large membership of several hundred – everyone, in fact, with land worth over £100 a year in the seven riverside counties, together with representatives of every riverside town and of Oxford University – it not surprisingly proved ineffective. Only with a further Act 20 years later was the Commission empowered to replace old flashlocks with poundlocks, and to borrow up to £50,000 (secured on lock tolls) for the purpose. Thereafter a belated programme of improvements slowly got underway, with a string of 10 new locks from Taplow to Mapledurham completed by 1778, and more by the 1790s. In this, Henley people were instrumental. The Commission included several scientifically minded landowners such as General Conway of Park Place and Sambrooke Freeman (d. 1782) of Fawley Court, while several of the locks around Henley were designed by their friend Humphrey Gainsborough, the town's Congregationalist minister

Figure 76 Humphrey Gainsborough (1718–76), who combined his role as Congregationalist minister of Henley with a profound practical interest in science and engineering. A friend of local landowners such as Thomas Hall, Sambrooke Freeman and General Conway, he played a leading role in road and river improvement around Henley. The portrait is by his brother Thomas, the celebrated painter.

(see above). Gainsborough collected the tolls from the keepers, and maintained an interest in the locks' operation to the end of his life: it was while returning from this task (and reportedly chatting about locks with local gentlemen) that he died suddenly in meadows near Henley in 1776.

A more intractable obstacle to improvement was self-interest. Despite the enthusiasm of most Henley landowners, those further downstream feared that new poundlocks would flood their lands, and repeatedly opposed their construction. An anonymous letter in 1794 urged them 'to form ... an invincible phalanx' against 'the present alarming junto of the Commissioners', and on one occasion a group of 60 hostile landowners was said to have swamped a Commission meeting which was discussing the building of new locks below Taplow. The beleaguered Commission faced further challenges from promoters of canals, who accused it of not doing enough and threatened to bypass the river, though here, too, self-interest was paramount. During the early 18th century, when engineering work on the River Kennet turned Newbury into a major inland port, the people of Reading responded with a remarkable show of orchestrated violence, fearing that the improvements would damage their town. Works were smashed, and bargemen using the new cut (among them the Henley bargemaster John Usher) met with death threats and hostile stone-throwing mobs. Fifty years later, Reading's inhabitants took a rather different view of a proposed canal from Reading or Sonning to below Maidenhead, which they believed would benefit the town. Opposition this time came from proprietors and traders in the places which would have been catastrophically bypassed, including

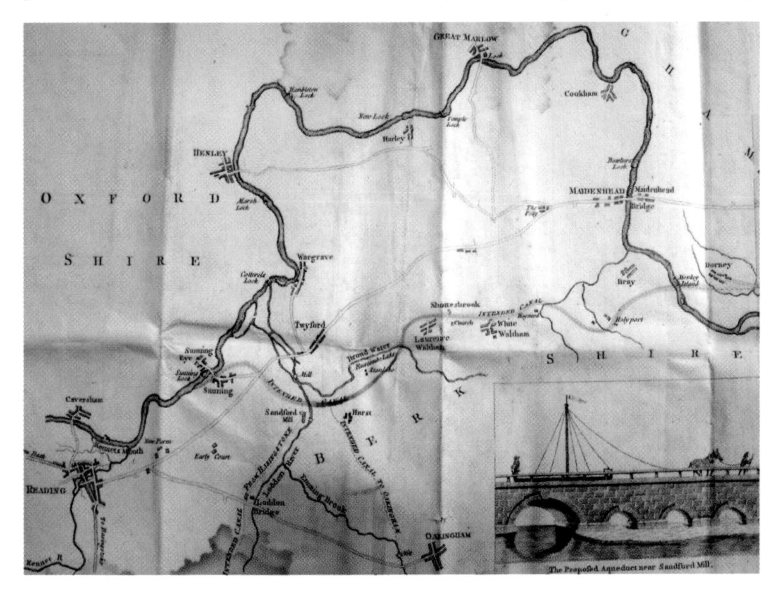

Figure 77 Part of the proposed canal from Sonning (above Henley) to Monkey Island (below Maidenhead), which would have bypassed the large northern loop in the Thames and diverted barge traffic away from Henley, Marlow and Maidenhead. The proposal led to bitter antagonism between those who stood to gain and those (including the Thames Commissioners and inhabitants of the bypassed towns) who stood to lose. A related scheme proposed a canal from the mouth of the River Kennet at Reading.

Henley. Similar battles between canal companies, riverside landowners and those responsible for the Thames rumbled on into the 19th century, fought through a series of polemical and often abusive pamphlets in which public and self-interest can be hard to disentangle.[119]

Barges and Bargemasters

As vessels became larger, barging seems (like many industries in the period) to have become more capital-intensive. By mid-century barges capable of carrying up to 200 tons were becoming commonplace (Panel 8), with the very largest bargemasters running at least one or two vessels and sometimes three or four. Clearly such a venture required substantial capital and could be extremely lucrative. John Burton, a pamphleteer strongly opposed to the huge increase in barge size, complained that 'a few overgrown barges ... engross the whole business of the country adjacent', allowing masters to inflate prices. The bargemaster 'considers himself rather as a Merchant than a Carrier ... refusing to carry goods but on his own terms'.

But this was also a high-risk venture. Particularly on the unimproved river it was not uncommon for vessels to run aground or sink with complete loss of their cargo, bringing dire consequences for the bargemaster or 'cost-bearer'. The Henley bargemaster Walter Powney was one of three in the town to place a notice in the *Oxford Journal* in 1784, warning that they would not be held responsible for loss of goods if their barges were sunk by accident. Nonetheless Powney was bankrupt four years later, for reasons which were not given.[120]

For Henley no comprehensive list of 18th-century bargemasters has been found, though the town seems to have followed the general pattern. Those identified were all substantial townspeople, and often expanded into related activities. Successive members of the Usher family were not only bargemasters but landlords of the *White Horse* inn, which adjoined Henley bridge and the waterfront. Others set up as coal merchants or acquired interests in Henley's wharfs. William Soundy, for instance, whose father was a maltster, advertised in 1791 as a bargemaster, wharfinger and ironmonger, and a few years earlier acquired rights in a coal and coke business at Henley's Bridge Wharf. Yet others had property in the town, among them John Smith (d. 1715), who left his 'boats, tackle, sails [and] oars' to his sons together with houses on New Street and Friday Street. Their own homes were presumably respectable and well furnished, though not much is known about them as there are few probate inventories for this period. William East (d. 1774), however, lived in a brick house at the lower end of New Street, towards the river.

How many bargemasters operated from Henley at any one time is difficult to establish. Probably it was never more than half a dozen or so, with several families (such as the Ushers, Smiths and Jacksons) continuing for several generations. Alongside them were bargemasters from neighbouring towns, who also operated through Henley: men like William Mills of Reading, or the Marlow master William Langley, who in the 1790s ran three barges of between 66 and 146 tons between Henley and London. In some instances women continued the family business after their husband's death. Sarah Jackson was described as a bargemaster and publican in 1774, though at the time she was in Oxford Castle for debt.[121]

Such bargemasters owned the boats and fixed the contracts, and in some instances may have physically captained the vessel. But working such huge barges required significant amounts of skilled labour, and the larger body of bargemen recorded in and around the town presumably worked for them. Though tough physical labour this, too, was a 'lucrative' occupation according to William Mavor, requiring 'not only strength and activity but considerable experience and local knowledge'. Unfortunately we have no Henley bargemen's inventories for the 18th century to test this, and only very few wills, making it difficult to know more. One who died in 1711 had a feather bed and a 'great chest' and was owed £44, though a near contemporary lived in a small rented cottage, and made only a few negligible family bequests. Even less is known of the 'halers' who hauled boats upstream (Panel 8), and the wharf-side labourers

Figure 78 The waterfront south of New Street around 1813, with the former *Anchor* pub in the foreground. Statements by Henley people in the 1780s paint a vivid picture of the bustling activity along this stretch, with barges being constantly loaded and unloaded. However, the road flooded frequently, and was newly embanked around 1785. Fortune's or Eylsley's wharf is just off to the left.

Halers and Horses: Working Western Barges

From the 17th century to the early 20th the typical vessel on the middle and upper Thames was the 'Western barge', so called because they operated inland west of London Bridge. Like the barges shown in paintings of the 1690s (Figure 41), those of the 18th and early 19th centuries were wide and flat-bottomed, but substantially bigger. By the 1760s some measured nearly 130 feet long by 18½ feet wide, and could carry 180 tons or more. From 1751 they were required to have their tonnage and place of origin painted on the side, and to have a draught (their depth below the water) of no more than four feet, though both regulations were regularly flaunted by bargemasters keen to cram the largest possible cargo into their vessels. Such massive sizes declined slightly by the early 19th century, partly because new poundlocks and canals could not accommodate them. The largest barges required a crew of six men and a boy, the steersman 'assisted by bargemen who, with large ashen poles from 14 feet to 19 feet in length, with incredible dexterity, keep the barge in the proper navigation channel' (Figure A).

Until the late 19th century most barges had a sail to help the downriver journey, with masts which could be lowered to fit under bridges. Most were square-rigged like those in Siberechts' paintings, though from the 1790s smaller triangular sprit sails (which were less efficient but easier to handle) gradually replaced them. Barges travelling upstream or over particularly difficult stretches had to be hauled manually, which in the 18th century was still sometimes done by teams of men

Figure A *Despite its similarity to the traditional Western barge, the vessel shown approaching Henley bridge in this drawing of 1834 is an 'improved' Kennet or Thames-and-Severn canal-type barge, with rounded prow and a spritsail mounted towards the front. The bargemen are using long ashen poles to help keep it off the shallows.*

Figure B *Halers (far right) hauling a Western barge upstream to Henley in the 1690s, as shown in a detail from Jan Siberechts' painting of 'Henley with Rainbow' (Panel 7). During the 18th century haulage by horses gradually became more common: an Act of 1771 provided that halers put out of work through use of horses or by injury and old age could apply for relief to the Thames Commissioners, who might authorise payment of up to 4s. a week. (© Tate, London 2009)*

Mr. WILLIAM LANGLEY, of Great Marlow, Bargemaſter, being examined, ſaid, that he navigates the River from Henley to London a Barge of One hundred and Forty-ſix Tons, a ſmall One of Seventy-ſeven, and another of Sixty-ſix; that it generally takes Two Horſes to draw the One of 146 Tons from Putney to Richmond, with the ſmall Barge in Tow Three Horſes; from Richmond to Hampton Court moſtly Ten Horſes with the ſingle Boats, Twelve with the ſmall One in Tow; from Hampton Court to Weybridge Twelve, and Fourteen with the ſmall One in Tow; from Weybridge to Windſor Fourteen, and Seventeen with the ſmall Barge in Tow in the Winter Streams; from Windſor to Hambleton Bank Ten Horſes, with the large One Twelve; from thence to Boulter's Lock Twelve Horſes, either ſingle or double; from Boulter's Lock to Headſor Twelve; from Headſor to Cookham, Ten Horſes; from Cookham to Spade Oak, Four Horſes, being a very eaſy Strain; from Spade Oak to Marlow Ten Horſes; and from Marlow to Henley Eight: that the worſt Paſſage is Tangier Flat, a Quarter of a Mile below Windſor, a very dangerous Place, and at Sunbury Flat Accidents

Figure C *Part of the statement made to a parliamentary inquiry in 1793 by William Langley, a Marlow bargemaster who operated between Henley and London. Langley reported that 'it generally takes two horses to draw the [barge] of 146 tons from Putney to Richmond'; Weybridge to Windsor required 17 horses in winter 'with the small barge in tow', and Marlow to Henley required eight.*

known as haulers or 'halers'. An eye-witness account described their back-breaking work:

> Coming upstream the barge was towed by 5 or 6 men; each had a leather breast-strap with a small harness rope which he could attach to the tow-rope. Hauling a loaded barge upstream was no light task and, at a rapid, it was desperate work, the advance being only foot by foot. The men bent forward and sometimes, if the barge happened to give a shear in a stream, they almost lay on the ground, and waited till she could recover herself.

By the 1730s towing with horses was becoming more common, though the number needed on different stretches varied considerably. In 1809 the agriculturalist William Mavor reported that a 128-ton barge needed just one horse for the downward journey, but between eight and 14 upstream. Like halers, horses seem to have been available for hire *en route*, though bargemasters presumably made advance arrangements for regular journeys. Improving the quality of towpaths formed an important part of the Thames Commissioners' work, and was mentioned in government legislation as early as 1730.

Journey times in the 1790s remained conditional on weather and water levels, though Mavor claimed that floods hindered Thames navigation for no more than 20 days a year on average, and that the river was less prone to freezing than a stagnant canal. Upstream journeys from London to Marlow or Henley generally took around three to four days, not all that different from in the 15th century; the nine days taken to Oxford (or eight days downstream from Lechlade) was, however, a huge improvement on earlier. Nonetheless, in exceptionally bad conditions the journey from London to Oxford could still take eight weeks.

Sources: Wilson, DG, *The Thames: Record of a Working Waterway* (1987), 35–54; Mavor, W, *General View of the Agriculture of Berks* (1813), 432; Burton, J, *Present State of Navigation on the Thames Considered* (1767); Vanderstegen, W, *The Present State of the Thames Considered* (1794); *Report from Committee ... into Improvement of the Thames* (Parl. Paper 1793, xiv); Acts 3 George II, c.11; 24 George II, c.8; 11 George III, c.45.

who helped to load them; halers seem to have been billeted along the river, and none are explicitly recorded living in Henley.[122]

Bargemen landed and loaded their goods along much of the Henley waterfront in the 18th century. Long before then the stretch between New Street and Phyllis Court had been developed as a large commercial wharf called Fortune's, Hawkins's or Eylsley's, after a succession of 17th- and 18th-century tenants. By the 1760s there was a pub there called the *Ship*, and in the 1780s this was the only Henley wharf to have a crane. The Stonors of Stonor Park had another wharf south of Friday Street, though in the 1690s that seems to have been little more than a large open area in waterside meadows, where timber and other goods were stacked for loading. The stretch between Hart Street and New Street, where the road sloped gently to the river, had no formal landing facilities, but statements made by inhabitants in the 1780s show that barges habitually stopped there, and that the whole frontage was a hive of bustling activity. Barge tackle was regularly laid on the shore for several days while barges were cleaned and blacked, and freight of all kinds was piled up there awaiting loading or collection. Often it was left overnight, either rolled into gateways or covered with tar cloths, and guarded by a night watchman who received 6d. a night. Coal was unloaded by hand, the sacks carried on men's backs, while imported grain was either loaded onto carts or carried into Barrett March's adjoining granaries. Conversely, farmers selling grain frequently carted it to the waterside for loading onto barges. Barges outside the *Red Lion* were tethered to 'stumps' or posts set in the water, though the campshot there extended no more than 150 feet along the waterfront – roughly the length of a single barge.[123]

IMPROVING HENLEY

By 1800, then, those approaching Henley did so through a landscape transformed by the engineering improvements of the nascent industrial age: well-made roads punctuated by toll houses and coaching inns, and carefully managed waterways negotiated through a growing series of poundlocks. From their barges and coaches travellers would have seen further symptoms of the 18th century's mania for improvement, in the newly landscaped (and often scientifically managed) country estates of houses like Fawley Court or Park Place. Predictably, such changes did not stop at the town boundary but transformed the town itself, opening up and improving its streets, giving it a smart, more modern waterfront, and perhaps most strikingly producing the elegant new bridge of which the town remains justifiably proud.[124]

In the early 1780s travellers approaching Henley along Gainsborough's new road down White Hill entered the town not over the current bridge, but over an increasingly ramshackle timber affair which had been repeatedly patched up (see Panel 1). The most recent occasion was in the mid-1770s after storms swept part of it away, but that was not the first time: in 1712 the bridge was said to be 'very slight and ... frequently down', and between 1754 and 1756 the corporation had to supply a ferry. Part of the problem was that the only funds for its upkeep came from the corporation's 'bridge rents' on certain properties in the town, which had been established during the Middle Ages and which were now woefully inadequate. Deciding that enough was enough, in 1780–1 the corporation applied for an Act of Parliament allowing them to charge tolls in support of a new stone bridge, a procedure similar to that for establishing turnpike trusts. William Hayward, a respected Shrewsbury architect, was appointed in 1781, and the new bridge was completed in 1786, built immediately along the north side of its predecessor. The old bridge remained in use until the new one was ready to take traffic.

Figure 79 Carvings of Thamesis and Isis over the bridge's central arch are personifications of the river. The sculptor was Anne Damer (1749–1828), whose father General Conway took a close interest in the bridge design and may have amended it. The plaster and terracotta cast shown here is contemporary.

But the bridge's creation was not trouble-free. For some neighbouring landowners, the incentive to replace the bridge was not only economic but aesthetic. Sambrooke Freeman, the architecturally minded owner of Fawley Court and Henley manor, became so offended by the old bridge's appearance that in 1769 he arranged for it be covered with boards representing a bridge at Florence (probably the 16th-century Ponte Santa Trinita), and as soon as word was out of the corporation's intentions local gentry insisted on becoming involved, seeing this as a natural extension of the landscaping of their own estates. The result was a protracted battle over representation on the trust, the design of the new structure, and even its location. Freeman, who like any well-educated 18th-century gentleman really did know something about architecture, drew up his own plans for a bridge which he insisted should be sited at the end of New Street, where it would be seen from Fawley Court. The corporation successfully overturned that idea on the entirely reasonable grounds that it would divert traffic away from the market place. Nonetheless, General Conway of Park Place attended every meeting at which the bridge was discussed, and may well have influenced the design: certainly it was his daughter, the sculptress Anne Damer, who carved the heads of Thamesis and Isis which grace the bridge's central arch. The final result won the approbation of no less a figure than Horace Walpole (a close friend of Conway), though Hayward himself tragically died before the bridge was completed. The debt was not finally paid off until 1873, when the tolls ceased.[125]

The Act of 1781 provided not only for the building of the bridge but for other improvements to the town: new paving, lighting and guttering, and above all replacement of the narrow twisting route through the centre with 'commodious avenues', which required demolition of buildings near the river, removal of part of the churchyard, and the clearing away of the accumulated medieval clutter in the middle of the market place. This was, in fact, merely a continuation of a process which had started in the 1760s, with the corporation's clearance of medieval houses in the middle of Hart Street and removal of the medieval town cross, apparently in connection with road improvement and turnpiking. The approach to the bridge past the church was widened in 1781–2, and the Middle Row in the market place (including the medieval guildhall) was demolished in stages in the early 1790s, creating the impressive open area which still dominates the town west of the crossroads. Its upper end was closed off in 1796 by an imposing new town hall in classical style, designed by the Henley builder and alderman William Bradshaw; the site was that of a former market house, and the corporation stipulated that the new building should include a covered arcade on its ground floor to attract local farmers on market day. Coincidentally the old gabled manor house at Phyllis Court, by then little used, was also swept away around 1786, to

Figure 80 The opening up of Henley's market place followed the Bridge Act of 1781, and culminated in the completion in 1796 of a new town hall. The new building replaced both the medieval guild hall to the east, and an earlier market house on the same site. The two-storeyed portico harks back to designs by the 16th-century Italian architect Andrea Palladio, and was probably transmitted through pattern books.

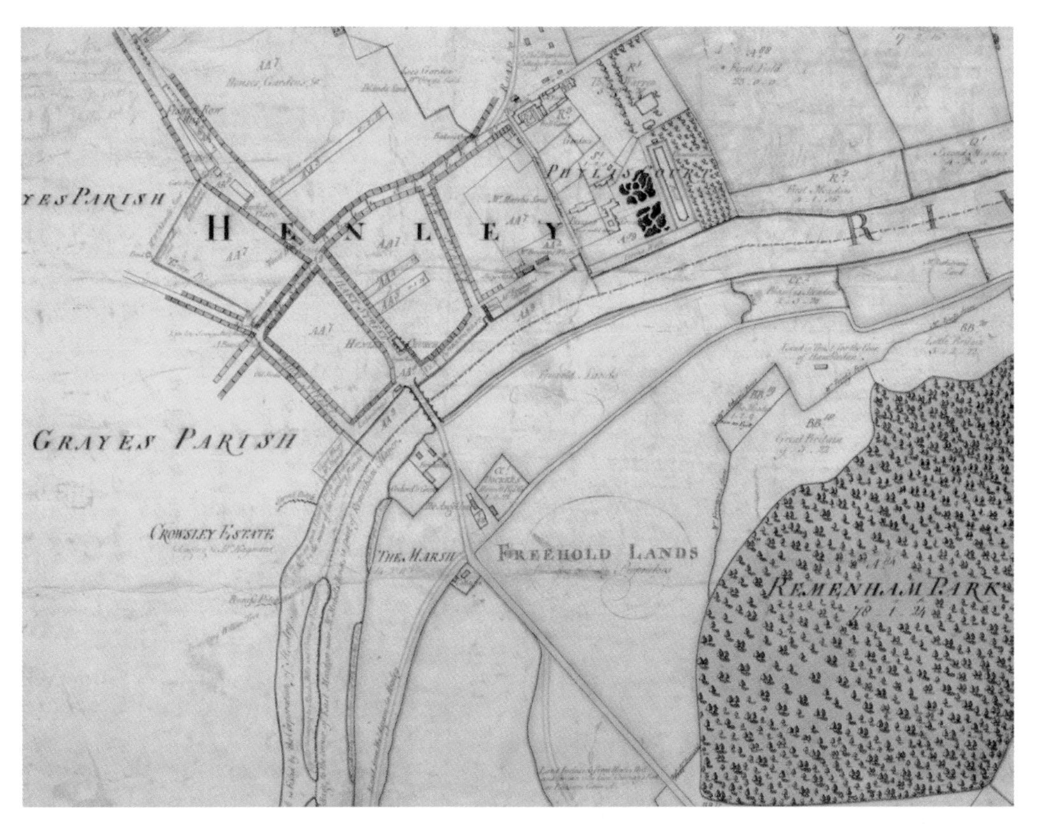

Figure 81 Henley c.1788, shown on a map of the estates belonging to Strickland Freeman of Fawley Court. The medieval Middle Row in the market place is still shown, though similar buildings in the middle of Hart Street have gone. North of the bridge is the 'new embankment', with 'Mr Freeman's wharf' beyond it; south of Friday Street is the Stonors' 'upper wharf'. Phyllis Court is marked as 'now pulled down'. At bottom right, Humphrey Gainsborough's straight new road runs down White Hill to the new bridge, its curving earlier course (by then taken into Park Place's grounds) still visible. North is tilted 45 degrees to the right.

be replaced by the present building in the 1840s. The process of clearance and rebuilding continued into the 19th century, when a further Act (in 1808) allowed for widening of the central crossroads. Duke Street, however, remained an exceptionally narrow thoroughfare until 1872–3, still lined on its western side with ancient timber-framed houses.[126]

Improvement of the waterfront proved trickier, since owners of Henley manor claimed it as part of their property, and refused to allow any development without compensation. This had already caused controversy earlier in the century, when John Smith, a Henley bargemaster, built a landing place between Hart Street and New Street, only to have it torn down on the orders of Sir William Whitelocke. The roadway there flooded frequently, however, and as part of the bridge scheme the corporation decided to press ahead with a new embankment flanked by a riverside wall. The result was a series of lawsuits with Strickland Freeman of Fawley Court (Sambrooke's nephew and heir), who demanded £5,000 compensation, and separately sued Barrett March, the owner of the *Red Lion* granaries, for landing goods there. That the town was already in conflict with Freeman over fishing rights can hardly have helped matters, but armed with the 1781 Bridge Act, which authorised new roads to the bridge, the corporation seems to have won its case. The new embankment duly appeared on an estate map drawn up a few years later (Figure 81), commissioned – ironically – by Strickland Freeman.[127]

A Changing Town

Intentionally or not, the new embankment north of Hart Street seems to have altered the nature of the waterfront along that stretch. March's granaries continued into the 19th century, but bargemen found the frontage less convenient as a landing place, and increasingly used the neighbouring wharfs beyond New Street and above the bridge. The transformation says much about Henley's dual nature in the 18th century, fuelled by the transport revolutions of the period. On the one hand it remained a town built largely on the river trade, as its malthouses and the bustling waterfront, with its barges, river workers and alehouses, clearly show. On the other it was emerging as a social centre, its grand coaching inns and function rooms catering for a privileged and sophisticated clientele, and its newly broadened streets and new public buildings designed to appeal to those used to the latest London and Bath fashions. Alongside both strands, as in any town, lay a darker and more impoverished underside, reflected in the building of a large new workhouse on its western edge at the top of West Street.

What, then, can we learn about the broader life of the town in the 18th century? It is to this that we now turn, beginning with the people who lived and worked there, before moving on to its social and cultural life and the rebuildings which transformed its appearance.

Chapter 8 The 18th-Century Town

Henley in the 18th century was a town balanced between two worlds: the old familiar one of commerce, river barges, granaries and malthouses, and the nascent social one of grand coaching inns, assembly rooms, and glittering social events. Both remained central to the town's wellbeing, but with the success of coaching and the spread of new social fashions, the balance began to shift. By the 1840s shops and services catering for a well-heeled resident and visiting population had already become dominant, part of an ongoing process which in various ways has continued to the present day. How were these changes reflected in the life of the 18th-century town, and in the related transformation of its streets and buildings?

TRADES, CRAFTS AND SERVICES

The previous chapter concentrated on coaching and expansion of the river trade. But as in earlier periods, many or most of the town's population were not directly involved in either. Reconstructing how people earned their livings is not straightforward, since before the 19th-century censuses there is no single source to give an overview of trades and occupations. Nonetheless, the evidence of wills suggests the broad outlines, combined, from the late 18th century, with printed trades directories listing the town's main trades and businesses. Two main trends are visible. First was the emergence

Figure 82 Hart Street in 1826, showing some of the changes which transformed Henley during the 18th century. Smart classical façades of brick or stucco rub shoulders with older gabled frontages, the pavements are newly laid, and the street itself, leading to the graceful bridge completed in 1786, is newly widened. A century earlier, the stagecoach would have had to negotiate a tortuous course around medieval buildings in the middle of the narrow, unmade road. The church, too, has a classical pediment (since removed) over its west door, a new clock installed in 1733, and an extended south aisle rebuilt in 1789 and 1819–20.

of large-scale commercial brewing, encompassing the beginnings of what later became Brakspears' Brewery. Second was the gradual but inexorable expansion of the retail and service economy, as Henley – partly but not entirely on the back of coaching – began its transformation into a fashionable social centre.

Brewing and Malting

The development of 'common' or commercial brewing was a phenomenon shared by many provincial towns in the 18th century. Brewing was traditionally a domestic activity, but with rising demand it made sense for specialists with the necessary skill and capital to produce in bulk. Most supplied inns and pubs within a narrow radius of perhaps 10 miles, pretty well the limit for transporting beer for sale before the coming of the railways. In Henley the existing malt trade made this a particularly attractive option, and several of the town's early brewers were maltsters or innkeepers who moved gradually into the brewing side. Both the Brooks and the Sarney families, who respectively set up businesses on Bell Street and New Street, were established as maltsters, while the brewer Robert Cluett (d. 1744) owned the *Black Horse*, and Charles Brigstock (d. 1753) was lessee of the *Rose and Crown*, both in Market Place. Brewing was a high-risk business, but the rewards could be substantial. All these men became prosperous and respected townspeople who figured prominently in town life: Brigstock, for instance, served several times as warden or mayor, and left bequests worth over £600. Two later brewers were listed as gentry in 1793.

Figure 83 Portrait thought to show Robert Brakspear as a young man, probably a few years after he settled in Henley. With his uncle Richard Hayward, Brakspear established the brewing firm which, as W.H. Brakspear & Sons, continued in Henley until 2002.

Of particular significance for the future of Henley's brewing industry – though this would not have been clear at the time – was Robert Brakspear (1750–1812). The son of an impoverished Faringdon tailor, Brakspear set up as an innkeeper and brewer in Witney before joining his uncle Richard Hayward in the Bell Street brewing and malting business set up by the Brookses. The late 18th century was a period of intense competition among south Oxfordshire brewers, and Brakspear faced rivalry not only within the town but from growing businesses at Wallingford, Watlington and Reading, all keen to extend their influence through the acquisition of pubs across the area. Through tireless dedication and not a little luck Brakspear ended his career a wealthy and respected man, with interests in over 30 pubs in and around the town, and a beneficial merger negotiated between his Bell Street business and that of his rivals on New Street. It was, however, his son William who ensured the survival of the family business, based in New Street and known later as W.H. Brakspear & Sons.[128]

Figure 84 An 18th-century brewhouse, from Croker's *Complete Dictionary of Arts and Sciences* (1764–6). Workers are mixing malt and water in mash tuns, before adding hops and boiling the mixture in a copper. Malting took place elsewhere: in Brakspear's case, behind 76 and 78 Bell Street. Brakspear's output in the late 1790s averaged 6,250 barrels a year, minute by London standards, but still a large quantity.

Henley's 18th-century brewers ran their own malthouses, and sometimes (like Brakspear) rented extra capacity. But independent malting continued, some of it presumably for local brewers and some of it for London, whose brewing industry dwarfed that of places like Henley. As purpose-built malthouses took over from domestic kitchen chimneys and ovens, the overall number of maltsters in the town may well have fallen, as suggested by a sharp fall in the number of maltsters' wills after the 1720s. Even so there were 13 maltsters in Henley in the 1790s, and if anything overall production probably went up rather than down.[129]

Shops, Crafts and Services

Important though these developments were, they remained small-scale. Henley's 18th-century brewing industry never employed particularly large numbers, and the town failed to develop into an industrial or manufacturing centre. By contrast the service and retail sector became steadily more important, as shopkeepers and craftsmen catered for a growing social elite and for the passing coaching traffic. The development of Henley's coaching inns was outlined above, and alongside them traditional suppliers such as butchers, bakers, tailors, drapers, shoemakers, and saddlers or harness-makers continued to expand. As the 18th century progressed, they were increasingly supplemented by more specialised shopkeepers. Grocers, originally traders in spices, dried fruits, sugar and more general foodstuffs, were recorded from soon after 1700, selling mostly imported items brought upstream by barge; in the 1790s there were no fewer than 18 grocer's shops

Figure 85 The Hart Street house (centre) of Francis Blandy, the Henley lawyer poisoned by his daughter in 1751. The house, with its projecting 'Ipswich' windows, was by then decidedly old-fashioned, and was rebuilt in the 19th century: the symmetrical house next door, with its door hood and decorative pilasters, is much more typical of Henley's 18th-century town houses. Like other 18th-century lawyers and professionals in the town, Blandy was closely involved in municipal affairs, and served for several years as town clerk.

in the town, which by then probably sold imported tea, coffee and cocoa as well. Brandy merchants were mentioned from the 1770s, and confectioners soon after. Other shops and services included booksellers and stationers, watchmakers, hairdressers, a peruke (or wig) maker, and specialist clothing suppliers such as a mantua maker, specialising probably in silk fabrics. These were not the sorts of services found in the 18th-century countryside, but they were most certainly what inhabitants of a sophisticated provincial market and coaching town expected to find, and clearly they flourished. In 1841 there were milliners and haberdashers, glass and china dealers, and a perfumier, alongside clock- and watchmakers, tea dealers, butchers and bakers, and (still) 18 grocers.

Similar trends were apparent in the growing body of professionals settled in Henley, where they could not only enjoy the ambience and social facilities of a fashionable country town, but make a decent living from the local 'respectable' classes. A trades directory in the 1790s listed four clergy, five surgeons or druggists, and three lawyers, along with five schoolmasters or mistresses employed at a number of private schools and academies. An earlier Henley lawyer was the prominent solicitor and town clerk Francis Blandy, who in 1751 was notoriously poisoned by his daughter at the instigation of her unscrupulous army-officer lover. A bank was co-founded in 1791 by the brewers Richard Hayward and Robert Brakspear, with their relative Mr Fisher.

Alongside these people worked the more traditional craftsmen and retailers required in any town or village: blacksmiths, coopers, ironmongers and the like. Small-scale leather-working and textile manufacture continued in the form of the odd currier, tanner or weaver, presumably supplying the local market. Rather better represented – unsurprisingly given the scale of rebuilding in 18th-century Henley – were the various building trades, encompassing significant numbers of carpenters, bricklayers, masons, glaziers and plumbers. Last but not least was a significant agricultural element, though as in the 19th century many of those directly involved in agriculture may have lived on the peripheries of the town or in the parish's rural part, towards Badgemore and Assendon. Inhabitants listed in the 1790s included four farmers, a 'yeoman', a nursery and seedsman, and four corn chandlers or mealmen, while in the 1840s (the first date for which we have such information) the town and parish contained nearly 80 agricultural labourers. The agricultural element was further reflected in the Thursday market and four annual fairs, which continued for sale of livestock, poultry, fish and grain, and were clearly bustling events. 'All the country some miles round' heard of an impromptu royal visit to the area in 1785 because 'it happened to be market day at Henley'.

Largely invisible beneath these prominent tradesmen, craftsmen and professionals was the vast bulk of the town's labouring population. The truly poor – those who through infirmity, indigence or misfortune could no longer support themselves – float occasionally into the records of poor law administration, and are discussed below. Hints about the rest of the 18th-century populace are contained in the earliest of the 19th-century census enumerator's books, which for 1841, alongside the sorts of people mentioned above, list over 320 domestic servants (mostly women), and over 200 unspecified labourers – in all nearly a third of those whose occupation was given. Another 40-odd women eked a living as laundresses or washerwomen. Reading back such evidence into the 18th century is questionable, but in broad outline this undoubtedly tells us something about the 18th-century town, which must similarly have included large numbers of servants, general labourers, and people at subsistence. A more transient fringe population is hinted at in the sad report of a 'travelling woman' found dead at Northfield End in 1774.[130]

HENLEY AS A SOCIAL CENTRE

The development of such a large service and retail sector reflected the presence of consumers with disposable income. Some were coach travellers stopping off on the way to somewhere else; others were permanent (or at least seasonal) residents in and around the town, attracted by the combination of swift communications with London and the area's natural beauty. The early 19th-century writer James Brewer highlighted Henley's location 'near the base of

Figure 86 General (later Field-Marshal) Henry Seymour Conway of Park Place, one of several high-ranking local landowners who played a significant role in Henley's social and cultural life in the later 18th century. The portrait is by Thomas Gainsborough, whose brother Humphrey (Henley's Congregationalist minister) enjoyed close relations with Conway and other local gentry.

a cluster of hills in one of the most agreeable windings of the River Thames', adding that the 'beauty of [its] situation' had 'induced many private families to construct ornamental houses'. The town's prosperity was further 'evinced in the improvements progressively taking place in the habitations of traders of every rank'. Numerous other visitors painted a similar picture, singling out the 'elegant villas' among the 'lofty beech-woods and extensive plantations'.[131]

As earlier, some of Henley's wealthiest and most fashionable figures were landowners living in neighbouring country houses. Several were of high social rank. Park Place, across the river in Remenham, was owned from around 1738 to 1751 by the Prince of Wales, who used it as a country retreat for hunting parties; his successor was the celebrated soldier and politician Henry Seymour Conway (d. 1795), who retired there as a country gentleman, indulging a passion for landscaping and pursuing literary and other cultured interests. Decades later a visitor still remembered 'the brilliant society of Field-Marshal Conway's house', which included the likes of Horace Walpole, the philosopher David Hume, and the poet Thomas Gray. Part of the same circle were the Freemans of Fawley Court, where John Freeman (d. 1752) and his son Sambrooke (d. 1782) pursued similar interests, expanding their estates and reshaping both the house and its grounds with the help of such cutting-edge figures as the landscape gardener 'Capability' Brown and the architect James Wyatt. Their roots, as we saw earlier, were in commerce, and the same remained true of several other landowning families in the area: the Grotes at Badgemore House, for instance, who were London bankers of Dutch origin and acquired their Henley estate around 1785. Others included the Hodges family at Bolney Court in Harpsden, who like

Figure 87 Sambrooke Freeman's re-landscaping of the grounds at Fawley Court included the construction of an ornamental temple on an island in the Thames, designed by the leading architect James Wyatt, and originally used for fishing parties. The building later became associated with the Royal Regatta course, which started nearby.

the Freemans owned slave plantations in the West Indies. William Caesar, 'a black belonging to Anthony Hodges Esq', was buried at Harpsden in 1778, having presumably been kept as a manservant.[132]

Many of these landowners became involved in Henley life, serving as bridge commissioners, for instance. But Henley's well-to-do were not confined to surrounding country estates. By the time of the first surviving census in 1841 no fewer than 183 Henley residents (over 11 per cent of those whose occupations were given) were of 'independent means', and another 15–20 were in leading professions. This alone explains the large number of domestic servants in the town, and in social and consumer terms prosperous tradesmen or manufacturers like the Brakspears were on a similar level. Though the census evidence is late, the picture fits well with that derived from wills, trades directories and visitors' descriptions in the 1770s to early 1800s, and helps to explain how Henley was gradually transformed into a town of smart sophisticated streets: a place in which those accustomed to London or Bath fashions might feel at home despite the town's undoubted provincial air. A further indicator is the number of private academies and boarding schools catering for the sons and daughters of the 'gentry' and the well-to-do. In 1793 Henley had at least three boarding schools 'for young ladies' and another for 'young gentleman', alongside the endowed Grammar, Periam and 'Greencoat' schools.[133]

Figure 88 Caroline Powys (*née* Girle), whose diaries paint an evocative picture of the glittering social life enjoyed by Henley's privileged classes in the later 18th century. Her brother-in-law Thomas (with whom she and her husband lived at Fawley Rectory) was a chaplain to George III, giving the family an entrée to the highest social circles.

Charity balls and concerts in the town were mentioned from the 1750s, held sometimes in the town hall and sometimes in the more up-market inns. One in 1777, 'for the benefit of M. Vanscor, a dancer at Drury Lane', was held at the *Bell*, and a gentleman's club met regularly at the *Red Lion* by the 1790s. These can be traced through local newspapers, but the social round among Henley's privileged classes is most evocatively captured through the diaries of Caroline Powys, whose brother-in-law the Revd Thomas Powys was rector of Fawley and a chaplain to George III. Powys described the glittering events she attended in minute detail. By far the grandest was a 'gala week' in January 1777, sponsored by the tenant of Phyllis Court, Lord Villiers. Plays (featuring local gentry in key roles) were staged at a specially improvised theatre at Bolney Court, and grand suppers and balls running into the small hours were held at the *Bell Inn* and at Fawley Court, where 'ninety-two [including prominent members of the aristocracy] sat down to supper'. The diaries also detail the more routine social round. Like many of their class the Powyses usually spent the spring season at Bath, where they frequented the fashionable Assembly Rooms and mingled with aristocracy. Back in Henley they flung themselves into a winter season of assemblies and other events:

> On Friday [17 October 1788] began our winter Henley ball, and was a very full one, the whole neighbouring families making it a point to attend. Got home about four, as there is always a supper and dancing after. We were very gay this autumn, having a very tolerable set of strollers [actors] at Henley; most of the ladies bespoke plays, as Lady Ailesbury, Mrs Damer, both Mrs Freemans ...

In and between was a more *ad hoc* round of dinners, balls, and near-daily visits which evokes the world of Jane Austen (a distant relative), 'for except in the most important point of late hours, our most agreeable and sociable neighbourhood never suffer their friends to pass a day solo'. The Powyses were particularly close to the Conways and Freemans, with whom they enjoyed a 'delightful' water party on the Freemans' pleasure boat in 1795. Ten years earlier Mrs Powys left an entertaining account of an impromptu royal visit to Sarah Freeman at Henley Park. The king and his party, she reported, 'talked incessantly, seemed vastly pleased, and knew every family and their concerns in this neighbourhood ... better than [Mrs Freeman] did herself.'[134]

Amateur dramatics played an important role in these social gatherings, and performances by travelling players in the town seem to have been frequent. A purpose-built theatre on New Street opened in 1805, and Mrs Powys was soon there, declaring an actor in Sheridan's 'The Rivals' to be 'as capital a performer as any I've seen in London or Bath'. Nonetheless audiences gradually declined, and from 1813 the building was put to other uses, to be resurrected as the Kenton Theatre only in the 20th century. During its short life its character evidently changed, and certainly not all its early patrons were as genteel as the Powyses: in 1812 a Newbury

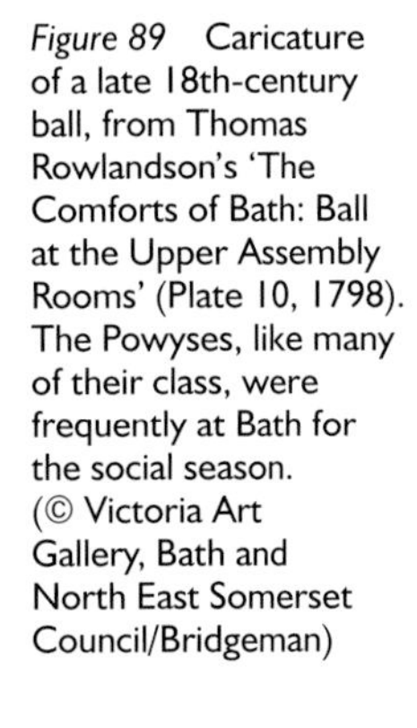

Figure 89 Caricature of a late 18th-century ball, from Thomas Rowlandson's 'The Comforts of Bath: Ball at the Upper Assembly Rooms' (Plate 10, 1798). The Powyses, like many of their class, were frequently at Bath for the social season. (© Victoria Art Gallery, Bath and North East Somerset Council/Bridgeman)

Figure 90 Design for a fish wagon by Henley's Congregationalist minister Humphrey Gainsborough, whose engineering and scientific interests were shared by local gentry. The system of pistons was to maintain airflow, keeping the fish fresh while it was transported. Gainsborough's design for a condensing steam engine led to disputes with James Watt over whose design came first.

bargeman admitted having 'wantonly' thrown 'a quart mug with beer in it from the gallery into the pit', and was prosecuted by the manager. The incident is a reminder that for the bulk of the town's population the world of balls and assemblies was a distant one, and that for most, entertainment remained centred on the town's numerous pubs and alehouses, with their bowls and skittles and card games. Even at such well-appointed inns as the *White Hart* illegal back-room gambling seems to have been common, sometimes for very high stakes.[135]

A different facet of 'polite' society in and around Henley were the cultural and scientific interests of some of its leading figures, embracing not only architecture, landscape gardening and progressive farming, but new technologies and experimental science. Prominent in these circles were Sambrooke Freeman and General Conway, Thomas Hall at Harpsden Court, and the Congregationalist minister Humphrey Gainsborough, whose interest in road and river improvement has already been mentioned. Gainsborough, described in an obituary as 'one of the most ingenious men that ever lived', was an engineer of note, whose numerous inventions included a tide mill, a condensing steam engine, a refrigerated fish wagon, a drill plough, and timepieces. He enjoyed warm support from local landowners who shared his interests, with whom he corresponded and swapped ideas. Hall in particular, as a fellow Congregationalist, seems to have supported him in practical ways, and may have provided a workshop at Harpsden. The spirit of scientific enquiry and technological innovation, so typical of the period, found other local expressions too, in Robert Brakspear's methodical experimentation with brewing techniques, for instance, and his use of new instruments such as a thermometer and hydrometer. Such shared interests seem to have promoted genuine friendship and mutual regard, though probably within strict limits. Gainsborough called Freeman his 'good benefactor', and his relationship with the local elite probably always remained that of respected protégé rather than genuine social equal.[136]

TOWN GOVERNMENT AND THE POOR

In 1722 the corporation was revamped under a new royal charter, which confirmed and broadened its powers. The new body was headed by a mayor, assisted by nine fellow aldermen, a recorder, and 16 burgesses. All were members of Henley's trading and professional elite, the mayor (like earlier wardens) appointed for one year, and the aldermen and burgesses generally for life. Other officers included a town clerk, two serjeants-at-mace, and a

Figure 91 (Right and below) Part of the new parish workhouse built at the top of West Street in 1790, replacing an earlier one on New Street. The arcaded range (with an inscription over one of the arches) dates from that period; adjoining buildings were added after 1834, when it became the Union workhouse. In the 20th century the site became Townlands Hospital.

largely honorific high steward. The corporation was empowered to make byelaws and hold a weekly court of record, which could hear debt cases involving sums of less than £10: a useful facility in a trading town like Henley. As earlier, it controlled the market and bridge and administered the town's substantial charities and ancient bridge rents, appointing two 'bridgemen' who doubled as churchwardens.[137]

But as in most towns the corporation was not the only organ of government. Vestiges of manorial jurisdiction continued, while the parish vestry – largely composed of the same leading townspeople as the corporation – retained responsibility for church and parish affairs. Among these was responsibility for poor relief, which as in most towns and villages came to dominate the vestry's affairs from the later 18th century.

The overall costs of poor relief can be traced from the 1770s through parliamentary reports, and Henley's experience was typical: between 1776 and 1803 expenditure on the poor rose from £687 to nearly £2,600 a year, reaching a peak of nearly £4,000 10 years later. This was part of a national phenomenon, reflecting rising population, increased mobility, and rising bread prices, and throughout the 18th and early 19th centuries the town's prosperous classes wrestled with how to tackle the problem and keep down the poor rates. A workhouse on New Street (on the site of the Kenton Theatre) was set up in 1726 under recent legislation: people seeking parish relief through illness, age or unemployment had no choice but to go there, though the vestry gradually relaxed the requirement later on. For much of the 18th century responsibility for the workhouse and those in it was leased to a workhouse keeper at fixed rates, though there was some attempt to impose minimal standards: in 1779, for instance, the vestry dismissed a keeper for failing to keep the inmates clean or teach them reading and writing, and for not conducting them to church or saying prayers. From the 1780s the poor were occasionally inoculated against smallpox, primarily to stop it spreading through the town.

A new purpose-built workhouse was opened on the town's western edge in 1790–1, much of the cost advanced by the wealthy innkeeper Barrett March until the debt could be paid off. But as poor-relief costs rose, so did the rates, much to the dislike of a growing body of inhabitants. The new workhouse scheme was presented as a means of reducing taxes, and in 1815 (at a time of especially high prices) there were committees and public meetings to see how expenditure might be reduced. By then over 370 adults (12 per cent of Henley's population) were on some form of parish relief, 88 of them in the workhouse, and 200 through regular weekly payments. The problem was only finally removed by the sweeping away of the old poor-law system in 1834, to be replaced by new Poor Law Unions.[138]

RELIGION IN HENLEY

What of Henley's religious life in this period? As earlier, religious nonconformity played a significant (though never dominant) role in the town. The Independent or Congregationalist group, whose origins were described in Chapter 6, continued to thrive, and by the early 18th century was increasingly respectable. A report in 1715 estimated the congregation at 400–500 including 21 'gentlemen' and several county voters, with the rest made up of tradesmen, farmers, and labourers. A purpose-built meeting house on the Reading road (just over the parish boundary in Rotherfield Greys) was opened in 1719 on the site of the current building, and by the time that Humphrey Gainsborough arrived in 1748 the Congregationalists seem to have been a generally accepted part of Henley life, their nonconformity broadly tolerated even by the town's Anglican clergy. Gainsborough himself moved in the most eminent circles, as we have seen, and died 'universally beloved and respected', having declined several offers of preferment in the Established Church if he would agree to be ordained. His determination to harness technological advance for the good of his fellow men was a direct expression of his nonconformist principles.[139]

Figure 92 The Congregationalist meeting house on Reading Road, built in 1719, reflected the size and relative prosperity of its membership. Members came not only from the town but from as far away as Wallingford, Checkendon, Stoke Row, Twyford, Marlow and Watlington, and included prominent local gentry such as the Halls of Harpsden Court. The building was replaced in 1907.

Other nonconformist groups fared less well, probably because of the Congregationalists' dominance. The Quaker meeting house at Northfield End continued, but with falling numbers, while John Wesley's attempts to establish Methodism met with mixed success. At his first visit in 1764 he claimed to have 'found a wild, staring congregation ... void both of common sense and common decency', and, though he later softened his judgement, in 1783 he lamented that the Henley Society had 'sank into nothing'. Even so a meeting room was licensed before 1805, and soon after the rector reported around 70 Methodists in the town. Roman Catholicism, despite the presence of the Catholic Stonors a few miles away, remained almost non-existent, with only a handful of adherents during the 18th century and no priest in regular attendance.[140]

The Anglican Church, meanwhile, settled into a pattern familiar in many 18th-century parishes – though better served than some, by a succession of relatively conscientious rectors who mostly lived in Henley. The routine involvement of the town elite was reflected in erection of private pews and galleries, repairs and alterations to the church fabric, and occasional gifts of furnishings or plate: Richard Jennings of Badgemore, for instance, gave a pewter almsdish in 1711, while in 1774 Sambrooke Freeman paid for the setting up of a gilt ball on the church tower. Corporation members had lockable private pews at the front of the church, where they sat in order of rank. Rectors occasionally complained that too many people skipped church for 'motives too vague and various to enumerate', a problem exacerbated by inadequate seating as the population rose. But on the whole – and leaving aside the continuing strength of nonconformity – the 18th century proved an uneventful period for the church in Henley, free from the religious controversies which marked the preceding centuries and, to a lesser extent, the succeeding one.[141]

A 'HANDSOME AND CAPACIOUS' TOWN: 18TH-CENTURY REBUILDING

Changes in Henley's social and economic life were matched by equally far-reaching changes in the town's appearance. The improvements which transformed its streets and waterfront were described in the previous chapter, and in the 1790s impressed the compilers of the *Universal British Directory*, who found its thoroughfares 'widened, paved, and lighted ... [with] few traces of its antiquity ... to be seen'. But improvements were not confined to public spaces. Many of the town's private houses were also modernised as part of a long and continuing process, which saw the increasing replacement of timber with brick, and of vernacular traditions with classical design. The beginnings of these trends are traceable from the 1670s, and were mentioned in Chapter 6. But in the 18th century they acquired an entirely new momentum, transforming the town and – as in neighbouring places such as Marlow or Wallingford – giving it a visual character which it still retains.[142]

Figure 93 Though brick and classical detailing were commonplace in Henley by the 1720s, more old-fashioned traditions co-existed for a time. This design for a pair of houses in Henley is dated 1712, but shows a gabled, timber-framed building more typical of the 17th century.

Classicism and Brick

As a small town, Henley did not see the large-scale speculative building that created the new urban landscapes of Bath and Dublin, London's West End, or the New Town of Edinburgh. Instead, rebuilding occurred piecemeal on the initiative of individual owners or occupiers, who generally employed local men both to design and to build their houses. The architectural profession in a modern sense did not really exist before the end of the century.

In areas of timber building such as south Oxfordshire, local builders usually emerged from the carpentry trade. During the late 17th and early 18th centuries they gradually assimilated what has been called the Classical Language of Architecture: a language whose 'grammar' depended on universally accepted rules of proportion, and whose 'vocabulary' (columns, pilasters, pediments and the like) derived ultimately from the buildings of Ancient Greece and Rome. Inigo Jones was the first Englishman to use this language with precision and mastery, and some of his domestic designs of the 1630s foreshadow much of what was built in Henley and small towns throughout England in the 18th century.[143]

The rebuilding of London after the Great Fire and the concurrent development of the West End gave added impetus to the adoption of this new style (see Chapter 6). Even so, and despite its close London connections, Henley was quite slow in taking it up. Gabled timber houses of traditional type with wood-mullioned windows were still being built in 1712, judging from a drawing of a pair of houses belonging to (or built by) a Mr Jennings – conceivably the master carpenter Richard Jennings, who worked for Sir Christopher Wren at St Paul's Cathedral and owned an estate at Badgemore. But by the 1720s – a time of much building activity throughout southern England – brick had become the favoured building material in and around Henley, and it soon ousted timber in all but the humblest buildings.[144]

One of Henley's first entirely new brick-built classical houses was the Old Rectory on the waterfront, south of the bridge (Figure 94) . It stands on the site of a gabled timber house shown in one of Siberechts' views, and has a symmetrical front of seven bays and two storeys, with large white-painted sash windows, a projecting eaves cornice with dentils, and a hipped roof – features widely used in and around London in the late 17th century. The windows (which have been replaced) are almost flush with the wall, an indication of a relatively early date, and the dates 1701 and 1715 are scratched on bricks. Unfortunately the inside has few original features, and the back was later rebuilt. The original owner

Figure 94 The Old Rectory on the waterfront typifies the London classical styles widely adopted in Henley by the early 18th century, with its symmetrical brick façade, tall sash windows, hipped roof, and decorative dentil cornice (the tooth-like projections under the eaves).

is unknown (as with most of Henley's 18th-century houses), but its prominent position by the river suggests that he may have been a maltster or timber merchant. A later occupier was the brewer James Brooks, before the house was adopted as a rectory in the 1820s. Other houses of similar type soon followed, among them Nos 26/28 Hart Street (built as a single house) and No. 55 New Street, which carries the date 1715 on a rainwater head. A smaller and possibly slightly earlier example is Queen Anne Cottage on Friday Street, built by the tanner Henry Wheeler or his son Benjamin next to their workshop. That has a regular classical brick front of five bays and a pedimented doorcase.[145]

Much of the visual appeal of Henley's early 18th-century houses stems from their varied brickwork (Panel 9). The Old Rectory is of dark red brick, but 26/28 Hart Street and 55 New Street used silver-grey vitrified bricks from Nettlebed or its vicinity, with red brick for the window and door surrounds. At No. 18 Hart Street – a three-storeyed house built possibly for a maltster, since part of an 18th-century malting floor survives behind – the front wall is made up almost entirely of grey-brick headers, but the windows are joined together vertically by bands of red brick, and the tops of the windows are of 'gauged' (i.e. individually cut) brick with very little mortar showing. The windows are set four inches behind the wall surface to minimise fire-risk, as stipulated by the 1709 London Building Act, and the same is true at Nos 15/17 opposite, now part of the *Catherine Wheel.* At the rather later 32 Bell Street, one of the largest houses in the town, red-brick stretchers alternate with blue-grey headers to create a chequered effect, with the glazed or vitrified headers glistening in the sunlight. The most elaborate brickwork is at No. 13 Reading Road (Panel 9), a narrow-fronted three-storeyed house of *c.*1730 on the southern edge of the town. Here classical detailing is picked out in delicately cut brick, in a feat of virtuoso craftsmanship unmatched elsewhere in Henley.[146]

The roof at 13 Reading Road is hidden behind a blind parapet, of a type that became popular in London after the 1707 Building Act outlawed wooden cornices as a fire risk. A similar arrangement exists at 39 Hart Street (Longlands), built probably around 1730–40. Its façade is of yellow-brown brick, more typical of London than Henley, and is relatively sober (Figure 95). Countess Gardens, at the northern end of Bell Street, is of similar design and slightly larger. Usually dated *c.*1740, it too has arched windows in gauged brick, but its pedimented doorcase with its correctly-proportioned Doric pilasters and frieze reflects the influence of the Palladian-inspired pattern books which began to appear in the 1720s. These helped builders keep up with metropolitan-driven fashion, and their widespread use helps explain the parallels

Figure 95 Classical brick façades at 39 Hart Street (right) and Rupert House and Countess Gardens (left). Both show London influences, with their curved window heads (popular in London from c.1715), their pronounced string-courses or plat-bands demarcating each floor, and (at 39 Hart Street) the raised pilaster-strips at the corners, and the strongly emphasised keystones over the windows.

between the domestic architecture of Henley and that of other provincial towns. An equally accomplished pattern-book doorway, this time of the Ionic order, adorns the adjacent (and probably near-contemporary) Rupert House.[147]

A group of mid-18th-century houses in the Market Place gives a good idea of the variety permissible within the broad dictates of Georgian classicism. The most impressive is No. 20 (Panel 9), built, like most 18th-century Henley houses, on the site of an earlier timber-framed house, and retaining some of its fabric. The façade is crowned by a pediment, and inside is a handsome staircase with carved scrollwork under the treads. The house looks as if it was built around 1750, and in the 19th century it was home to the surgeon James Brooks and his descendants. No. 17 opposite, a narrow-fronted house dated 1749 on a rainwater head, is quite different, with a wooden cornice of a kind that must have seemed old-fashioned at the time. Different again are Nos 37–41 to the west, narrow-fronted and dated by a rainwater head to 1755, but with roofs largely concealed behind a parapet. A passage beside No. 37 leads to a 19th-century malt-kiln, a reminder that most of Henley's houses were still workplaces as well as homes. Two re-sited plaques there have the date 1778 and the initials RJH, possibly for the maltster Joseph Rackstraw.[148]

Interiors

The mercantile and professional elite who built Henley's larger 18th-century houses not only wanted space in which to conduct their business or profession; they also needed rooms for polite entertaining. Usually these were placed in the front of the house, as at 55 New Street (mentioned above), which stands close to the

Henley's Ornamental Brickwork

The visual appeal of Henley's 18th-century buildings stems partly from the way in which different types of brick were combined for decorative effect. Early brickwork in the area was mostly dark red, reflecting a high iron content in the local clay, though dark grey-blue bricks (produced by over-firing in the kiln) were sometimes used for patterning (Panel 6). But in the early 18th century combinations of different coloured bricks became increasingly fashionable, and as demand increased new techniques were developed. Extra heating produced a glazed (or 'vitrified') effect, while a grey glazed surface might also be achieved by adding salt during the firing process. Red and vitrified grey bricks were sometimes combined to produce a chequer pattern, or could be used to much grander effect, as at 20 Market Place (Figures A and B).

The 'bond' (i.e. the way in which the bricks are laid) was also varied for effect. By 1700, English bond (alternate courses of headers and stretchers) had generally been supplanted by Flemish bond, in which headers and stretchers alternate in each course. But sometimes a more costly all-header bond was used to give a special air of distinction to a façade (Figure A).

Another indicator of wealth and status was the use of specially sawn 'gauged' bricks for detailing (e.g. in keystones and window arches), and of individually moulded bricks for architectural features such as cornices. A striking example is 13 Reading Road, where the unknown builder introduced classical Doric pilasters and a dentil cornice of moulded bricks (Figure D). Gauged brickwork also aimed for an especially smooth effect, achieved by the addition of fine sand to the clay before firing, and by carefully cutting the bricks to make as fine a mortar joint as possible (Figure C).

Such extravagance slowly disappeared in the second half of the 18th century, as neo-classical restraint replaced Baroque ostentation. This often meant covering the brickwork with stucco (or render) to produce the desired effect of smoothness (e.g. Figs 98–9). But a smooth effect could also be created in brick, especially when it was of a uniform redness and the mortar was concealed by tuck-pointing (Figure A).

Figure A *Brick façades could be varied by combining different coloured bricks in varying bonds. The Flemish bond at 54 New Street (top right) is accentuated by use of blue-grey headers and red stretchers, a pattern particularly popular in the late 18th and 19th centuries. The more expensive header bond at 18 Hart Street (bottom left), with all the bricks laid end-on, uses exclusively blue bricks to good effect. Tuck pointing (bottom right) gave the illusion of a smooth regular surface by giving the finished brickwork (including the pointing mortar) a red colour wash, then incising the joints, and pointing up the narrow grooves with lime putty. The effect, when new, would have been quite startling. An Act of 1725 ruled that bricks should be 2½ inches thick, slightly thicker than those of earlier centuries.*

Figure B *20 Market Place, built probably around 1750, where the use of red and grey brickwork creates the illusion of tall pilasters forming part of a temple-like classical portico.*

Figure C *This large, flared window arch at 39 Hart Street consists of soft red 'rubbed' or 'gauged' bricks, made of smooth clay and fine sand. The bricks were sawn to achieve the desired wedge shape before being rubbed smooth. They are pointed up with fine lime putty.*

Figure D *Classical detailing at 13 Reading Road, where slender brick pilasters flank the reception rooms on the two upper floors. The dentil cornice (the decorative projection at roof-level) is similarly of moulded and delicately cut brick, rather than wood. The top-floor windows have decorative aprons below and curved brick keystones above, adding a further note of bravura.*

river and was presumably built by someone involved in water-borne trade. The house is two rooms deep, with an off-centre entrance leading into a passage-like hall with reception rooms on each side, each heated by a chimney on the side wall. Behind the hall is the staircase, with the kitchen to one side and what may originally have been a study or office on the other. The arrangement was matched at No. 53 next door (dated 1729 on a rainwater head) and at No. 86 (The Old Brewery House) opposite, built probably in the mid-18th century by the maltster and brewer Benjamin Sarney, who married the daughter of a wealthy London upholsterer. It can also be seen at Countess Gardens, where the main reception rooms (which retain their original panelling) are separated by a narrow entrance hall with an archway at the far end, leading to the staircase.[149]

Figure 96 18th-century staircases at 39 Hart Street (top) and 20 Market Place (bottom), both with elegant turned balusters.

A variant is 39 Hart Street (Longlands), where the pedimented wooden doorway again leads into a passage between the two front parlours. Here, though, the kitchen was in an older timber wing at the back, leaving more space for the staircase: an important status symbol in many 18th-century town houses, leading to bedrooms and sometimes to a formal dining room over one of the downstairs parlours. Here it rises around three sides of a well, and has slender wooden balusters, three to each tread and each of a different pattern. A similar staircase survives at 20 Market Place.

These houses provided an increasingly comfortable domestic environment for Henley's middle classes. Their furnishings are reflected in an inventory of the surgeon William Young (dated *c.*1834), who lived at Rupert House. His goods, worth the very substantial sum of £658 14s., included plate, linen and china, horses and carriages (a 'chariot' and a phaeton), and wine worth £52, including twenty dozen bottles of port. The ground-floor reception rooms – dining room, breakfast room and drawing room – had substantial mahogany furniture and a variety of side tables, sofas and 'lounging chairs'. There were two bedrooms on the first floor, each with a four-poster bed and dressing room, and three more on the top floor. At the back of the house was a well-equipped kitchen with an adjoining 'wash house', used to store pots and pans and china. The surgery, by contrast, contained little apart from some scales, two pestles and mortars and 'a few drugs and bottles various'.[150]

Cottage Accommodation and the Workhouse

This sustained rebuilding of Henley also affected houses at the lower end of the social scale. Some were simply given new windows and a new coating of plaster, hiding the timber framing. But as the population rose there was need for more accommodation, and on

Figure 97 An early cottage row at 17–29 Friday Street, remodelled from older (partly medieval) buildings in the 1730–40s by the local builder Benjamin Bradshaw. Despite the regular front, the varied rooflines are a clue to the earlier buildings within.

Friday Street several dilapidated houses and malthouses belonging to the corporation were redeveloped as cottage rows in the late 1730s and 1740s, probably for artisans or craftsmen. The developer was the carpenter and builder Benjamin Bradshaw (d. 1768), who later served as mayor, and who is the earliest Henley builder whose work can be identified. At Nos 17–29 he converted three late-medieval timber-framed houses into a row of six, with a new brick façade, old-fashioned casement windows and a red-tile roof. Two adjacent houses at Nos 31–33 received a similar treatment.

Even so, much of the working population continued to live in cramped and dilapidated older housing, often in squalid conditions. A writer in 1813 commented on the 'mean and incommodious ... ancient tenements' in courts and yards off the main streets, and though most such houses have been swept away five one-up and one-down timber dwellings still survive on a burgage plot behind Anne Boleyn Cottage on New Street (Nos 58–78). Only from the 1820s did piecemeal suburban development start to provide new artisan and working-class housing for the fast-rising population (see Chapter 9).[151]

The largest building project aimed at the poor was the new workhouse of 1790–1 (Figure 91), built on corporation land at the town's western edge. Responsibility for this fell to William Bradshaw (*c.*1728–1801), a prominent townsman and builder who may have been Benjamin's son, and who also designed the new town hall and oversaw construction of the new bridge (Chapter 7). Built for £1,600 by the Henley bricklayer John Strange (who ran the *King's Arms* in the Market Place), the workhouse is externally less grim and more domestic-looking than one might expect, with walls of grey and red brick, a central block with a round-arched loggia, and two projecting wings which contained the work rooms and dining room. As first built it housed 150 poor. An early inmate was the poet Samuel Taylor Coleridge, who in 1794 (at the age of 22) was briefly sent here by the Light Dragoons after he joined up under a false name. His punishment was to nurse a fellow recruit in the 'pest-house', a ward for infectious diseases.[152]

Later Rebuilding

Figure 98 The long, remodelled frontage of the *Bell Inn* (far left), Denmark House, and the neighbouring cottage terrace. The stuccoed exteriors conceal the older timber-framed buildings behind, and created an impressive northern approach to the town. The *Bell* was one of Henley's most fashionable coaching inns, long used for high-class social gatherings.

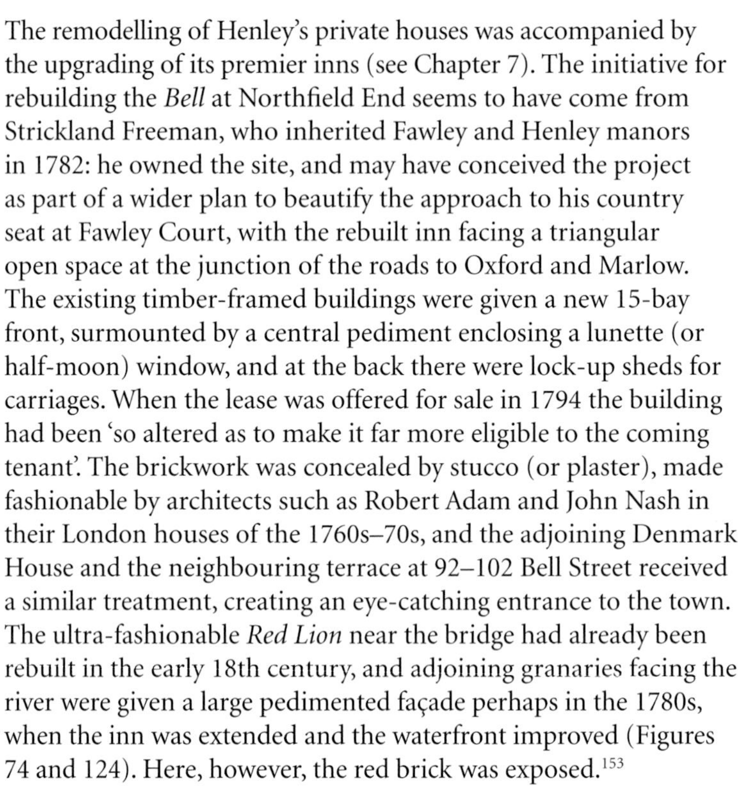

The remodelling of Henley's private houses was accompanied by the upgrading of its premier inns (see Chapter 7). The initiative for rebuilding the *Bell* at Northfield End seems to have come from Strickland Freeman, who inherited Fawley and Henley manors in 1782: he owned the site, and may have conceived the project as part of a wider plan to beautify the approach to his country seat at Fawley Court, with the rebuilt inn facing a triangular open space at the junction of the roads to Oxford and Marlow. The existing timber-framed buildings were given a new 15-bay front, surmounted by a central pediment enclosing a lunette (or half-moon) window, and at the back there were lock-up sheds for carriages. When the lease was offered for sale in 1794 the building had been 'so altered as to make it far more eligible to the coming tenant'. The brickwork was concealed by stucco (or plaster), made fashionable by architects such as Robert Adam and John Nash in their London houses of the 1760s–70s, and the adjoining Denmark House and the neighbouring terrace at 92–102 Bell Street received a similar treatment, creating an eye-catching entrance to the town. The ultra-fashionable *Red Lion* near the bridge had already been rebuilt in the early 18th century, and adjoining granaries facing the river were given a large pedimented façade perhaps in the 1780s, when the inn was extended and the waterfront improved (Figures 74 and 124). Here, however, the red brick was exposed.[153]

Prosperity from coaching and the long-established malting, brewing and river trades presumably explains a new upsurge in house-building from the 1780s to the early 19th century. Two houses in New Street were described as 'lately built' in 1786, and two years later a 'newly improved' house with two parlours, four bedrooms, a brewhouse and garden was offered for letting by William Shennan, a building surveyor with premises at Eylsley's wharf. Those houses have not been identified, but a reference to three newly built houses in Bell Street in a rental of 1785 may apply to Nos 46–50, a group of three-storeyed houses of grey and red brick, each of four bays. They are severely plain with little or no external decoration, again reflecting London legislation – the 1774 London Building Act forbade external woodwork and insisted on windows being placed yet further behind the wall surface, something that occurred here and in later Henley houses.[154]

Stucco made a further appearance at No. 71 Bell Street, which has an Adamesque fan-like motif over the main first-floor window and an attractive glazed fanlight over the main doorway. No. 9 Northfield End (Figure 99), a little to the north, is also stuccoed, though here the new façade hides an earlier timber-framed building. Both houses have low-pitched roofs of Welsh slate, which in Henley replaced tiles as the main roofing material in the late 18th and early 19th centuries – a development made possible by improvements in river navigation and the opening of the Thames and Severn Canal. Stucco was also used on the façade of the so-called Assembly Room in Bell Street, probably built around 1800 as an auctioneer's showroom, and remained fashionable well into the 19th century. Examples include the terrace called Albion Place in West Street (Nos 6–14), Northfield House, and W.H. Brakspear's slightly later bow-fronted house on New Street, built next to the family brewery and used later as the brewery office. There, however, the stucco has been removed.[155]

The new theatre so admired by Caroline Powys (above) replaced the former workhouse on New Street in 1805, built on charity land administered by the corporation. The site was developed on building leases by the brandy merchant Samuel Allnutt (responsible for the theatre) and the bargemaster Robert Kinner, who arranged for the construction of the two adjoining houses with their distinctive arrangement of windows set in relieving arches. The theatre's promoters were Sampson Penley and John Jonas, who managed several provincial theatres, but the building itself was 'designed, planned and executed' by a Henley man, William Parker, who seems to have taken over William Bradshaw's business after Bradshaw's death in 1801. Mrs Powys thought the theatre 'a very nice one indeed', but the building has been heavily altered, and nothing survives of the original interior.[156]

Figure 99 These stuccoed houses at Northfield End (opposite the *Bell Inn*) reflect the street's social status by the late 18th century. No. 9 (left) is a remodelling of an earlier timber-framed house, the Venetian windows on its first floor a popular 18th-century motif. Northfield House next door, with its handsome bow front, was built in 1812 for Richard Ovey, one of a long-established Henley family who also who owned No. 9.

Further rebuilding in the centre accompanied street improvements under the amended Bridge Act of 1808 (see Chapter 7). Bell, Duke and Hart Streets were still 'extremely narrow ... out of repair, [and] not lighted', making it awkward for carriages to pass safely, particularly at night. The streets were resurfaced so that the water could drain away, and the blocks on the two eastern corners of the central crossroads were reconstructed with low-pitched, Welsh-slated roofs and rounded corners, to widen the roadway. A similar approach was adopted at the junction of Thameside and New Street (where the former *Anchor* pub was shortened in length and its north corner rounded), while near the bridge a new three-storeyed house with a curved façade replaced the old Longland

Figure 100 Henley's central crossroads in the 1890s, looking north up Bell Street. The curved frontage on the right resulted from road widening around 1808, part of a continuous process of improvement running back to the mid-18th century. The water fountain (now near the churchyard entrance) was given in 1885.

Almshouses after 1829. Replacement almshouses, stuccoed and in neo-Tudor style, went up on the churchyard's west side in 1830, necessitating the demolition of two early 18th-century brick houses. Sixteen years later the Messenger and Newbury almshouses on the churchyard's east side were also rebuilt, giving the churchyard its present appearance.[157]

The Changing World

As visitors like James Brewer recognised, the Henley of 1820 – with its smart brick or stucco houses, its broad paved streets, and its fine classical bridge and town hall – was a very different place from that painted by Jan Siberechts just over a century earlier. Nor were the changes only physical. True, the river trade with London continued much as it had in Defoe's day, as the town's barges, malthouses and bustling waterfront testified; but at the same time Henley was undoubtedly coming up in the world, its coaching, upmarket inns and unrivalled setting attracting a new type of visitor. With the new century, those twin planks of Henley's success were to be suddenly and unexpectedly challenged by an invention which, for a time, seemed set to all but destroy its economy, causing it to 'drift back', in the words of one historian, 'into a languid rural torpor'. How Henley met that challenge to emerge triumphant, and the changes which followed in its wake, form the subject of the next chapter.

Chapter 9 New Beginnings: Railway and Regatta 1830–1914

In retrospect the railway appears a great Victorian triumph, and ultimately proved Henley's saving grace. But in its earliest days it was seen very differently by the vested interests whose hegemony it threatened, among which coaching and water transport figured large. Bypassed until 1857, for nearly two decades Henley suffered the negative consequences of the railway on its staple trades without receiving any of the benefits.

But with the belated securing of a railway link the town continued its interrupted development into a social centre and inland resort. Central to its success was the self-conscious cultivation of the Regatta and of the sophisticated, high-class image which it projected, an image communicated to the world through contemporary literature and word of mouth. It is to this story that we now turn, concluding with a picture of the working town which underpinned the glittering surface, and with a look at the ways in which Henley's changing fortunes were reflected in its 19th-century buildings.

A 'USELESS AND MISCHIEVOUS PROJECT': RAIL, RIVER AND ROAD

The first public railway (from Stockton to Darlington) opened in 1825, followed five years later by the Liverpool–Manchester line. This ushered in a frenzied and largely unregulated free-for-all, which by 1852 had created over 7,000 miles of track. For Henley, the most significant route was the Great Western Railway's line from London to Bristol (completed in 1841), which included stations at Twyford (opened 1839) and Reading (1840). The line bypassed Henley itself until 1857, however, when a branch finally opened from Twyford.[158]

The impact of the railway on the Thames river trade was marked and immediate, fulfilling fears expressed as early as 1834 when the Thames Commissioners asked the City of London 'what steps have been taken towards opposing that most useless and mischievous project the Great Western Railway'. By 1849 toll income from river traffic below Staines had fallen by a half, and despite piecemeal attempts to cut costs the Commission found it increasingly difficult to perform basic maintenance. In 1866 it was finally wound up, to be replaced by a new Thames Conservancy which since 1857 had been responsible for the lower river.[159]

Figure 101 Fashionable crowds arriving at Henley station for the annual Royal Regatta in 1907. The rail link, opened in 1857, allowed the Regatta to develop its full potential, attracting crowds of over 34,000 by the 1890s.

This did not spell the end of commercial barge traffic on the Thames, which continued to carry a substantial body of freight (particularly coal) into the early 20th century. In 1905 well over a million tons was carried on the river. Much of it, however, was confined to the lower reaches, and the story of Thames barge traffic remained one of gradual decline, balanced by a corresponding increase in the volume of pleasure craft. By 1887 tolls from pleasure boats on the river accounted for 76 per cent of the total, compared with under 30 per cent twenty years earlier, and by 1906 there were over 11,000 registered rowing and sailing craft on the Thames, along with 863 launches and 173 houseboats. Henley's experience largely mirrored this general picture. Robert Webb & Sons, barge builders and timber merchants, ran a weekly barge to London into the 1880s, and a handful of barge workers were recorded into the early 20th century. Nonetheless by the 1890s the town's river trade was dominated by pleasure boats, and in 1893, when increased railway goods-rates prompted renewed enquiries about river transport, this turned out to be impractical in the absence of sufficient trade for a regular weekly run.[160]

The impact on coaching was even more dramatic. In 1830 around 26 long-distance coaches a day passed through Henley (many of them from the *White Hart*), but in 1852, some 12 years after the opening of the GWR, there was only one daily service to London and a twice-weekly one to High Wycombe. This was supplemented by an omnibus to Twyford station, whose driver, in a vain attempt to hold back the clock, 'kept up the dress and dignity of earlier times'. By the 1860s those services too had ceased, replaced by local shuttles between Henley station, the *Catherine Wheel* and the *Red Lion*. The most immediate impact was presumably on the inns which had invested so heavily in coaching. The *Red Lion* closed (temporarily) in 1849 and the *Bell* in the early 1850s, although whether this followed directly from the collapse of coaching is not entirely clear. Certainly inns like the *White Hart* and *Catherine Wheel* appear to have weathered the storm.[161]

The effects on the town more generally are difficult to quantify, but for a place so reliant on trade, retail and services, and with virtually no manufacture other than malt and beer, the prospects must have looked bleak. The effects were felt by 1848, when a town petition against the new national income tax claimed that diversion of traffic to the railway had 'very materially decreased' the town's trade and increased 'the burthen of the poor'. The town's troubles were reflected in a marked slowing of population growth, which from 1801 to 1831 had seen a rise of over a fifth to 3,618 (excluding the area south of Friday Street). Thereafter, population growth even in the expanding southern suburbs slowed considerably until the 1860s, approaching early 19th-century rates only in the 1880s–90s when the total (including the suburbs) reached 5,600. House building followed a similar pattern.

Figure 102 Henley's population growth 1801–1911, based on the national census. The dark blue line shows population in the ancient borough (north of Friday Street); the light blue line includes the southern suburbs (data available only from 1851). The columns show numbers of houses. The slow-down from the 1830s reflected economic difficulties, alleviated from the 1860s after the opening of the railway. Sharp growth from the 1880s (when national population growth was slowing slightly) marked Henley's flowering as a resort and commuting centre, fuelling the first really significant expansion of the town since the Middle Ages.

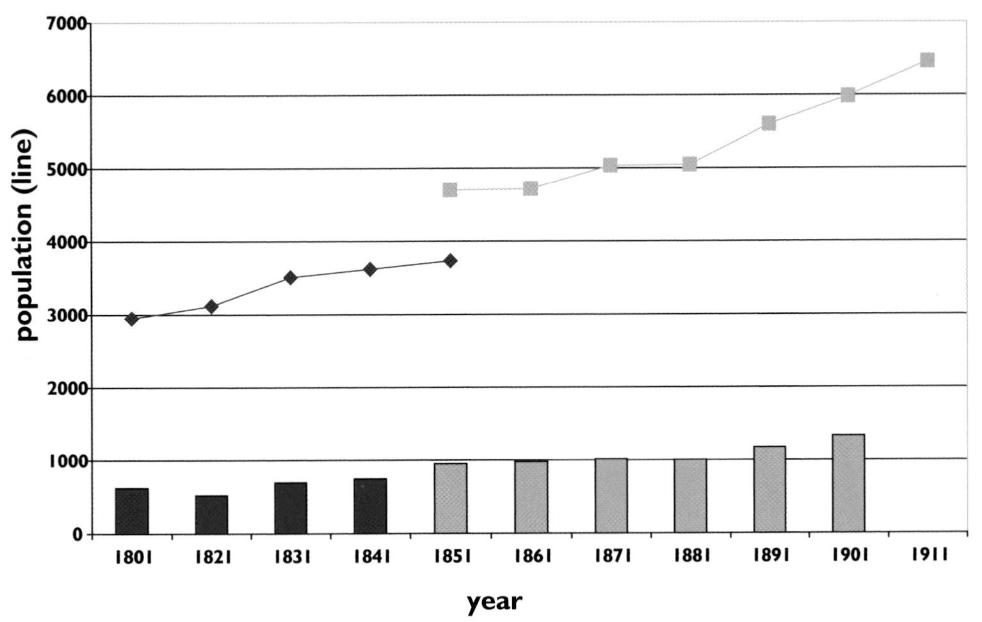

The crisis, in fact, went much deeper than a temporary loss of trade. Bypassed for the first time in its history by the most important transport routes, Henley looked set to become an inconsequential backwater, endangering not only income from coaching but the town's burgeoning appeal as a fashionable social centre. The banker George Grote, who inherited his family's Badgemore estate at Henley in 1830, sold up soon after because of the five-hour journey-time to London, an event which must have set alarm bells ringing: as a relative later noted, he 'would have been inclined to fix his residence at Badgemore, but in those days 40 miles from the City was too great a distance for a mercantile man'. Another resident (born in 1840) recalled Henley as 'a quiet little town', its sole connection with the outside world the Twyford omnibus – a far cry from the bustling world of the late 18th-century coaching town.[162]

Nonetheless, there were those in Henley who recognised that its greatest asset was its setting, and that its best hope was to capitalise on its reputation as a resort and social centre. This was the thinking behind establishment of the Regatta in 1839 (below), and was an aspiration flagged in the various town guides published locally from the 1820s. By the 1840s–50s there was only one way of promoting that ambition, and that was by embracing the railway.

Figure 103 Henley station from the south-east in 1928, the nearby *Imperial* and *Royal Hotels* clearly visible. Station Road was laid out by the GWR, and was originally gated; the curve on its north side marks the site of the original turntable, which was moved when the station was improved in 1903. The land west of the station was yet to be built on when this photograph was taken.

A town meeting called by the mayor in 1852 to press for a branch line was supported by local gentry and landowners, a 'considerable number' of farmers and corn dealers, and 'a great majority of the tradesmen of the town', and when the line from Twyford was finally opened in 1857 it was celebrated by bell-ringing and a large public breakfast in the town hall for GWR representatives. In a public address Lord Camoys (of Stonor Park) anticipated 'a new era of prosperity' for the town, adding that the railway 'would be the means of making numbers acquainted with the delightful scenery of the neighbourhood, to whom, but for this branch railway, it would never be known'. Henley was back on the map.[163]

A RESORT TOWN

With the securing of the railway, leading townspeople set out to capitalise on Henley's reputation as an attractive and sophisticated resort. Key to this was its promotion as a scenic jewel only an hour from the heat of the capital – a theme which recurs time and again in literature of the period. Successive *Guides* played up its setting on 'one of the finest reaches of the Thames, flanked by gentle hills or cliffs covered with hanging woods', and surrounded by scenic walks and drives. By 1896 it was being promoted as a haven for commuters and 'the toiler in the metropolis ... a bourne of peace and rest after the worries of business'. By then there were 28 passenger trains to and from London even in winter, with far more in summer and further improvements expected – although improvements proved divisive when they were thought to threaten Henley's greatest asset. In 1897 the corporation supported plans for an extension of the line through to Marlow, anticipating more visitors and trade. The move provoked howls of protest from well-heeled residents and seasonal visitors who feared a 'vulgarised' Henley 'marred by the kind of hideous eyesore which the Great Western Railway are seeking to erect', while a leading councillor acknowledged that the line might 'detract from the superb scenery' which was Henley's 'stock-in-trade'. The scheme was quietly dropped.[164]

The resurrection in the town's fortunes was reflected in renewed building and suburban expansion, as confidence and prosperity returned and local builders and developers recognised the opportunities. The new suburbs which they created (and which by 1900 extended virtually to the Rotherfield Peppard boundary) are described below, and continued the interrupted transformation of the town begun in the 18th century. Some of the new housing was occupied by professionals and by the upper-middle classes, of whom many had private means: in 1901, more than half the 80-odd householders with independent income lived in the southern

Figure 104 Friar Park on the town's western edge, built *c.*1890 for the solicitor Frank Crisp in a spectacularly eclectic style. Though London-based, Crisp played a philanthropic role in Henley life and regularly opened the grounds to the public. The picture is from a hand-tinted postcard dated 1909.

suburbs. A similar number of professionals included clergy, solicitors, surgeons and schoolteachers, along with the odd artist, writer, or musician. Other suburbs catered for better-off artisans and tradespeople or for the lower-middle classes. At a higher social level, the building of villas and larger houses spilled beyond the southern suburbs and the Fair Mile into the surrounding countryside, the most spectacular example being Friar Park on the town's western edge (Figure 104). Other professionals or businessmen moved into nearby country houses such as Greenlands, home from 1871 of the stationer and Conservative politician W.H. Smith (posthumously Viscount Hambleden). The influx marked the beginnings of a creeping gentrification which gradually transformed not only Henley but the whole of the south-west Chilterns.[165]

To a degree this represented a continuation of Henley's earlier social role, its natural beauty and proximity to London now enhanced by the railway. But at the heart of its social renaissance was a two- or three-day summer 'water picnic' which probably did more than anything to secure its 19th-century reputation for elegance and fashion: the Henley Royal Regatta.

The Regatta

The origins of the Henley Regatta lie in the first Oxford–Cambridge university boat race, held on a course from Hambleden to Henley in 1829. Amateur rowing clubs and competitions were becoming increasingly fashionable, and the Thames was a popular venue, both at London and higher upstream. Cambridge's initial challenge was for a rowing match 'at or near London', but the venue was switched to Henley soon afterwards, almost certainly at Oxford's instigation. The Henley reach must have been well known to Oxford rowers, and provided a good clear stretch on neutral ground, easily accessible from London, yet in a scenically attractive setting.

The event created 'an unusual bustle' in the town, with every room booked and visitors flooding in from far afield. Later Oxford–Cambridge matches were held in London, but similar one-day events (sometimes called 'regattas') followed sporadically at Henley throughout the 1830s, the main impetus coming apparently from London clubs and the universities. Henley's inhabitants were quick to spot the economic potential, providing stands and adding music and fireworks on an *ad hoc* basis, and from there it was a short step to establishing an annual event, locally managed for the benefit of the town. Leading townsmen and neighbouring gentry set up a subscription in 1838, and the 1839 regatta (featuring university and Eton College boats as well as town crews) proved a popular and commercial success. Thenceforth, despite growing competition from similar events elsewhere, it became an established part of the social and sporting calendar, held generally over two days, and from 1886 over three. A glowing report in *The Times* in 1844 expressed widely held sentiments:

> Of all the towns in England there is not one to which, as regards a flourishing Regatta, Henley ought to yield the palm of pre-eminence ... Placed in the midst of scenery the most delightful, with a beautiful reach of water admirably calculated for such sport ... it can form no matter of surprise that this annual event should constitute one of the chief attractions of the season.[166]

From the outset the Regatta attracted a fashionable clientele. The *Oxford Journal* noted the 'beauty and fashion' crowding the river banks in 1837, and later reporters took to listing the various nobility spotted in the grandstands, or watching from their carriages on the bridge. The university element, too, remained

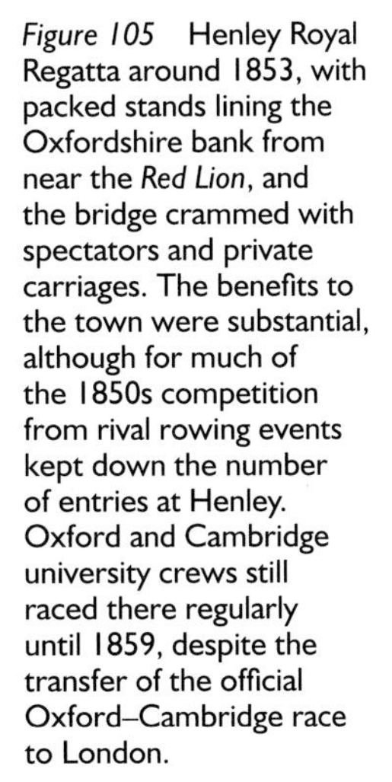

Figure 105 Henley Royal Regatta around 1853, with packed stands lining the Oxfordshire bank from near the *Red Lion*, and the bridge crammed with spectators and private carriages. The benefits to the town were substantial, although for much of the 1850s competition from rival rowing events kept down the number of entries at Henley. Oxford and Cambridge university crews still raced there regularly until 1859, despite the transfer of the official Oxford–Cambridge race to London.

important, though in these early days it was not always so genteel. Alfred Rowland, son of the Congregationalist minister, recalled hoards of Oxford undergraduates and 'others of a far lower grade' driving over on dogcarts, provoking drunken rowdyism, town and gown riots, and worse.

> Sometimes they took letters from the names over the shops and mixed them, wrenched off knockers from the doors, flung the gate of the turnpike on the bridge into the river, ordered a big supper with plenty of drink, and finished ... by overturning the tables and smashing all the glass and crockery ...; seldom did a regatta pass without ... the ruin of some senior girls in the Sunday school.

Not surprisingly Rowland's father set himself against the event, only to have his manse windows smashed more than once in retaliation.

The Regatta's early management was through a body of stewards made up of local gentry and the mayor, with a separate Committee of 14 drawn mostly from leading townsmen. Given the costs of staging the spectacle, profits were slim at best. But the impact on the town seems to have more than compensated, and not only at Regatta time. When financial difficulties threatened the event in 1849, some 225 Henley tradesmen petitioned the stewards to persevere, crediting the Regatta with introducing the town 'to the notice of thousands', and promoting 'so great an influx of visitors during a considerable portion of the year' that it significantly offset 'the injury [which] the trade of the town has sustained from various causes'. The support of influential gentry paid further dividends in 1851, when the town corporation decided to seek royal patronage to help boost the Regatta's ailing finances. Following an approach from Lord Camoys (one of the Regatta's founding stewards) Prince Albert duly agreed to become patron, turning the event into a 'Royal Regatta'. Its new status seems to have considerably heightened its social appeal, even though the Prince himself never attended.[167]

Figure 106 'Betty', a programme seller at the Regatta in 1902. The event boosted employment throughout the town, which even outside the Regatta season became increasingly geared to a service economy.

With the opening of the railway in 1857, the town was fully equipped to exploit the Regatta's potential. The first permanent Regatta building (a boathouse) was completed in 1864, and a visit by the Prince of Wales and the kings of Denmark and Greece in 1887, instigated by Lord Camoys' son and successor, lent the event the ultimate fashionable approval. In 1895 over 34,000 were said to have visited over the three days, and 'it would be impossible to estimate the whole concourse of people attending, for miles round every house is full to repletion with guests'. An evocative description of the Regatta at its height was published soon afterwards by Emily Climenson, author of the 1896 *Guide to Henley*:

> For weeks before the Thames Conservators are nearly driven wild with assigning places for house-boats and steamers, extending now in a line from near the bridge to Regatta Island ... Forty years ago the Regatta was the rendezvous of ... the immediate neighbourhood ... Today it is the world's water picnic. All sorts and conditions of men and women resort to it in thousands, many not caring a straw for the races, but for the charms of the scenery, the kaleidoscopic glow of colour and form, represented by every variety of craft ... the stalwart men, brilliant in their coloured flannels, the beautiful women, ... the creature comforts which are indeed abundant, lavish hospitality being Regatta order from high to low.

Rather less romantic was the pollution accompanying this annual concentration of houseboats, whose occupiers habitually dumped uneaten food and the contents of their water closets directly into the Thames. An article in the *Lancet* described the river's appearance in 1886 as 'simply scandalous', with 'decomposing salad leaves, some rotten fruit, ... lobster shells ... and a dead roach'.[168]

Amidst the social whirl, the rowing itself might easily be overlooked. Rowing men were not even represented on the management committee until 1881, and only in 1894 did a rower (the appropriately named H.T. Steward) become chairman. Yet

Figure 107 A typical crush of pleasure boats at the 1896 Regatta, viewed from one of the luxury houseboats which lined the banks for weeks on end. Some were up to 70 feet long, with 10–12 beds and a kitchen: 'to all intents and purposes a house'.

from the first the Henley Regatta excited considerable excitement among the rowing fraternity, and as its social standing grew, so too did its reputation among the burgeoning number of rowing clubs, particularly after the introduction in 1886 of a new and fairer course. By then, with the first entries from the United States, it was becoming an international event, and in 1908 it received the ultimate accolade when Henley was chosen as the venue for the Olympic Regatta, held two weeks after the Royal Regatta itself. The honour was to be repeated 40 years later, making Henley the first town in the world to stage two Olympic Regattas.[169]

Boating and Leisure

With a reputation so far flung, the Regatta's importance in advertising Henley to a wider world can scarcely be exaggerated. But for the town to succeed as an all-year resort more was needed, and Climenson's *Guide* (like those before it) rams home the extent to which the town had become geared to servicing a genteel tourism extending way beyond the Regatta. Boat hire was widely catered for, from the modern steam and electric launches available from the *Red Lion* or at Marsh Lock through to small punts and rowing boats. Professional fishermen could be hired to guide visiting anglers and, as earlier, Henley boasted a range of accommodation to suit every pocket, supplemented by a variety of cafés and restaurants. Some were long-established inns such as the *Red Lion* (re-opened in 1859), which following a remodelling in 1889 re-emerged as one of the town's most fashionable hotels.

Figure 108 The 'grand coffee room' of the refurbished *Red Lion* around 1897. Emerging as one of Henley's premier coaching inns in the 18th century, the *Red Lion* enjoyed a renaissance during the late 19th and early 20th centuries, particularly after its extension and remodelling in 1889.

Others were newcomers like the *Oxford Temperance Hotel* at Market Place or the newly built *Henley Restaurant* (opened 1893) at the corner of Hart Street and Duke Street, with its 'airy, well-furnished bedrooms' and 'a good bath room offering a hot or cold bath – a luxury when heated from rowing, cycling etc'. Such facilities clearly paid off. Rectors in the 1880s and 1890s reported (mostly with disapproval) the increase in visitors and pleasure seekers over the summer months, and from around 1900 day excursions from London by rail added further to the transitory population.[170]

Meanwhile the town's indigenous social life thrived, with an ever-growing number of polite clubs and societies typical of many small 19th-century towns. As in the 18th century occasional concerts and lectures were held in the town hall or other venues, and a gentleman's literary and reading society existed by the 1830s. Increasingly there were upper-class sporting clubs for cricket, tennis, and (later on) golf. Conservative and Liberal Clubs, both effectively doubling as gentlemen's private clubs, were set up in 1886 and 1894 respectively, while in 1890 a Freemasons' Lodge acquired imposing purpose-built premises on Reading Road, the site donated by W.D. Mackenzie of Fawley Court. Philanthropic residents like the Mairs at Phyllis Court or Frank Crisp at Friar Park engaged with the town in various ways, sometimes throwing their houses and gardens open on special occasions. The grounds of Phyllis Court, in particular, became a favourite viewing point for the Regatta, before the house itself was acquired for the private Phyllis Court Club in 1906.[171]

THE WORKING TOWN

Trades, Services and Industry

As in the 18th century, the polite world of Henley's middle classes, property owners, and seasonal visitors was underpinned by a working town geared increasingly to retail and services. Boat operators, innkeepers and restaurateurs have already been mentioned, and with shopkeepers made up a substantial part of the working population: in 1901 well over a fifth of householders made their living from retail or services in one form or another, among them innkeepers, butchers, bakers, shoemakers and clothes retailers. As earlier, shopkeepers not only provided staple goods but catered for Henley's prosperous consumers. Those listed in 1901 included five watchmakers or jewellers, two glass and china dealers, four hairdressers (one of whom also ran a 'fancy business'), and two tobacconists, along with a musical instrument dealer, a piano maker, and two chemists or druggists. Building trades

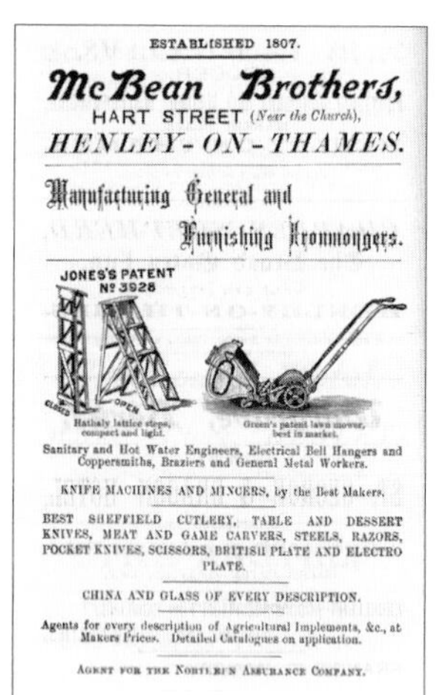

Figure 109 A page from the 1896 *Guide to Henley*, advertising Bean Bros ironmonger's on Hart Street. The firm doubled as 'sanitary and hot water engineers [and] electrical bell hangers', and sold cutlery, china and glass.

accounted for another 18 per cent of householders' occupations, and domestic or private service (housekeepers, manservants, coachmen) for five per cent – although as most domestic servants lived in other people's households, the total number of those in service was considerably higher. A handful of traditional craftsmen (blacksmiths, ironmongers and saddlers or harness-makers) rubbed shoulders with workmen in more modern jobs, including railway workers, stationary engine drivers, and gas workers or fitters. Another six per cent of householders were professionals including clergy, doctors, lawyers, bankers, schoolteachers and auctioneers, again continuing the 18th-century trend.[172]

By contrast, Henley remained (in Emily Climenson's words) 'not much given to manufactures, except beer and boats' – in sharp contrast to towns like Witney or Banbury, with their growing industrial base. Brakspears' Brewery, expanded by the founder's son William Henry Brakspear (d. 1882), employed perhaps 100 men, and in 1895 (under William's sons Archibald and George Edward) became a public limited company, largely to help finance its takeover of the smaller Greys Brewery on Friday Street. The workforce seems to have enjoyed genuinely good relations with its employer. W.H. Brakspear was typical of the successful Victorian entrepreneurs found in many small towns: strict, upright and hard-working, but genuinely paternalistic and with a profound sense of public duty, which saw him serve four times as mayor and as a JP. An obituary called him one of Henley's 'oldest and most respected townsmen', and on the day of his funeral shops were closed and blinds drawn as a mark of respect, the church bells sounded a muffled peal, and a

Figure 110 W.H. Brakspear & Sons' former malthouses north of New Street, built in 1899 as part of an expansion of the site. Under W.H. Brakspear production focused increasingly on New Street, where a steam engine was installed in 1865. By 1880 the brewery was producing over 14,000 barrels a year, small-scale compared with London breweries, but more than twice the number produced 70 years earlier. By then, independent malting in the town had all but disappeared.

Henley in the Censuses

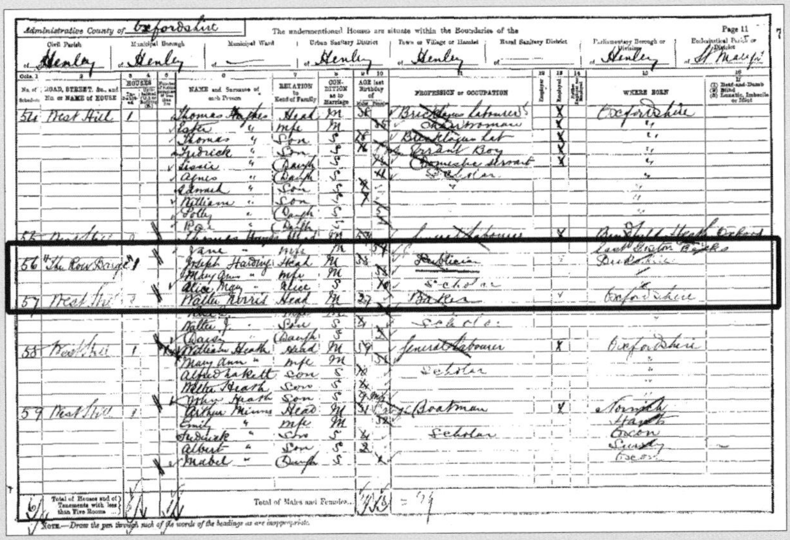

Administrative County of Oxfordshire — The undermentioned Houses are situate within the Boundaries of the — Page 11

Civil Parish of Henley | Municipal Borough of Henley | Municipal Ward of — | Urban Sanitary District of Henley | Town or Village or Hamlet of Henley | Rural Sanitary District of — | Parliamentary Borough or Division of Henley | Ecclesiastical Parish or District of St Mary's

No. of Schedule	Road, Street, &c., and No. or Name of House	Houses	Name and Surname of each Person	Relation to Head of Family	Condition as to Marriage	Age last Birthday of Males	Age last Birthday of Females	Profession or Occupation	Where Born
54	West Hill	1	Thomas Hughes	Head	M	56		Bricklayers labourer	Oxfordshire
			Kate "	Wife	M		55	Charwoman	"
			Thomas "	Son	S	18		Bricklayers lab	"
			Fredrick "	Son	S	16		Errand Boy	"
			Lissie "	Daur	S		15	Domestic servant	"
			Agnes "	Daur	S		11	Scholar	"
			Edward "	Son	S	[illegible]			"
			William "	Son	S				"
			Polly "	Daur	S				"
			[illegible] "	Daur	S				"
55	[illegible]		Thomas [illegible]	Head	M	[illegible]		[illegible] Labourer	[illegible] Heath Oxford
			Jane "	Wife	M		[illegible]		[illegible] Berks
56	"The Row Barge"	1	Joseph Harding	Head	M	33		Publican	Berkshire
			Mary Ann "	Wife	M		[illegible]		"
			Alice Mary "	Daur	S		10	Scholar	"
57	West Street		Walter Norris	Head	M	27		Baker	Oxfordshire
			[illegible]	Wife	M				"
			Walter J. "	Son	S	[illegible]		Scholar	"
			Daisy "	Daur	S		[illegible]		"
58	West Street	1	William Heath	Head	M	57		General Labourer	Oxfordshire
			Mary Ann "	Wife	M		56		"
			Alfred Hakett	Son	S	10		Scholar	"
			Walter Heath	Son	S	[illegible]			"
			John Heath	Son	S	9 mo			"
59	West Street	1	Arthur Minns	Head	M	31		Boatman	Norwich
			Emily "	Wife	M		32		Hants
			Frederick "	Son	S	8		Scholar	Oxon
			Albert "	Son	S	2			Surrey
			Mabel "	Daur	S		[illegible]		Oxon

Total of Houses and of Tenements with less than Five Rooms — 6 — Total of Males and Females

Note.—Draw the pen through such of the words of the headings as are inappropriate.

Figure A *Part of the 1891 census for Henley, detailing households on West Hill (now West Street). The* Row Barge *pub (outlined) was occupied by Joseph Harding, publican (aged 33 and born in Berkshire), with his wife Mary Ann and their 10-year-old daughter Alice Mary, who was a school girl (or 'scholar'). Near neighbours included labourers and a boatman. West Hill was then a poor part of Henley with a reputation for roughness, perhaps partly because of the workhouse at its upper end.*

Before the 19th century no single historical source gives a systematic overview of population, employment or social structure, whether in towns and villages or at national level. From 1801, however, we have the benefit of the national censuses taken every 10 years, by which governments kept track of changes in demography, employment, and society.

In the 19th century information was gathered by enumerators who visited every household in a given area, entering information on official forms in (theoretically) a standardised way. The resulting data was summarised in Parliamentary Reports, and from 1841 onwards the enumerators' books themselves survive, detailing the occupants of every house with their name, age, family relationship, employment, place of birth, and a range of other information.

The statistical possibilities of this information are almost endless, encompassing family organisation, migration, public health, fertility and economic change. Evidence for particular places can be related to the national picture in ways not always possible for earlier periods, while at local level, censuses allow us to build up a detailed picture not only of particular towns but of particular streets or areas within them, seeing how their character changed over time.

The original enumerators' books are preserved in The National Archives at Kew, and are released for research after 100 years. TNA and most local studies libraries have microfilm copies, and for Oxfordshire most censuses from 1841 to 1901 are available on CD from the Oxfordshire Family History Society. Searches for family names can be undertaken through a growing number of genealogical websites, though as these do not generally give access to the census as a whole they are of limited use for wider historical research. For Henley population data, see Figure 102.

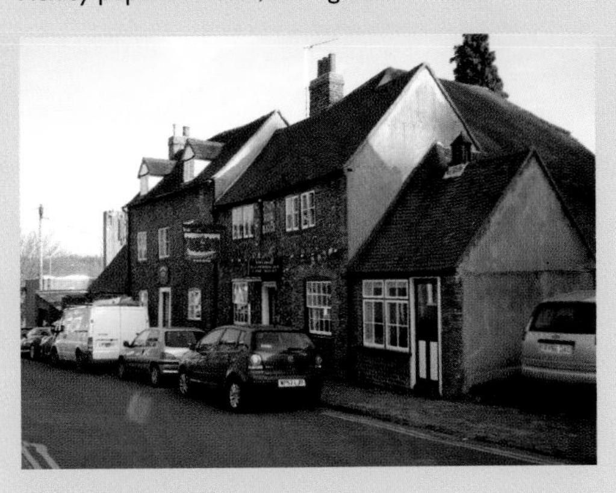

Figure B *The* Row Barge *pub today.*

'large concourse' too big to fit into the cemetery chapel (including all of the brewery employees) accompanied the coffin to the graveside.[173]

Boat-building was a more recent phenomenon, associated with Henley's 19th-century emergence as a resort. Tom Shepherd's business at the *Red Lion* opened in 1888, and the following year won an award at the Paris Exhibition for a pair of skiffs. Sales to Germany, Holland and South America followed, and by 1896 Shepherd was building an 80-foot steam yacht for 160 passengers, besides running three pleasure launches and hiring out smaller boats. Messrs Hobbs (established 1870), at the end of New Street, similarly built 'all sorts of river boats from steam launches to ... punts', while the London-based firm of Kerbey Bowen had a building works and charging station (for their electric launches) at Marsh Lock Island.

Other manufactures in 19th-century Henley were relatively small-scale, among them a silk-winding mill in Bell Lane (closed 1856), a foundry and paper-bag manufactory on Friday Street, and paper-making at New Mills near Marsh Lock. More significant for the future was the arrival in Henley around 1905 of Stuart Turner's light engineering firm, set up at Shiplake where Turner ran a steam plant for generating electricity. In its earliest decades the firm made model steam engines, gas and petrol engines, motor cycles, and domestic generation plants, continuing into the 21st century to become one of Henley's longest-running businesses.[174]

Alongside these activities, agriculture remained integral to the town's life. The Thursday market was still 'well attended by neighbouring farmers' in the 1850s, and a former mayor recalled the whole of Hart Street, Market Place and Gravel Hill 'thickly occupied by cattle, sheep and horses' at the annual Ascension Day fair. As late as 1901 at least four per cent of Henley's householders were agricultural workers, while market gardening developed particularly at Newtown, a little way south of Henley, where small allotments and nurseries were laid out near the Reading road before the 1840s. Over 50 'gardeners' were listed in 1901, a fair proportion of them market gardeners or nurserymen rather than domestic employees.[175]

The railway also served the working town. Brakspears' imported hops by rail, together with hogsheads, cases of spirits, and crates, while Henley's saw mills received large quantities of timber. Coal (formerly brought in by river) was particularly important: the coal merchants Messrs Toomer & Co., who supplied the gas works, expanded their facilities at Henley station in the 1870s and again in 1903, and ran their own fleet of wagons. Rail exports were less extensive, reflecting the town's limited manufactures; even so some 42,000 tons of goods passed through the station in 1903, together with 264 livestock.[176]

Social Provision and The Poor

As in many towns, the growth of 'polite' societies was balanced by a profusion of working-class clubs during the 19th century, many of them aimed at 'improving' the labouring population. As early as 1838 a gentleman's reading and literary society had a counterpart 'supported by the tradesmen', and by the 1890s there was a variety of church and sports clubs aimed specifically at 'mechanics', 'working men' and 'shop assistants'. Among them was a working men's rowing club founded in 1886, presided over by Archibald Brakspear and based at the *Little White Hart* on the waterfront, where it had its own boathouse. Other clubs included friendly societies to provide support in illness or old age, to which members paid subscriptions, and which had social meetings as well.[177]

Attempts at 'improvement' did not stop there, and in Henley the Temperance movement (dedicated to eradicating the evils of intoxicating drink) proved a bitterly divisive force – unsurprising in a place where brewers featured so prominently. The Henley Temperance Society (founded 1859) held meetings at the Assembly Rooms on Bell Street, and though allegations of habitual drunkenness among 'the poorer classes' may have been exaggerated, in the 1890s Henley certainly had 51 pubs and 11 other outlets for a population of only 5,600. The pro-Temperance builder and alderman Charles Clements claimed to know of 'many cases amongst my own men where [on a Saturday half-day] they do not reach home till 7 or 8 or later in the evening, with very little of their wages left to go to their wives', while on Saturdays 'quite small children are taken in with the wives and mothers to drink'.[178]

A further means of improvement was education, and like most 19th-century towns Henley saw a marked increase in schooling for all ages. The Church established an Anglican National School in the former New Street theatre in 1817 (moved later to new buildings at the top of Gravel Hill), while an Anglican infant school for the southern suburbs was opened around 1850, and succeeded in 1893 by a National school nearby. As so often, the schools' sectarian approach created tensions with the Nonconformist community, prompting the Congregationalists to establish their own non-sectarian British School. Meanwhile the Grammar and Greencoat schools continued in reorganised forms, the former relocated to the former *Bell Inn* at Northfield End. Inspectors' reports suggest that most schools were generally well run, although in 1848 a master at the National school was 'summarily dismissed for taking improper liberties with the girls'.[179]

Yet despite the improvements, a significant proportion of the 19th-century working population continued to live in cramped

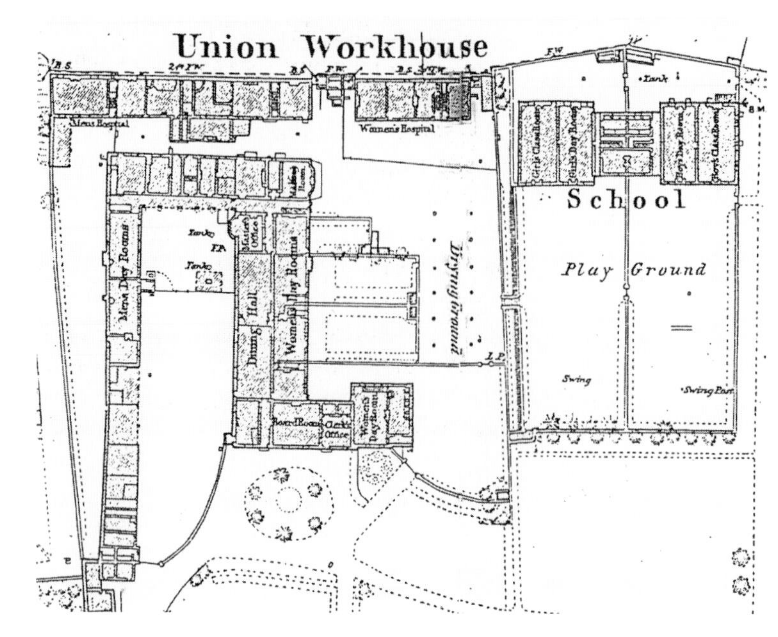

Figure 111 Henley Union workhouse at the top of West Street, shown on the Ordnance Survey map of 1879. The U-shaped block on the left incorporated the parish workhouse of 1790, which was extended after 1834. At top left are the men's and women's hospitals, and in the U-shaped block the men's and women's day rooms, the dining hall, and (towards the bottom) the added board room. The schoolrooms (right) were added in 1873, replacing an earlier school.

and unsanitary conditions (below). Formal responsibility for the poor lay from 1834 with Henley Poor Law Union, created that year during a national shake-up of poor relief; the town's existing workhouse became a Union workhouse for Henley and 23 surrounding parishes, and was subsequently extended. Additional help came from parochial charities and the friendly societies already mentioned, along with voluntary bodies like the District Visiting Society (for relief of the sick and poor), or the Henley Parochial Work Society, which supplied 'deserving' women with needlework which was subsequently sold to the poor. Allotments let to 'industrious labourers' were claimed in 1850 to have 'proved of much benefit to the working classes', the social attitudes behind such ventures clearly reflected in the *Town Guide*: 'It is pleasing to add the poor are loud in their expression of gratitude for this attention to their comforts and look forward to ... winter, satisfied ... that the plan much alleviates their sufferings'.[180]

GOVERNMENT, POLITICS, AND RELIGION

Otherwise, national reforms in local government were slow to make their mark in Henley. In 1835 it was one of the few corporations unaffected by the Municipal Corporations Act, on the grounds that existing arrangements were popular with the townspeople, and were thought adequate for a small provincial town not expected to grow much. New powers over public health and building regulations were acquired in 1864 with the setting up of a Local Board (under recent legislation), and the old, increasingly moribund, system was finally swept away in 1883, to be replaced by a new corporation comprising a mayor, four aldermen and 12 councillors. The offices of high steward, recorder and bridgeman were abolished. Soon after, the town's expansion was recognised in a series of boundary changes, bringing in the extensive southern suburbs south of Friday Street, but jettisoning the parish's rural parts to create a separate parish of Badgemore (Figure 112).[181]

As in any small town, personal rivalries surfaced from time to time. Particularly strident in the late 19th century was the conflict between the predominantly Liberal (and sometimes Nonconformist) pro-Temperance lobby, exemplified by the builder, alderman and magistrate Charles Clements, and the Conservative interest associated with brewers like Archibald Brakspear. Already

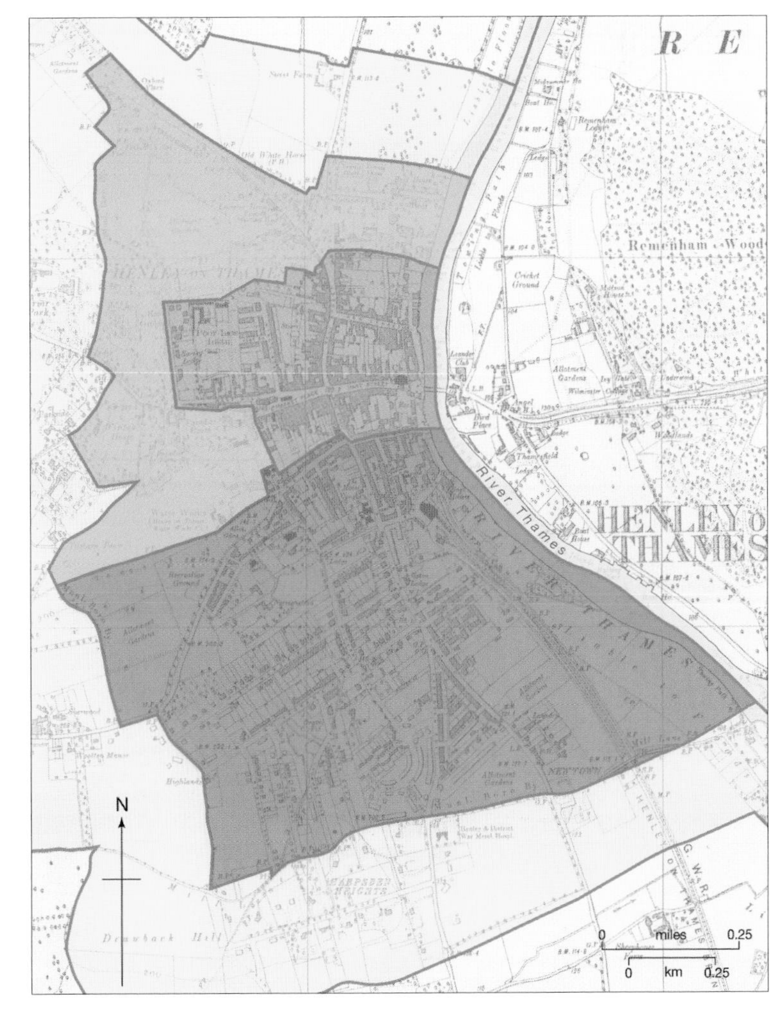

Figure 112 Henley's suburban growth prompted a series of boundary extensions (superimposed here on a map of 1938). The orange central area shows the ancient borough, to which the blue and green areas were added in 1892. From 1905 that expanded area became a single civil parish (the blue area having remained part of Rotherfield Greys parish until 1894). The surrounding yellow areas are part of a further extension in 1932.

Figure 113 Henley borough council in the old town hall, 1895. The mayor (standing) is Alderman W. Anker Simmons; to his right is Charles Clements (1845–1920), a leading builder, Liberal, and Temperance reformer who clashed with the Conservative brewing interest. Clements himself served six times as mayor, and ended his career a widely respected figure.

at loggerheads over several issues, in 1889 Clements contested Brakspear's election to the new County Council in 'the hardest and most thoroughgoing election which ever took place in Henley', losing by only 43 votes. Eight years later Clements sparked controversy by attacking the town's brewers and licensing laws before a Royal Commission, and not until 1901 were the pair finally reconciled. Many such battles were fought out in the local Henley press, of which one of the earliest incarnations was the Conservative *Henley Advertiser* (established 1868). The more Liberal *Henley Free Press* (set up by the Congregationalist minister Joseph Jackson Goadby) followed in 1885, only to be taken over by the Henley Conservative Association seven years later and subsumed in the *Henley and South Oxfordshire Standard.*[182]

Figure 114 The Congregationalist (now United Reformed) church on Reading Road, built in 1907 on the site of the earlier meeting house. The distinctive tower was partly paid for by Frank Crisp of Friar Park, a wealthy lawyer and Liberal whose grandfather John Filby Childs was a leading Congregationalist campaigner.

The town's religious life, too, had its tensions, which were not confined to difficulties between Anglicans and Dissenters. In the 1850s moves towards greater ritual in the parish church met with warm approbation from some and 'a spirit of opposition' from others, though by then Henley was generally well served by conscientious rectors. One, T.B. Morrell, oversaw a major restoration of the parish church in 1852–4, while his predecessor James King donated a grand 18th-century house by the river as a new rectory in 1830, and supported establishment of the new church of Holy Trinity (consecrated in 1848) to serve the expanding southern suburbs. Nonconformity, meanwhile, continued to flourish, although in the 1850s almost a third more people still attended the two Anglican churches than the town's four nonconformist chapels combined. The largest group remained the Congregationalists, who in 1907 built a striking new chapel of brick and stone on the site of its predecessor, the tower partly paid for by Frank Crisp. The Quakers, too, replaced their meeting house in 1894 following a marked revival, while new chapels were built by the Wesleyans in 1874 (on Duke Street) and the Baptists in 1878–9 (on Gravel Hill). A Roman Catholic church was built near the railway station in 1888–9.[183]

REBUILDING AND EXPANSION

The First Suburbs

Henley's rapid population growth in the early 19th century was fuelled largely by immigration from the countryside and, though unspectacular compared with that of towns like Banbury or Reading, created a demand for new housing which left a permanent mark on the town. Speculative local builders began to put up new working-class houses after the Napoleonic Wars, a time of considerable building activity nationally, and building continued until the 1840s: between 1811 and 1821 the number of inhabited houses in Henley and Greys increased from 522 to 696, with a smaller increase to 747 in the 1820s. The building of these houses may have helped attract poor immigrants to the town, but seems also to have alleviated some of the worst overcrowding. Between 1811 and 1821 the average number of people per inhabited house actually fell from 5.6 to 4.9, despite the fact that the population rose by some 400. These new properties were also valuable investments, satisfying a demand in the 1830s for 'small and neat houses' with an annual rental value of between £20 and £40. This demand continued until the town's mid-century stagnation.[184]

The largest concentrations of new housing were in West Street and Gravel Hill, both on rising ground west of the Market Place, and further south in Greys Road and Greys Hill. Sixteen brick cottages were erected on West Street's northern side before 1829, and by 1851 there was a large population of labourers here, many of them agricultural workers with large families. Most of the new houses in this area were two-up-and-two-down terraced cottages of brick, sometimes stuccoed, and some, especially in West Street, degenerated into little better than slums. But there were a few larger and better-built houses in and around Greys Hill, which in 1829 was 'a much admired site for building', suitable both for cottages and for larger houses with basements and water-closets, which could be purchased or rented by 'genteel families'. One is Church House, a plain brick villa at the foot of the hill; another, cheek-by-jowl with artisan cottages, is the attractive semi-detached pair at Nos 22–4, with linear ornament in the manner of Sir John Soane on the stucco facing, and a pretty iron veranda. This

Figure 115 Early suburban development met contrasting local needs. Left: cramped working-class cottages on West Street, some of which degenerated into little better than slums. Right: more genteel housing at 22–24 Greys Hill, with stucco and ironwork decoration.

Figure 116 Holy Trinity church, built in 1848 as 'a poor man's church' for the expanding southern suburbs. Its architect, Benjamin Ferrey (a friend and biographer of Pugin), lived on the Fair Mile for several years, and restored Henley and Harpsden churches.

essentially late-Georgian style of building continued into the 1860s, judging by 62–6 Market Place, a terrace of three three-storeyed houses built by the Henley Building Company in 1864, and the adjacent row of two-storeyed cottages at 2–32 Gravel Hill (1866).[185]

Given the fragmented nature of land-holding in these parts of Henley, it is not surprising that there was no uniform control over building. Instead, small parcels were sold piecemeal to individual builders. One was the bricklayer John Strange (1778–1845), whose father had built the parish workhouse (Chapter 8). Presumably he was responsible for Strange's Row on West Street, and for a terrace in a yard at 70–76 New Street, which carries his name and the date 1823. Some later houses were put up by Robert Owthwaite (1804–87), whose long and varied career included cabinet-making and auctioneering. Owthwaite was also the builder of Holy Trinity church (1848), intended as 'a poor man's church' for the 'vast accumulation of houses' nearby, and went on to become the dominant developer in Henley in the succeeding decades.[186]

Despite the town's mid-19th-century stagnation, some new middle-class houses also went up around the fringes. Phyllis Court was rebuilt in 1837 in a routine Italianate style, and leased to a succession of resident gentry before becoming a country club in 1906. More interesting architecturally was Rotherfield Court, a large, red-brick, spikily Gothic house built in 1861 for the rector T.B. Morrell, on a secluded wooded site at the top of Gravel Hill. Probably it was designed by the prolific Anglican church architect Henry Woodyer. Surrey Lodge (1866), in the Hop Gardens west of Townlands, is Gothic too, but smaller, while Fonthill next door (probably *c.*1880–90) exemplifies the later shift to 'Old English' detailing, with copious tile-hanging and ornamental brick chimneys – a style which had a huge influence in Henley. Rather different in character are Oxford Villas, large semi-detached houses built on the Fair Mile in the early 1860s. Loosely

Figure 117 Rotherfield Court, a relatively rare example in Henley of 19th-century domestic Gothic. Subsequently extended by the Makins family and taken over by Henley Grammar School in the 1920s, it now forms part of Henley College.

Italianate in style, they would be more at home in Ealing than in Henley, and seem to anticipate a suburban development that, when it occurred, took place to the south rather than the north of the town. Equally untypical of Henley, and of slightly later date, is River Terrace, a block of seven three-storeyed stuccoed houses of distinctly urban or even metropolitan character, overlooking the Thames south of Friday Street. Built by the Henley Building Company on land bought from Lord Camoys in 1866, they failed to attract permanent wealthy residents, and some of them later became up-market lodging houses.[187]

Improving the Town

Corresponding efforts to tackle Henley's physical infrastructure – slum housing, poor sanitation and narrow streets – did not seriously begin until the 1860s, several decades later than in large cities. Alderman Simmons, four times mayor, wrote in 1919 of the town as he remembered it in that decade: 'There was no water supply – everyone pumped from their own well – scarcely a house in the town possessed a bathroom, and the nightly rumble of the sewage carts … was a reminder of the cess pool system of drainage'. Matters began to improve with the appointment of a Local Sanitary Board in 1864, and in 1865 the Board adopted model by-laws framed by central government to rectify some of the worst abuses. These led to provision of effective sewerage, the clearance (albeit slowly) of the noxious courts and yards behind the main streets, and the framing of regulations insisting on minimum standards for new building and for the width of new streets. A piped water supply was installed in 1880–2, and by 1890 the Medical Officer of Health could report that only 53 houses were still unconnected to sewers. The gift in 1885 of a Gothic drinking fountain in the market place (since removed to the churchyard entrance) marked this significant development (Figure 100). The most important street improvement took place in 1872–3, when Duke Street was widened by the local builder Charles Clements. A picturesque row of timber houses on its west side was replaced with new brick structures designed by the local partnership of Frederick Haslam and William Wing, surveyor to the Henley Local Board. In 1893 the block at the corner of Duke Street and Hart Street was rebuilt on a larger scale, and in 1892 the southern corners to Greys Road and Friday Street were rounded, again by Clements. New three-storeyed shops and offices were built there in 1896 and 1899, completing a process of street improvement begun in the early years of the century (Chapter 8).[188]

Figure 118 The corner of Duke Street and Greys Road as rebuilt in the 1890s, 20 years after Duke Street was first redeveloped following the demolition of its entire west side.

New public buildings reflected improvements in social provision. One of the new Duke Street buildings was a 'School of Science and Art' or Working Men's Institute (1873–5), of which

Wing, a keen local historian, became Hon. Secretary. The new National school of 1848–9 on Gravel Hill, flint-built in the plain neo-Tudor style used in the new almshouses around St Mary's churchyard, provided a purpose-built elementary school for 500 boys and girls, its gabled classroom wings placed either side of a two-storeyed central part which contained housing for the teachers. Henley's other new 19th-century schools generally used flint as well, among them Holy Trinity infant school, which recalls a medieval hall with its projecting porch and single schoolroom under a steep-pitched roof. Possibly it was designed by Benjamin Ferrey, the architect of Holy Trinity church and restorer of St Mary's, while the new lower grammar school south of Hart Street (built 1856) was designed by James Brooks, known later as a designer of Anglican churches in London. The workhouse, meanwhile, was extended following its transformation into a Union workhouse, first by the Reading architects Richard and John Billing in 1835, and later by Haslam and Wing, who respectively added a school in 1873 and more wards in 1886. The Oxford architect William Wilkinson designed a police station for the foot of West Street in 1868, and the same year a new cemetery was opened at the far end of the Fair Mile, its two chapels (for Anglicans and nonconformists) by J.S. Dodd of Reading.[189]

Late 19th-Century Housing Developments

Large-scale domestic building did not resume until the 1880s, by which time agricultural depression in surrounding rural parishes was prompting new waves of immigration. Combined with increased life-expectancy, the need to re-house former slum-dwellers, and rising real wages, this created a demand for speculative artisan housing which transformed the town's southern part. By 1896, Emily Climenson was noting that 'a quite new town is springing up, with avenues of ... artisans' cottages'.[190]

The first of these new streets was Queen Street, linking Friday Street with the railway station. First laid out in 1879 by Robert Owthwaite (who also chaired the Sanitary Board), it was slowly developed in the 1880s with 'cottages of a superior class', on plots 15ft by 60ft with small front and back gardens. Most of the houses have bay windows, and all have rear extensions for the kitchen and scullery: amenities absent from earlier working-class housing. The façades, of red brick from local brickworks, were often enlivened by bands of blue and white or buff brick, and further enriched with terracotta detailing bought 'off the peg' from local manufacturers. Many more houses of this type went up under the direction of two brothers, Thomas and William Hamilton, the dominant builders

Figure 119 Above: The corner of Harpsden and Reading Roads, part of William Hamilton's suburban development in the 1890s.

Below: Stone frieze at 22 Queen Street, showing scenes from the life of Dick Whittington. The house was occupied and probably built by William's brother Thomas.

of working-class housing in late Victorian and Edwardian Henley. William's first recorded development was in Albert Road (south of Greys Road) in 1883, and in 1892 he took leases of a triangular plot at the corner of Reading and Harpsden Roads south of the station. This led to the growth of what was in effect a self-contained suburb of artisan housing, with its own pub (the *Three Horseshoes*) in the 'Old English' style favoured by Brakspears' Brewery. Thomas Hamilton, meanwhile, was developing Kings Road (west of Bell Street) and the connecting York and Clarence Roads, and in 1896 laid out Park and Marmion Roads next to his brother's housing development in the Reading Road. His houses were generally better built than William's, which were criticised for having walls of only half the required thickness, and insufficient lime in the mortar. But both brothers' houses still survive, and when William died in 1931 he owned some 200 houses in the town, and was the largest ratepayer. Less typical (and unusually ornamental) were cottages put up at 47/49 Gravel Hill by the Henley Cottage Improvement Association in 1890, another response to a growing need.[191]

Housing for the growing number of middle-class residents was provided in Caxton Terrace (1885) in Station Road, and on the higher ground south of Holy Trinity church. Robert Owthwaite acquired 104 acres west of Reading Road in the 1850s, but the time was not yet ripe for building and the ground was not laid out until after his death in 1887. Two parallel streets – St Mark's Road and St Andrew's Road – climbed the hill, with another (Vicarage Road) bisecting them and a shorter street (subsequently named Hamilton Avenue) further north. More streets were laid out higher up once development acquired momentum after 1900. Restrictive covenants ensured that shops and pubs were kept at bay, and the area eventually acquired an exclusive social character that it has never lost. Here there was no single developer, the plots being sold off by Owthwaite's trustees to individual purchasers, of whom many were builders. Development occurred very slowly, and by 1897 only the lower ground near the Reading Road had been covered. Larger houses higher up began to appear soon afterwards, some of them by George and Richard Wilson (of whom the latter married Thomas Hamilton's daughter). Some of their stone-fronted houses include inventive decorative detailing of Art Nouveau character, and one semi-detached pair (31/33 St Mark's Road) carries Richard's initials. Such houses were bought as investments and let to people like George Orwell's parents, whom the writer deftly characterised in *The Road to Wigan Pier* as members of a 'lower upper middle class'.[192]

The most spectacular *fin-de-siècle* house in Henley was Friar Park (Figure 104), built *c.*1890 as a luxurious weekend retreat for

Figure 120 Middle-class housing on Norman Avenue, developed by the Henley builder Charles Clements from *c.*1885. The rich and varied profusion of fanciful detail recalls Friar Park (Fig. 104), although claims that Clements incorporated unused building materials from there are probably unfounded.

the London solicitor Frank Crisp. Designed by the little-known Robert Clarke Edwards, it is an architectural fantasy in red brick, stone and terracotta, mixing English, French and Flemish motifs in lavish, undisciplined profusion. But the house achieved fame (and even notoriety) mainly on account of its 62-acre grounds, complete with topiary, 25 glasshouses, a gnome-ridden grotto, and a rock garden overlooked by a miniature Matterhorn. Crisp also supported (and perhaps influenced the designs for) the new Congregationalist church of 1907, which is architecturally a cousin of Friar Park, its lantern-like tower still announcing the approach to the town from the Reading direction. And it was another Nonconformist, the builder Charles Clements, who between *c.*1885 and 1901 developed Norman Avenue just south of the Congregationalist church: a street of eccentrically detailed red-brick houses whose ornamentation and carved stonework again recalls Friar Park. Here, the Henley middle-class house reached its architectural apotheosis.[193]

Riverside and New Commercial Buildings

As the Regatta grew in popularity, the banks of the Thames were gradually transformed by new boatyards, boathouses and hotels. The *Royal Hotel* (south of River Terrace) went up in 1869 on the initiative of Robert Owthwaite, but was not a success; the site was taken over by Brakspears' Brewery, and in 1899–1900 the hotel was rebuilt in a conventional neo-Tudor style by the prolific Reading architect G.W. Webb. Probably this was a response to the building in 1896 of the more ostentatiously 'Old English' *Imperial Hotel*, designed by the London architect William Theobalds. Positioned opposite the railway station, its extravagant half-timbering was well placed to catch the eye of the thousands of visitors pouring into the Regatta by train.[194]

Meanwhile the character of the river front north of the bridge was changed by the building of inns and boathouses. In 1888–9, a year after the Prince of Wales's visit to the Regatta, Tom Shepherd's boat-building shed went up on the site of the granaries immediately north of the *Red Lion*. The inn itself was the object of 'large and judicious expenditure' on improved facilities in 1889: the *Daily Telegraph* enthused in 1897 that it was 'no longer an old world coaching inn, but a fashionable hotel' complete with billiard room, reading room and two coffee rooms (Fig. 108), and yet more alterations were carried out in 1899 by William Wing, an enthusiastic oarsman. More boathouses, suitably gabled and bargeboarded, were built in the 1890s by Hobbs & Sons on the site of the boat and timber yards north of New Street, and in 1897 the ultra-fashionable Leander Club put up new headquarters, complete with boathouse, close to the bridge on the Berkshire bank of the river. Then in about 1900 Brakspears' completed the ensemble on the Henley side by rebuilding the *Little White Hart* as another 'Old English' extravaganza, its gabled roof-line enlivened by terracotta dragons made at the works of S & E Collier in Reading. A permanent regatta grandstand went up next to the grounds of Phyllis Court in 1913.[195]

The rebuilding of Henley's riverfront was accompanied by the provision of new public, commercial and industrial buildings. Brakspears' embarked on a pub-building spree following a major expansion of the brewery itself, which started in 1886 with the building (by Wing) of a Mineral Water Factory in New Street, and ended in 1899 with new maltings on the opposite side: Henley's most impressive example of industrial architecture (Fig. 110). In

Figure 121 The *Imperial Hotel* (built 1896) opposite the station, a neo-Tudor extravaganza designed to catch the eye of the thousands of visitors arriving by train. One of several hotels, inns and boathouses rebuilt in the period, it may have inspired the neo-Tudor *Royal Hotel* nearby (rebuilt 1899–1900).

Figure 122 The Masonic Hall in Reading Road, built in an eclectic red-brick style in 1892.

1891 Wing also rebuilt the rival Greys Brewery in Friday Street, taken over by Brakspears' in 1896 and later demolished. The street's semi-industrial character was reinforced by the building of a plain brick factory, used variously for printing and paper-bag manufacture. Two handsome new banks went up in the 1890s: the present National Westminster in the Market Place in 1891, and Barclay's (by W. Campbell Jones) in Hart Street in 1892. Both employed the gabled neo-Tudor or 'Old English' style used later at the *Imperial Hotel*, and both out-Tudored the town's genuine 16th- or early 17th-century vernacular of buildings such as Speaker's House at the other end of Hart Street. By contrast, in 1892 the talented Reading architect William Ravenscroft designed the new Masonic Hall in Reading Road in a freely handled version of the eclectic red-brick style which contemporaries called 'Queen Anne'.[196]

Finally in 1899–1901, following more than two decades of successful municipal activity, came the most impressive of Henley's public buildings: the new town hall. It was designed by H.T. Hare, one of the most successful architects of public buildings in late Victorian and Edwardian England. Hare had recently completed the new town hall in Oxford, but here he abandoned its rich neo-Jacobean style in favour of a more restrained 'Wrenaissance' manner, looking back to the comfortable red-brick style of Henley's Georgian houses, but with a suitably imposing pedimented façade to the Market Place. Inside, and especially in the public hall upstairs, is a rich display of Edwardian Baroque ornament, particularly in plaster. Its style is a typical expression of civic pride in an era which, with hindsight, can perhaps be seen as Henley's heyday.[198]

Figure 123 Completed in 1901 to mark Queen Victoria's Diamond Jubilee four years earlier, the town hall (by H.T. Hare) is one of Henley's grandest buildings: a visible expression of municipal pride and confidence. The red brick echoes the area's Georgian houses, but the grand pedimented front is unique within the town.

Towards the Modern Age

The Victorian and Edwardian periods, then, saw Henley's final transformation into a fashionable social resort, known across the world for its annual Regatta, and boasting an eclectic range of impressive new buildings to match its new-found prestige. At the same time it remained a typical small market town, albeit one geared overwhelmingly to services and retail rather than to manufacture.

In so many respects, the privileged and fashionable world of the Edwardian Regatta was about to be swept away by the cataclysm of the First World War. And yet, despite the profound social and technological changes of the 20th century, the story of Henley's more recent development is overwhelmingly one of continuity rather than of any sudden or radical change in direction. How did Henley fare in the modern age?

Chapter 10 Modern Henley

Like any town in the 20th and early 21st centuries, Henley has experienced far-reaching changes. Among the most obvious are unprecedented physical expansion (altering not only the size but the character of the town), the disappearance of old social hierarchies, the decline of agriculture, and the rise of the motor car, not to mention the impact of two world wars and occasional periods of national recession. Yet even so, early 21st-century Henley probably has more in common with its late 19th-century predecessor than many Oxfordshire towns. How has the town altered since 1914, and what factors have conditioned the rate of change?

HENLEY BETWEEN THE WARS

As with every town and village across England, the First World War left its mark on Henley. Large numbers of townsmen enlisted in the local Oxfordshire and Buckinghamshire Light Infantry, and no fewer than 186 were killed: 339 if we include casualties from the immediate area. Royal Engineers were briefly billeted in the town,

Figure 124 The waterfront in 2008, with the *Red Lion* on the left, and its former granaries, boathouses and boat-building premises (now shops) in the centre. The gabled building on the right was the *Little White Hart* inn, rebuilt *c.*1900 and used by the Henley United Rowing Club.

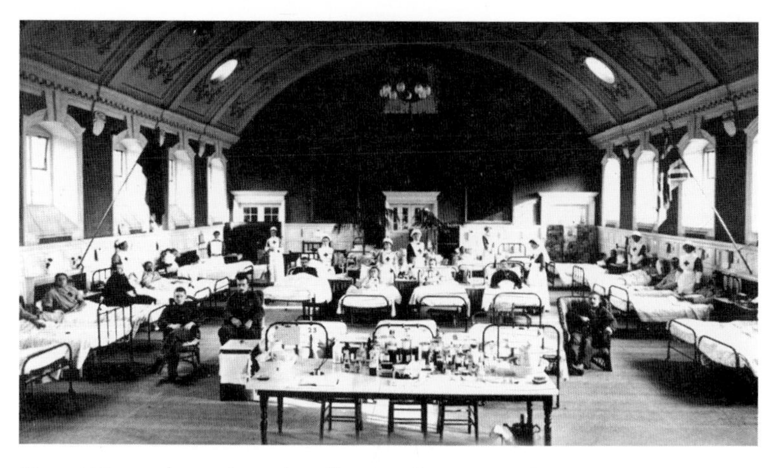

Figure 125 At the outbreak of war in 1914 the town hall's upper floor became a Red Cross Hospital with 24 beds, increased to 52 later on through conversion of the council chamber and two other small rooms. The initial cost was met by Robert Brakspear and other local benefactors.

Stuart Turner's engineering firm took on government contracts, and the town hall became a Red Cross Hospital, run mostly by local volunteers. The Regatta was, of course, suspended, to be revived in 1919 with a special four-day 'Peace Regatta'. More permanent memorials included a War Memorial Hospital a little way south of the town, paid for by public subscriptions and opened in 1923.[198]

But by then, despite the inevitable scars, Henley was already settling back into its earlier pre-war pattern. Its economic structure in 1935 was not fundamentally different from before the First World War, with a continuing emphasis on services and retail, and relatively little industry. Out of well over 300 local businesses, nearly half were shops selling groceries and provisions, shoes and clothing, or a wide variety of goods ranging from watches and china to furniture, radios and tobacco. Other services ranged from banks and law firms to dentists, doctors, chemists, photographers, dry cleaners, laundries, hairdressers, and (in one instance) a masseuse. Modern needs were reflected in the presence of three electricians, and of ironmongery firms like Champion & Co. on Bell Street, which specialised in central heating and hot water supply. Manufacturing, as earlier, was largely confined to Brakspears' Brewery, the boat builders Hobbs & Sons and Arlett & Sons, Smiths' paper bag business at New Mills and Friday Street, and Stuart Turner's engineering firm, now accompanied by a more recent engineering concern, Heckman & Sons, at Bell Street and Market Place.[199]

In other respects, too, traces of the old pre-war world survived into the 1930s. Most of the country houses around Henley, so important for its social and economic life in the past, continued in private hands up to the Second World War and beyond, providing local employment and a market for local goods and services. Farming, too, still permeated town life. The livestock market continued in the 1920s when it was moved from the market place to the yard of the (*Old*) *White Hart*, and in the 1930s tradesmen listed in Henley still included several dairymen, a horse slaughterer (at 56 Market Place), a nurseryman on Greys Road, and two seed merchants. A less welcome reminder of the past was the continuing economic hardship endured by some of the town's working population during the national economic difficulties of the 1920s–30s. The town council discussed measures to relieve local unemployment as early as 1921, and soup kitchens remained part of town life in the 1920s as they had been in the 1890s. Winter was especially difficult, when (as an elderly resident later recalled) 'the owners of the big houses went up to their town houses in London and their servants went with them'.[200]

Yet alongside this, Henley's role as a fashionable tourist, leisure and (increasingly) commuting centre continued, facilitated now not only by the railway but by the motor car. A 1928 publicity brochure for the prestigious Phyllis Court Club claimed that it was already 'one of the principal motoring and sports centres in the south of England', its accessibility along pleasant country roads allowing London-based members to lunch, dine, or spend the weekend there, and others to use it as a base for commuting or for recreational motoring. Ambitious building schemes (not all fully realised) aimed to make it 'the most luxurious and entertaining Club rendezvous outside London, ... comparable with the best of the great Country Clubs of America and the East'. This was one of Henley's more exclusive attractions, but it was by no means unique. *Salter's Guide to the Thames* (published in 1936) praised the town's recreational facilities and physical assets in terms little different from Climenson 40 years earlier, listing boating 'in the most charming reaches of the Thames', 'delightful walks and drives amidst river, woodland and common scenery', numerous local golf courses, and the leisure facilities (tennis, bowls, putting) available at the 'public

Figure 126 The main lounge of the Phyllis Court Club in its inter-war heyday, shown here in a hand-tinted postcard. Founded in 1906, by the 1920s the Club was one of the area's premier sporting, motoring and country clubs, and continues today. The building replaced the ancient manor house in the 1840s, then as now offering fine views of the Regatta course.

riverside gardens' at Mill Meadows, by then run by the borough corporation. A local trades directory listed no fewer than 12 hotels or guest houses and five cafés or tea rooms, one of them (Ye Olde Elizabethan House on Hart Street) connected with an antiques business patronised by Queen Mary on one of her frequent visits to the town. And, as earlier, there was a significant upper-middle-class population of well-heeled professionals or residents with private income, among them the 144 people listed as 'private residents'. Many, as before the war, lived on the town's northern fringes at Northfield End or the Fair Mile, or in the now well-established Victorian and Edwardian suburbs to its south and west.[201]

Underpinning Henley's continuing attractions were the improvements in its infrastructure common to most places in the period: resurfaced roads (begun before the First World War), improved and extended street lighting, and the gradual extension of the sanitation and water supply established in the late 19th century. Mains electricity was introduced in the 1920s, supplied by the Thames Valley Electric Supply Co. Yet at the same time, the need to preserve Henley's character in the face of modernisation was starting to be articulated, presaging a trend which featured prominently in late 20th-century planning initiatives. As early as 1931 the Oxfordshire Regional Planning Committee commented that 'This district requires special consideration on account of its popularity as a boating centre, the importance of its world-renowned Regatta, and the beauty of the river and its surroundings', and that 'building should not be allowed to spread in a disorganised fashion ... The layout of new building sites should be such that the beauty and attractiveness of the town shall be enhanced'. Such attitudes were given popular expression in 1933–4 during a campaign to prevent replacement

Figure 127 Proposed cinema intended for Hart Street, designed by Verity and Beverley of London in 1933–4. The building would have destroyed the Georgian frontage of 18 Hart Street, and prompted one of Henley's first planning and conservation battles. The smaller Regal Cinema was eventually built on Bell Street, replacing the old Picture Palace (opened *c.*1911).

of the Georgian frontage of 18 Hart Street with a large new cinema in the modern style, prompting letters to *The Times*, while a separate proposal for a cinema on meadowland off Reading Road was opposed on the grounds that it would spoil amenities for an important residential part of the town. The new Regal Cinema was eventually opened on Bell Street in 1937, on the site of the earlier Picture Palace.[202]

Other major changes in Henley followed national legislation. The last vestiges of the old Poor Law system were dismantled in 1929, when the workhouse passed to the County Council as a so-called Public Assistance Institution – the first stage of its transformation into Townlands Hospital. The County Council took over the Grammar School (moved to Rotherfield Court) the previous year, while primary and infant provision was reorganised around the two National schools and a newly built infant school in Greys Road (1932). Religious life saw little fundamental change, though a new and larger Roman Catholic church was built in 1935–6 on Vicarage Road, while falling attendance at the Friends' Meeting House at Northfield End saw it used from the 1930s–80s as a youth hostel.[203]

As with the First World War, Henley's experience of the Second echoed that of numerous small towns. Despite its proximity to London – whose fires during the Blitz lit up the sky beyond White Hill – the town escaped any serious damage, though 72 townsmen were killed, their names added to the war memorial plaque mounted on the town hall wall. The community aided the war effort in the usual ways, accommodating an influx of evacuees, running Home Guards, raising money for a Spitfire (components for which were assembled at an underground factory at nearby Warren Row), and tolerating the removal of iron railings from buildings around the town. A more positive consequence was the opening of the town's first public library in the town hall, set up for children by a Red Cross librarian, but later extended to adults and taken over by the borough council.[204]

Building between the Wars

In contrast to the 19th century, when Henley's population virtually doubled, in the inter-war period it changed very little, falling from a peak of 6,836 in 1921 to just over 6,600 in the early 1930s. Not surprisingly, therefore, the years after the First World War saw a sharp decline in building activity. Housing development fell into two broad and contrasting categories: the provision of new rented council housing for the less well-to-do on the southern fringe of the town, and the building of owner-occupied houses, mostly to the south-west. The tendency, as in England as a whole, was for rented housing to predominate in the 1920s, when there were more or less generous government subsidies following the Prime Minister David Lloyd George's promise to build 'homes fit for heroes'. More private housing followed in the 1930s, when interest rates were low, mortgages plentiful and government funding more parsimonious.[205]

Henley's first council houses went up in and around Vicarage Road and Western Avenue (west of Harpsden Road) in 1919–22, using subsidies offered under the Addison Act of 1919. Some were designed by H.T. Hare, architect of Henley town hall, and, in contrast to the artisan terraces erected by the Hamilton brothers immediately before the war, were laid out to a low density on Garden City principles. They were built in the cosy Arts-and-Crafts manner of the first London County Council 'cottage estates', with steep tiled roofs and large gardens. Inside, however, they offered little or no more accommodation than the earlier terraces, and the relatively high rents meant that the poorest inhabitants could not afford them. To alleviate the continuing problem of slum housing, especially in Friday Street and the Greys Hill area, the Henley & District Housing Trust was founded in 1929, building its first houses in Peppard Lane the following year and a total of 28 by 1933, when it moved on to renovating older buildings. Another council estate went up at Mount View in 1932–6, north of the former workhouse. Even so, some poor housing remained in the old town's southern and western parts until after the Second World War.[206]

Compared with larger towns like Oxford and Reading, Henley saw relatively little private speculative building. The town was too far from London for lower-middle-class commuters, and there was enough new housing around the fringes of Reading (the nearest large centre of employment) to cater for those who worked there. Instead of streets of semi-detached houses, therefore, Henley

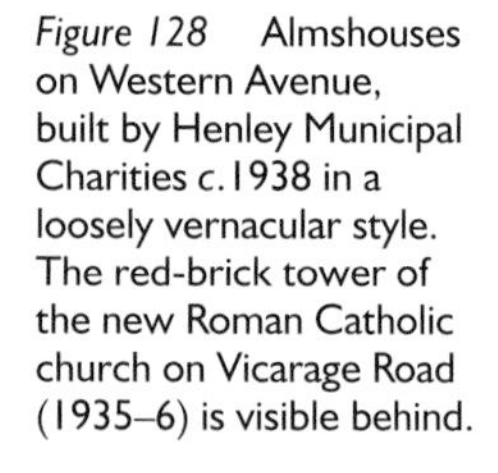

Figure 128 Almshouses on Western Avenue, built by Henley Municipal Charities *c.*1938 in a loosely vernacular style. The red-brick tower of the new Roman Catholic church on Vicarage Road (1935–6) is visible behind.

Figure 129 The Art Deco interior of the Regal cinema on Bell Street (1936–7), photographed shortly before its demolition in 1993. The 1930s Compton organ was acquired for the cinema by the Henley & District Organ Trust in 1971.

acquired detached houses in large gardens, catering for a more affluent clientele. Several are in the style dubbed 'Stockbroker Tudor' by the cartoonist Osbert Lancaster, who from 1953 lived at Leicester House (now demolished) in the Fair Mile. Owners of land to the north and west of the town saw no reason to encourage building, and such development as there was occurred mostly in Rotherfield Road (leading west from Harpsden Way), and at the top of St Mark's Road and St Andrew's Road.[207]

The extensive rebuilding of the town centre in the late 19th century meant that there was little scope for new public or commercial building. The War Memorial Hospital in Harpsden Way was designed by Charles Smith of Reading, but otherwise the only significant new public building was a handsome neo-Georgian post office built on the site of Southfield House in Reading Road in 1922, replacing an earlier one of 1895 opposite. Some pub façades were remodelled in a neo-Tudor style sufficiently authentic-looking to deceive the unwary, among them the *Argyll* in the Market Place and the frontage of the *Old White Hart* in Hart Street (1931), while in 1938 the *Old White Horse* at the town's northern approach in Northfield End was built in an attractive Arts-and-Crafts-inspired manner to designs by the Henley-based A.E. Hobbs. Other examples of 'Old English' remodelling included a shop at the southern end of Duke Street, its front rebuilt with old timbers in 1936, and a former granary at the east end of Friday Street. The modern world struck back, exceptionally for Henley, with the new Regal cinema in Bell Street, designed in 1936–7 by L.T. Hunt. Solidly brick outside and with an Art-Deco interior, it survived until 1993, when it was demolished amid considerable controversy.[208]

THE MODERN TOWN

Change and Continuity

In the 60-odd years since the end of the Second World War many Oxfordshire towns have changed virtually beyond recognition, partly as a result of planning decisions. Witney, Banbury, Bicester, Didcot and Carterton spring most readily to mind. Compared with them Henley has, in essence, changed relatively little, whether in size, economic infrastructure, or general tone and appearance. And yet profound changes there have obviously been, reflecting developments both in Henley and in the wider world.

Perhaps the most obvious is urban growth. Henley's population, only 6,621 in 1931, rose sharply from the 1950s: by 1961 it was 9,144, and by 1971 nearly 11,500, climbing again to 10,646 in 2001 after a slight fall in the 1970s–80s. During the same period the number of dwellings doubled from around 2,400 (in 1951) to over 5,000. The results were not only physical. Looking back in 1985, some of Henley's older inhabitants recalled its transformation from 'virtually a village' where everyone knew everyone else into a larger, more anonymous and more diverse place, 'still friendly', but with new people, new ideas, and less close-knit.[209]

Meanwhile the town's economy changed only slowly and in some ways less radically. Planning reports from the 1960s to 1990s repeatedly emphasised the importance of shops, services, tourism and commuting, a pattern familiar from the late Victorian era, and arguably with its roots in the 18th century. In 1966 by far the highest proportion of the working population (24 per cent) were professionals or managers, of whom many worked outside the town; the other largest groups were those in miscellaneous services (18 per cent), construction industries (17.5 per cent), and distributive trades (8 per cent), a pattern which the planners thought appropriate for Henley's size and character. The picture was similar a few years later, when over a third (mostly professionals) still worked outside the town, and as many as 11 per cent in London, the rest (62 per cent) living and working in Henley itself. The unusually high proportion of well-off professionals and commuters reflected not only the town's continued appeal but its continued accessibility, enhanced by the building of the M4 and M40 motorways and by the exceptional survival of the rail link to Twyford and London. In addition, Henley continued to serve as a shopping centre for a wide hinterland, offering a range of goods and provisions to those unwilling to struggle into larger towns like Reading or Slough.

A small industrial area between Reading Road and the river was developed piecemeal from the 1960s, partly to attract newcomers and partly to entice some existing businesses away from the town centre. By the 1990s it was one of Henley's main employment areas, hosting manufacturing and light industrial firms, offices, builders' merchants, and car showrooms. Otherwise, except for Stuart

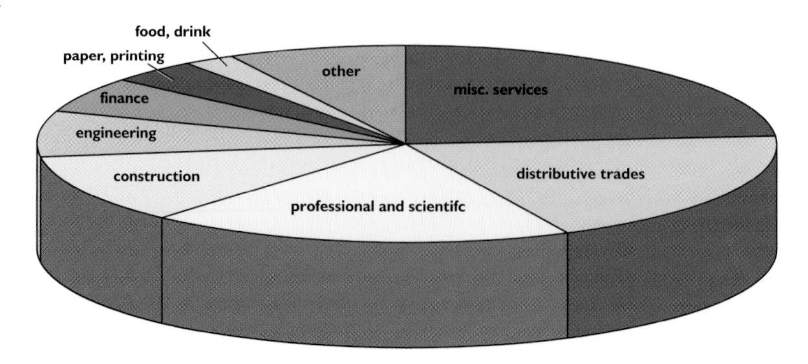

Figure 130 Employment in Henley in 1976, based on the 1979 District Plan. As earlier, the emphasis was on shops, services, and professional jobs, many of them outside the town. Manufacturing (including brewing and engineering) remained small-scale, though the sizeable numbers employed in construction continued an ancient tradition.

Turner's engineering works and Brakspears' Brewery, the main employment was still in shops and offices, town-centre provision ranging from Hallmark Cards' large purpose-built premises in Station Road to small offices over ground-floor shops. By then Stuart Turner's (employing around 150) specialised in industrial and domestic pumps, having ended its long-standing manufacture of marine engines and model steam engines. Brakspears', after a long period of restructuring, finally and unexpectedly closed in 2002, continuing as a pub-owning business but selling its brewing brand to a Witney-based firm – appropriate, perhaps, given Robert Brakspear's Witney origins. Up to a point this was balanced by important newcomers such as Perpetual plc, a major investment company set up in 1974. Its founder (Sir) Martyn Arbib took an active interest in the town, and in the 1990s (when the company won several prestigious awards) employed 120 people.[210]

Underpinning the continuities was an increasingly rigorous planning process, regulated from the 1940s by a torrent of central government legislation. As we have seen, the desirability of preserving Henley's character and attractiveness was stated as early as 1931, and from the 1960s successive County and District Council plans wrestled with how to balance conservation against the need to provide jobs, amenities and affordable housing, and to keep the town centre alive and vibrant. Large-scale industrial or housing development was generally accepted to be neither practical nor desirable, though when it came to specifics Henley, like many towns, experienced its fair share of planning controversies. In the 1980s the unsuccessful battle to save the Regal Cinema brought celebrities such as the former Beatle George Harrison (then living at Friar Park) onto the streets alongside local townspeople, and disputes over the redevelopment of the site by Waitrose supermarket dragged on for years. So, too, did Tesco's application for an out-of-town-supermarket off Reading Road, eventually opened in 1995. Such disputes became especially virulent against the backdrop of early 1990s recession, when the Henley Chamber of Trade claimed that the town centre was 'dying' because of the squeeze on small traders – a sharp contrast with the late 1980s, when a national TV documentary held up 'prosperous' Henley as a symbol of the north–south economic divide. Planning decisions were further complicated by the high proportion of older and retired people attracted to Henley, a characteristic which in 1993 was claimed (with a large dose of journalistic hyperbole) to be creating a 'twilight town'.[211]

Such dilemmas are probably intractable, though in recent years Henley seems to have trodden a moderately successful path through the labyrinth. In the early 21st century the town does indeed retain its historic character, its fine buildings, and its unparalleled setting, while nevertheless remaining a 'real' town with a vibrant shopping and commercial centre and a wide range of amenities, catering for the resident population as well as for visitors and tourists. The loss of Brakspears' in 2002 was a symbolic blow, but many other key firms continue: indeed, loyalty to the town and the benefits of being based there were among the factors which kept both Stuart Turner and Perpetual plc in Henley during the 1980s and 1990s, when both considered moves elsewhere. More recent national recession has inevitably left its mark, with no fewer than 34 town-centre shops reported vacant in March 2009. But whether that is a sign of long-term problems or (as seems more likely) just a temporary downturn is at present impossible to say.[212]

In other respects, too, the positives seem generally to have outweighed the negatives. The acute need to provide affordable housing for couples and first-time buyers has been at least partially addressed since the 1990s, although from 1988 to 2002 average house prices in Henley were nonetheless reckoned to have risen by a staggering 183 per cent, making them the second highest in England. Health Authority restructuring caused the controversial loss of the War Memorial Hospital in 1985, now almost certainly

Figure 131 The town centre in 2008, with Market Place partly pedestrianised, but traffic still flowing through. The wooded hills beyond the church and river are a reminder of Henley's ancient rural setting, still largely preserved against encroachment: even now the town retains a clear 'edge', particularly on the north and east.

to be followed by Townlands Hospital. On the other hand Henley's leisure amenities – more varied than in many towns of comparable size – include a new cinema, the revamped Kenton Theatre, a multi-purpose sports centre (opened in 1974), a new library (1981), and the award-winning River & Rowing Museum (below). Even the town's long-running traffic problems have been eased by partial pedestrianisation of the market place, although with access from the east still confined to the narrow 18th-century bridge, the larger problem remains.

The responsibility for meeting these challenges now lies primarily outside the town, the town council having lost many of its traditional powers under local government reorganisation in 1974. Nonetheless, the council continues (with other local groups) to play an important and sometimes controversial role, liaising with the myriad of local and national bodies which hold the key to Henley's future.[213]

River, Regatta and Tourism

What, meanwhile, of the river? Despite the long-term decline of heavy water transport, commercial use of the Thames continued beyond the Second World War, enjoying something of a renaissance during the war itself when merchant traffic above Teddington increased to over 600,000 tons a year. But the revival was short-lived, and by the early 1970s commercial traffic upstream had all but ceased. By contrast, use of the river by pleasure craft continued its inexorable rise, with the Henley stretch between Marsh Lock and Boulters Lock the busiest on the river. By 1979 traffic here was already reckoned to be at 'saturation point', with long lock queues on summer weekends, occasional conflict between anglers and motor launches, and regular use not only by rowers but by canoeists and sailing boats.

This was, however, just one aspect of a wider post-war development of tourism around Henley and the south-west Chilterns. In the 1970s Henley lay within the English Tourist Board's Thames and Chiltern Region, which received some 5 million tourist trips a year, with tourists spending around £100 million and 33,000 people employed in related jobs. Henley's share – outside Regatta season at least – was relatively small, though by then it was already well established as a base for exploring the area and as a stopping point for visitors to Oxford and Windsor, with five hotels, several B&Bs, and up to 27,000 overnight visitors a year. As with economic development and housing, planners sought to find a balance between encouraging tourism and improving facilities, while opposing development which might threaten the town's character.

Boat hire and river trips from Henley continued as earlier, while Mill Meadows by the river (run by the town council) remained popular with residents and visitors alike, with its leafy open spaces and its bowling greens, playground, refreshment facilities, and new multi-purpose pavilion (opened 1992). Tourism received a further boost with the opening in 1998 (by the Queen) of the prestigious River & Rowing Museum, a multi-million pound scheme supported by Martyn Arbib of Perpetual and other local sponsors.[214]

The Royal Regatta, meanwhile, despite periodic financial problems, ended the 20th century as a major business seemingly going from strength to strength. The immediate post-war achievement (according to one former rower and long-term steward) was 'to recreate the gracious, perfectionist, privileged yet popular ambience' of earlier Regattas, and later chairmen worked to modernise the event and win younger adherents while simultaneously retaining its traditional appeal. From the 1920s the organisation gradually acquired much of the land required for its stands and amenities, and in the 1980s corporate entertainment helped further boost its finances, so that by 1989 some 10 per cent of its income came from hospitality tents. By 2005 the total cost of mounting the Regatta amounted to some £1.76 million, with income exceeding this by £485,000. At the same time the Regatta has remained a major sporting event, attracting a record 386 entries (42 of them from the USA) in 1988, staging up to 100 races a day, and now held (since 1986)

Figure 132 Revellers at the modern Royal Regatta, held since 1986 over five days at the start of July.

over a five-day period. Nonetheless its appeal as a high-class social event remains paramount. In the words of the former steward quoted above, 'were it not for the immaculate lawns and flower beds, the Pimms and champagne bar, and the military band playing the Knightsbridge Suite and Iolanthe, the magic might fade and the cash registers cease to ring'.[215]

Post-War Buildings

The Regatta's continuing success was reflected in 1986 in the erection of a new Royal Regatta headquarters next to the bridge (see below), creating a strikingly modernist addition to the Henley waterfront. And in other ways, too, the changes of the last 60 years found physical expression in the town's buildings and physical fabric.

The Second World War initially put an end to even the limited amount of building activity which had characterised the previous twenty years. But with marked population increase from the 1950s, and a growing influx of professional and managerial middle classes attracted by easy transport and the congenial physical environment, Henley entered on a new housing boom. At first, as after the First World War, the emphasis was on council housing, as in the Gainsborough estate north and west of Greys Road (begun in 1946), or the nearby prefabs which remained occupied until the 1980s. Housing developments for owner-occupiers followed in the 1950s and 1960s: in Manor Road (1957–9), south of Greys Road, and later in Blandy Road (1963–4) and Deanfield Road (1968–70), continuing the south-western spread of the town that had begun in the 1930s. This necessitated the rebuilding of some older schools (Sacred Heart in 1958, Holy Trinity in 1965), and the provision of a new one at Valley Road in 1970. Soon after, another large development occurred to the north of Friar Park, in and around Crisp Road and Luker Avenue.

These were relatively low-density developments, creating a suburban environment that could be matched in any English town (and which were criticised as such). But with planning restrictions forbidding further outward spread, new high-density housing developments of flats and 'town houses' began to go up closer to the old town centre, most of them on the site of large 18th- and 19th-century houses and villas. Examples are Leicester Close (replacing Leicester House at Northfield End, *c.*1968), and Ancastle Green and Milton Close (1967–70) at the top of Gravel Hill, the latter on the site of the Brakspears' former home at Paradise (formerly Deanfield) House. For those with tighter budgets, Upton Close was built on the site of Upton House in Reading

Figure 133 Henley from the south-west in 1986. The triangle between Harpsden Road and Reading Road was part of the late Victorian and Edwardian development; further west and south are the 20th-century suburbs, including Western Avenue and Gainsborough Avenue. Industrial estates developed from the 1960s can be seen between Reading Road and the railway line (on the right, towards the river).

Road, conveniently close to the railway station. Such developments ensured that the town centre retained a resident population, and this was further encouraged by the gentrification of streets like Friday Street and West Street, as affluent newcomers replaced the older inhabitants who were decanted to estates on the edge of the town. One neighbouring country estate that remained inviolate was Friar Park, acquired by a religious order after the war before George Harrison bought it in 1971.[216]

The town centre itself retained its pre-war (and essentially pre-First World War) character largely intact, the increasingly vocal conservation lobby ensuring that schemes such as the proposed demolition and rebuilding of the *Catherine Wheel* in Hart Street in 1961 came to nothing. With one or two exceptions, modernist interventions were notably discreet, as with a house by the architect Francis Pollen (The Walled Garden) hidden away in Bell Lane in 1959, and a doctors' surgery with an ingenious circular plan fitted into a corner of the Townlands Hospital (former workhouse) site by Patrick Gwynne in 1968. Gwynne also designed Past Field (on Rotherfield Road) for one of the doctors in 1960 (extended 1966). As the national economy slumped in the 1970s the pressure to build decreased, apart from some new council flats at Mount View in 1978 (replacing earlier council houses), and a new Badgemore primary school on the edge of Friar Park opened the same year. The Oxfordshire County Architects' team who designed the Badgemore school rejected the flat-roofed modernism of the 1960s and early '70s in favour of neo-vernacular brick walls and pitched, tiled roofs, and pitched roofs were also a feature of the new public library built in 1981, close to the new Waitrose supermarket in Bell Street. The supermarket itself was rebuilt in a similar manner in 1994.[217]

Close not only to London but to the high-tech 'M4 corridor', Henley was well placed to benefit from the economic boom years of the 1980s and '90s. House prices were forced up not only by Henley's continued appeal to well-off professionals (both working and retired), but by continuing planning restraints, which prevented new building on the outskirts. Pressure consequently resumed on the central areas, especially where there were older, unlisted buildings or abandoned 'brownfield sites' ripe for redevelopment, whether for residential or commercial purposes. So in the 1980s, several years after malting had ceased at Brakspears' Brewery, the handsome maltings on the north side of New Street were turned into offices and eventually flats (Figure 110), and when brewing followed suit in 2002 the old buildings on the southern side became a hotel. Henley College (created in 1988) expanded southwards with the construction of a large new building in Deanfield Avenue in 1998, and the controversial Tesco supermarket at the town's southern extremity opened in 1995, built on former sports grounds which had to be relocated. A run-down area which received particular attention was that around the railway station, demolished in 1975 and

Figure 134 Perpetual House near the station, built in 1993–4 for the successful unit-trust company Perpetual plc. Designed to fit in with the surrounding conservation area, the building was welcomed for its beneficial impact on a 'rapidly deteriorating area'. The company has since moved to premises elsewhere in Henley.

Figure 135 The Royal Regatta Headquarters of 1986, one of two outstanding modern additions to Henley's townscape in the final decades of the 20th century.

replaced in 1984 with a nondescript and much smaller building, the site of the old station being given over to offices. In 1993–4 Martyn Arbib, as head of Perpetual, employed the Broadway Malyan firm to design a large new block of offices (Perpetual House) opposite the station, heavily post-modern in character, with pitched roofs and a massive central archway. Then in 1999 and 2006 red-brick blocks of flats went up opposite the junction of Station Road and Reading Road, transforming the frontage to the south of the Congregationalist Church.[219]

In the last decades of the 20th century Henley was fortunate to acquire two buildings which stood out from the normal rut of developers' architecture. The first was the Royal Regatta Headquarters, built in 1986 to the designs of Sir Terry Farrell, one of the leaders of the post-modernist tendency in English architecture. Replacing a pub (the *Carpenters' Arms*) and some boat-sheds on the Berkshire bank of the river, it echoes the design of a classical temple, with its pedimented river façade. But Farrell invested this ancient archetype with a new vitality, hollowing out the centre to form a club-room with a boathouse underneath, and introducing bright colours to enliven the brick structure. The building has something of the extrovert character of the town's late Victorian and Edwardian buildings. Then in 1998 long-standing plans for a museum matured with the building of the River & Rowing Museum in Mill Meadows, designed by the internationally acclaimed architect David Chipperfield. Here the prevailing motif is taken from Henley's connection with the river. The main, top-lit galleries loosely resemble boat sheds or even upturned boats, clad externally in timber, and attached by a covered bridge to a large, plain building housing exhibits relating to the town's history. The external effect is introverted and self-effacing, the building almost hiding itself among trees in its park-like setting. But inside it opens up to form a series of unexpected, light-filled spaces. Like the Regatta Headquarters it celebrates the past while unashamedly engaging with the present: a symbol perhaps of Henley's aspirations in the early years of the 21st century.[220]

Figure 136 Henley River & Rowing Museum, designed by David Chipperfield and opened by the Queen in 1998. The building fulfilled long-standing plans for a national rowing museum at Henley, and alongside galleries on river and rowing themes houses important collections on the history of the town and area.

Afterword

This book has been not only an exploration of a particular place, but a journey through time. Over its course we have traced Henley's development from its origins as a planned medieval town to its modern incarnation as a service and tourist centre, with its shops, small businesses, leisure facilities, and still largely unspoilt historic core and landscape setting. Through the unfolding story has flowed the Thames – boundary, power source, transport corridor and (latterly) playground – linking Henley and its Chilterns hinterland with the ever-important metropolis 60-odd miles downstream.

Why bother with the history of places at all? Examining towns like Henley in detail can certainly shed light on broader historical issues, and we have seen (for example) how from the Middle Ages Henley's economy and that of the surrounding countryside was inextricably linked with the demands of London, and how its role casts light on the changing history of Thames navigation and of water transport generally. No town or village can be properly understood in isolation, and this is especially true of a long-established market centre and inland port like Henley.

Even when looking to the future, the past is constantly present. Modern planners and architects recognise that they cannot hope to make informed and viable decisions without understanding how a town or building has evolved. It is pleasing to note, for instance, that almost without exception post-war planning documents for Henley have begun with a thumbnail summary of its earlier historical development. By improving our understanding of Henley's past we are also helping shape its future.

But perhaps the most important reason for exploring a place's history – and the most often overlooked – is that it helps us to understand and appreciate the world around us. Like the landscape itself, every town, village and hamlet is the sum total of its past. Henley is no exception, with its medieval market place and street plan, its impressive (though often hidden) medieval buildings, the polite Georgian frontages which recall the 18th-century age of balls and coaching, and its modern riverside – now bereft of granaries, but still lined with its Victorian and Edwardian boathouses, and (since 1986) with the gleaming Royal Regatta Headquarters. If this book inspires just a few of its readers to look at Henley (and indeed at other towns) with new eyes and deeper understanding, then it will have served one of its primary purposes.

Endnotes

The following abbreviations are used throughout the endnotes.

BL	British Library
Bodl	Bodleian Library
Briers	Briers, PM (ed.), *Henley Borough Records: Assembly Books 1395–1543* (ORS 41, 1960)
Burn	Burn, JS, *A History of Henley-on-Thames* (1861)
Cal Chart	*Calendar of Charter Rolls ... in the Public Record Office*
Cal Close	*Calendar of Close Rolls ... in the Public Record Office*
Cal Pat	*Calendar of Patent Rolls ... in the Public Record Office*
Cal Inq pm	*Calendar of Inquisitions Post Mortem ... in the Public Record Office*
Census	Census returns 1801–2001, published until 1911 as Parliamentary Papers
Cottingham	Cottingham, A, *The Hostelries of Henley* (2000)
Dir	Directory
HAHG	Henley Archaeological and Historical Group
HS	*Henley Standard*
Hepple and Doggett	Hepple, LW and Doggett, AM, *The Chilterns* (1994 edn)
Kelly	*Kelly's Directory of Oxfordshire*
NMR	National Monuments Record, Swindon
New DNB	*Oxford Dictionary of National Biography*
OHS	Oxford Historical Society
ORO	Oxfordshire Record Office
ORS	Oxfordshire Record Society
OS	Ordnance Survey
Oxf Jnl	*(Jackson's) Oxford Journal*
Oxon.	Oxfordshire
OxS	Oxfordshire Studies, Central Library, Oxford
Peberdy	Peberdy, RB, 'The Economy, Society, and Government of a Small Town in Late Medieval England: A Study of Henley-on-Thames from *c.*1300 to *c.*1540 (Leicester Univ. PhD thesis 1994)
Pevsner	Sherwood, J and Pevsner, N, *Buildings of England: Oxfordshire* (1974)
PO Dir	*Post Office Directory of Oxfordshire*
PRO	Public Record Office (in TNA)
Rec. Com.	Record Commission
TNA	The National Archives, Kew
Tyack, 'Rebuilding'	Tyack, G, 'The Rebuilding of Henley-on-Thames, 1780–1914', *Oxon. Local History*, vol. 3, no. 2 (Spring 1989), 67–89
VCH	Victoria County History

ORO and PRO wills are being transcribed by the Burford/Henley Probate Group, and made available on the Oxfordshire EPE website. Images of PRO wills are downloadable from The National Archives website.

Henley in Time and Place, pp.1–8

1 **Whitelocke:** BL Egerton 997, ff. 22v–23. **Regatta**: Chapter 9; Climenson, EJ, *Guide to Henley-on-Thames* (1896), 68–72.
2 **Landscape:** Hepple and Doggett; *VCH Oxon.* XVI (forthcoming). **Leland:** Toulmin Smith, L (ed.), *Itinerary of John Leland 1535–43* (1906–10), V, 71. **Defoe:** Cole, GDH and Browning, DC (eds), *Tour through the Whole Island of Gt Britain* (1962), I, 299. **Brick-making:** Hepple and Doggett, 108–9, 195–7.
3 **London, river trade, wool:** Chapters 3–7. **Pepys:** Hepple and Doggett, 177–8. **Defoe:** *Tour*, I, 299.
4 **Descriptions:** Moritz, KP, *Travels ... through Several Parts of England, in 1782* (1795 edn), 144–6; *Lewis's Topog Dict.* (1840), 409–10; Brewer, JN, *Topographical and Historical Description of the County of Oxford* [*c.* 1813], 324–5; *South Oxfordshire Local Plan* (South Oxon. District Council, December 1993), 70: copy in OxS. **Friar Park:** Chapters 9–10.
5 Chapters 3–8; Tyack, 'Rebuilding', 67.
6 Ackroyd, P, *Thames: Sacred River* (2007).

The Birth of Henley, pp.9–20

7 **New towns:** Beresford, MW, *New Towns of the Middle Ages* (1967).
8 **Roman roads and settlement:** Henig, M, and Booth, P, *Roman Oxon.* (2000), 36, 49–51, 74–5; Malpas, FJ, 'Roman Roads South and East of Dorchester', *Oxoniensia* 52 (1987), 23–33; Moloney, C, 'Excavations and Building Survey at Bell Street, Henley-on-Thames, 1993–4', *Oxoniensia* 62 (1997), 109–33. **Crossings:** unpublished town-plan analysis by Dr Antonia Catchpole of VCH Oxfordshire and EPE (2008).
9 **Benson estate:** Tiller, K (ed.), *Benson: A Village Through its History* (1999), 15–63; Blair, J, *Anglo-Saxon Oxon.* (1994), refs at 222; *Rotuli Hundredorum* (Rec. Com.), II, 37, 751; *VCH Oxon.* I, 374, 400, 411, 418, 423, 425. **Place name:** Gelling, M (ed.), *Place Names of Oxon.* (1953–4), I, 74.

10 **Pottery:** Pine, J, 'Excavation of Medieval and Post-Medieval Features at the Rear of 42c Bell Street, Henley, Oxfordshire', *Oxoniensia* 64 (1999), 272. **Manor house:** *Rotuli de Liberate* (Rec. Com.), 128–9 (probably Henley-on-Thames), and refs below. **Stephen:** Jenkins, JG (ed.), *Cartulary of Missenden Abbey*, I (Bucks. Archaeol. Soc. Records Branch 2, 1939), 16–17. **Droveways and green:** Catchpole, unpubl. town-plan analysis. **Rotherfield:** *Place Names Oxon.* I, 77.

11 **1177–9:** *Pipe Roll* 1178 (PRS 27), 117; 1179 (PRS 28), 94–5. **Bridge**: Panel 1. **Town foundations:** Beresford, MW, *New Towns of the Middle Ages* (1967); *VCH Oxon.* XII, 326. **Henley town, fair and guild:** *Rotuli litterarum patentium* (Rec. Com.), I (1), 4; *Cal Chart* 1427–1516, 7; Peberdy, 93–7.

12 See (e.g.) Palliser, DM (ed.), *The Cambridge Urban History of Britain, I: 600–1540* (2000), 153–86; Clark, D, Catchpole, A and Peberdy, RB, *Burford: Buildings and People in a Cotswold Town* (2008).

13 **Development and plots:** Catchpole, unpubl. town-plan analysis (2008), on which rest of section based. **Town ditch and Brook Street:** ORO MS Oxf. Dioc. c 748, ff. 1–3 (plan); *ibid.* BOR/3/A/IX/1/62; Briers, 160. **Badgemore boundary:** ORO BOR/3/A/IX/1/53 and 61, BOR/3/A/IX/1/267; Briers, 100. **Walls:** Peberdy, 21–2; Crocker, J, 'The Walls of Henley', HAHG *Jnl* 11 (Summer 1996), 16–21; Briers, refs at 244; deeds in ORO BOR/3/A/IX/1. **Grim's Ditch:** Crocker, J, 'An Attempt to Trace the Course of Grymes Dyke through Henley', HAHG *Jnl* (Feb. 1984); Henig and Booth, *Roman Oxon.* 28–9.

14 **Duke Street:** below, Chapter 9. **Friday Street:** Peberdy, 23, 30; ORO BOR/3/A/IX/1/1, 15–17; building surveys by R Gibson (Nos 17/19, 23/25, 31, 63, 67–71). **Parish boundary:** ORO tithe map; OS *Area Bk* (1879). **Squatter settlements:** Slater, TR, 'Planning English Medieval "Street Towns": The Herts Evidence', *Landscape History* 26 (2005), 19–36.

15 **Church:** *Rotuli Litterarum Patentium* (Rec. Com.), I (1), 4; *Rotuli Hundredorum* (Rec. Com.), II, 751; *Taxatio Ecclesiastica ... 1291* (Rec. Com.), 30. **Churchyard alterations:** ORO MS Oxf. Archd. Oxon. b 24, ff. 248–51 (1782); *ibid.* MS Oxf. Dioc. c 436, 235–62 (1831–3). **Rectory house:** Salter, HE (ed.), *Thame Cartulary*, II (ORS 26, 1948), 127; ORO BOR/3/A/IX/1/15–17; BOR/3/A/II/1, f. 7; Cottingham, A, 'The Rectory Garden Site', HAHG *Jnl* (April 1985), 1–6.

16 **Queenhithe:** *Cal Inq pm*, III, 462. **Wharfage:** Thomas, A H (ed.), *Calendar of Plea and Memoranda Rolls ... of the Corporation of the City of London at the Guildhall, 1323–64* (1926), 62–3, 87. **Granaries:** Peberdy, 31, 122, 242. **St Anne's chapel:** Briers, 27, 117, 173.

17 ORO BOR/3/A/IX/1/27–8, 53, 61, 64; *Cat. Ancient Deeds*, VI, 106–7, 435; Briers, 34; Peberdy, 26–7.

18 ORO BOR/3/A/IX/1/3–7, 18; Mellor, M, 'Pottery in the Oxford Region', *Oxoniensia* 59 (1994), 32.

19 **Manorial descent:** Burn, 219–73; *VCH Oxon.* XVI (forthcoming). **1296–7 repairs:** Midgley, LM (ed.), *Ministers' Accounts of the Earldom of Cornwall* (Camden 3rd ser. 66–7, 1942–5), I, 95. **1301 grant:** *Cal Close* 1296–1302, 426; ORO BOR/3/A/II/1, f. 12. **Fillets:** Burn, 267–81; *Cal Pat* 1338–40, 418; *Cal Close* 1341–3, 355; 1349–54, 597; *Cal Inq pm Henry VII*, II, 204. **Dereliction:** Burn, 235–6. **Countess Garden:** Briers, 69.

20 **Bell Street houses:** Chapter 4. **Town boundary:** Henley River & Rowing Museum, Fawley estate map (*c.*1788); OS Map 1:2500, Oxon. LIV.9 (1879 edn); ORO BOR/3/A/IX/1/51 and 58, confirming that Bell (Fillets) Lane was the manorial boundary by 1349.

21 **Property deeds:** ORO BOR/3/A/IX/1/53, BOR/3/A/IX/1/267; Briers, 100. **Gravel Hill houses (Nos 9, 11 and 13):** information from Ruth Gibson. (Cross wing of No. 13 dendro-dated to 1454).

The Medieval River Trade, pp.21–36

22 Thacker, FS, *The Thames Highway* (1968 edn); Naruhito, HIH Prince, *The Thames as Highway* (1989). **Anglo-Saxon Thames:** Blair, J, *Anglo-Saxon Oxon.* (1994), refs at 229; Blair, J (ed.), *Waterways and Canal-Building in Medieval England* (2007).

23 **Roads and haulage:** Harrison, D, *The Bridges of Medieval England: Transport and Society 400–1800* (2004); Langdon, J, *Horses, Oxen and Technological Innovation* (1986), 270–3. **Henley roads:** Gambier-Parry, TR (ed.), *Collection of Charters relating to Goring, Streatley and the Neighbourhood, 1181–1546* (ORS 13-14, 1932), II, 157; *Cal Inq pm* XX, 178; above, Chapter 2.

24 **Relative costs:** Peberdy, RB, 'Navigation on River Thames between London and Oxford in the Late Middle Ages: a Reconsideration', *Oxoniensia* 61 (1996), 320; Campbell, BMS, Galloway, JA, Keene, D and Murphy, M, *A Medieval Capital and its Grain Supply: Agrarian Production and Distribution in the London Region c.1300* (Hist. Geog. Research Series 30, 1993), 60–3.

25 Blair, *Waterways*, chapters 1–4 and 12.

26 **Bolney and Rotherfield:** *ibid.*, 70; above, Chapter 2. **Salt tolls:** Midgley, LM (ed.), *Ministers' Accounts of the Earldom of Cornwall*, II (Camden 3rd series 67, 1945), 95; Blair, *Anglo-Saxon Oxon.*, 86. **Henley as port:** *Rot. Litt. Claus.* (Rec. Com.), I, p. 60; *Cal. Liberate Rolls*, IV, 300, 309; VI, 78; *Rolls and Register of Bishop Oliver Sutton*, III (Lincoln Rec. Soc. 48, 1954), 182.

27 **1205:** Blair, *Waterways*, 260. **1234:** *Cal Pat* 1232–7, 51.

28 Peberdy, 'Navigation', 311–40; Blair, *Waterways*, chapters 1–2, 5 and 12; see also Davis, RHC, 'The Ford, The River and the City', *Oxoniensia* 38 (1973), 258–67; Prior, M, *Fisher Row: Fishermen, Bargemen, and Canal Boatmen in Oxford, 1500–1900* (1982), 108–13.

29 Campbell *et al.*, *Medieval Capital*, 47–9, 53–4, 62–3, 195; Harvey, PDA, *A Medieval Oxfordshire Village: Cuxham 1240 to 1400*, 103.

30 **Grain supply ('Feeding the City'):** Campbell *et al.*, *Medieval Capital*; Galloway, J A, 'London's Grain Supply: Changes in the 14th Century', *Franco-British Studies* 20 (1996), 23–34. **Cuxham:** Harvey, *Cuxham*, 92, 97, 103; Harvey (ed.), *Manorial Records of Cuxham c.1200–1359* (ORS 50, 1976 for 1974), Henley refs at 820. **Firewood:** Galloway, JA, Keene, D and Murphy, M, 'Fuelling the City 1290–1400', *Econ. Hist. Review* 49 (1996), 447–72 (misdating Filletts sale in TNA: PRO, SC6/1120/11). **Stonors:** Kingsford, CL (ed.), *The Stonor Letters and Papers 1290–1483* (Camden 3rd series 29–30, 1919), II, 5, 45–6, 65–6, 146, 175.

31 Peberdy, 106.

32 *Ibid.* 70–9, 105–6, 310–12; Campbell *et al.*, *Medieval Capital*, 47–8, 85–6, 101–4. **Salt hythe:** Sharpe, RR (ed.), *Calendar of Wills proved and enrolled in the Court of Husting, London* (2 vols, 1888–90), I, 414, 538. **Thames boats and bargemen:** Blair, *Waterways*, 128–9; Kingsford, *Stonor Letters*, II, 5, 45–6, 65–6, 72.
33 Peberdy, 78–88, 104–6, 113–23; Galloway, 'London's Grain Supply', 23–34.
34 Peberdy, 118–25, 148–9, 156–9, 166–82, 224–5, 239–43, 257–9. **Elmes and Oxford:** Peberdy, 'Navigation', 327. **London woolpacker:** *Cal Close* 1441–7, 281. **Southampton:** Coleman, O (ed.), *Brokage Book 1443–44* (Southampton Rec. Ser. 4 and 6, 1960–1); Stevens, KF (ed.), *Brokage Books 1477–8 and 1527–8* (Southampton Rec. Ser. 28, 1985). **Henley grain market:** Briers, 109, 178, 185–6.

A Medieval Trading Town, pp.37–60

35 **Park:** ORO BOR/3/A/II/1, f. 19; *Cal Inq pm* III, 465; *Cal Inq pm Henry VII*, II, p.204. **Badgemore estate:** Peberdy, 23–4; VCH Oxfordshire draft descent. **Phyllis Court and Northfield End:** Chapter 2. **Mill:** ORO BOR/3/A/IX/1/58, 100, 262; Briers, 36, 104, 212. **Bars:** *Cat. Ancient Deeds*, VI, 106–7, 364. **Buildings:** Gibson, R, 'A Late Medieval Manor in Bell St', HAHG *Jnl* 9 (Spring 1993); Chapter 4.
36 **General description:** Peberdy, 23–32, based on deeds in ORO BOR/3/A/IX/1 and Briers. **Middle Row:** Cottingham, 122–3; *Acts of Privy Council* 1578–80, 273–4; ORO BOR/3/A/V/BM/8, 633, 687. **Guild hall:** Briers, 93, 104, 108. **Butchers' fines:** Briers, 48, 124. **Dunghill:** ORO BOR/3/A/IX/1/450. **Barn:** *ibid.* BOR/3/A/IX/1/158. **Hemp Field:** Chapter 2. **Church:** VCH work in progress, based on structural evidence.
37 **Population:** Peberdy, 32, 64–5, 113–18, 160–6, 238–9. **Woodhall:** *ibid.* 122–3. **Buildings:** e.g. Bell Street nos 20, 61, 76, 81 (*Bear*), 93–5, *Bull*; Hart Street nos 20/2, *Old White Hart* front, Speaker's House; Market Place nos 5, 45/7 (Old Broadgates); New Street: Barnaby, Anne Boleyn and Tudor Cottages; Friday Street: Baltic Cottage; 29 Thameside. Fieldwork by Ruth Gibson, dating by Oxford Dendro Lab.
38 **Market days:** Peberdy, 41–4. **Wool:** *ibid.* 174–83. **Cuxham purchase:** Harvey, PDA, *A Medieval Oxfordshire Village: Cuxham 1240 to 1400* (1965), 66.
39 Peberdy, 212–15, 257–9, based on Briers.
40 *Ibid.* 49–64, 107–13, 150–60, 226–36.
41 *Ibid.* 14, 182–3; *Cal Chart* 1427–1516, 7; Briers, 48; Midgley, LM (ed.), *Ministers' Accounts of the Earldom of Cornwall*, I (Camden 3rd ser. 66, 1942), I, 91.
42 **Crafts and trades:** Peberdy, 66–80, 121–6, 183–4, 239–43. ***White Hart* and *Catherine Wheel*:** ORO BOR/3B/IV/CR/3; Weaver, JRH and Beardwood, A (eds), *Some Oxfordshire Wills* (ORS 39, 1958), 63. **Potters:** Mellor, M, 'Synthesis of Pottery in the Oxford Region', *Oxoniensia* 59 (1994), 32, 88, 200; ORO BOR/3/A/IX/1/5–7. **Craft guilds:** Briers, 121–2.
43 Peberdy, 123, 166–7.
44 *Ibid.* 83–5, 105–6; Rodwell, K (ed.), *Historic Towns in Oxfordshire* (1974), 201; PRO, E 179/161/9.
45 Peberdy, 80–8, 127–37, 185–91, 223–4, 243–57.
46 *Ibid.* 88–92, 144–8, 220–1, 254–5. **Court Rolls:** ORO BOR/3/B/IV/CR/1–18.
47 **Guild:** Peberdy, 92–7, 141–4, 195–224, 255–60. **Assembly Books:** Briers (transcribing ORO BOR/3/A/V/BM/1–4).
48 **Guild hall:** Peberdy, 28; Briers, 29, 93, 104, ORO BOR/3/A/V/BM/8, 699, 722; Act for Amending an Act for building a Bridge over the river Thames (1781); Reeves, I and Cottingham, A, *17th-Century Trades ... of the Inhabitants of Henley-on-Thames* (HAHG, 2003), Appendix, Figs 1–3 (including 18th-cent. plan of Middle Row).
49 **Lords:** Peberdy, 97–103, 138–41, 191–3, 254–5. **Moleyns:** *ibid.* 101–3; Fryde, N, 'A Medieval Robber Baron', in Hunnisett, RF and Post, JB (eds), *Medieval Records in Memory of CAF Meekings* (1978), 197–221. **Tolls claim:** Thomas, AH (ed.), *Calendar of Plea and Memoranda Rolls ... at the Guildhall, 1323–64* (1926), 62–3, 87. **Fair:** *Cal Chart* 1427–1516, 7; Briers, 48.
50 **1291:** *Taxatio Ecclesiastica Anglie et Wallie ... circa AD 1291* (Rec. Com.), 30. **Rectors:** Burn, 133–7 (not fully reliable). **Assistants:** e.g. Salter, HE (ed.), *Subsidy Collected ... in 1526* (OHS 63, 1909), 249; Hamilton Thompson, A (ed.), *Visitations in the Diocese of Lincoln 1517–31*, II (Lincoln Rec. Soc. 35), 65; Briers, 87, 164.
51 **Chapels of BVM and St Catherine:** ORO BOR/3/A/II/1, f. 7; *ibid.* BOR/3/A/IX/1/22, 25, 28, 33, 51 etc; *Cal Pat* 1381–5, 526; Briers, refs at 240; Burn, 126–7, 134, 149, 175, 178–9. **Weavers:** Weaver and Beardwood (eds), *Oxon. Wills* (ORS 39), 63. **Fraternity:** Briers, refs at 241; Burn, 183–6. **Elmes chantry:** ORO BOR/3/A/II/1, ff. 3 and v.
52 **Henley:** Briers (index refs for church, festivals, games). **Background:** Hutton, R, *The Rise and Fall of Merry England* (1994), 25–48, 66–7.
53 **Medieval buildings:** fieldwork and reports by Ruth Gibson, who arranged for dendrochronological dating of some buildings by Dr Daniel Miles, Oxford Dendrochronology Laboratory. Some reports are available in the National Monuments Record and Oxfordshire SMR.
54 **74–8 Bell Street:** HAHG Report No. 64 (1990, unpublished); Gibson, R, 'A Late Medieval Manor in Bell Street', HAHG *Jnl* 9 (spring 1993).
55 **Baltic Cottage:** HAHG Report; Vernacular Archit. Group *Jnl* 39 (2008); Oxford Dendro Lab report (2008).
56 **Burgage plots and subdivision:** ORO BOR/3/A/IX/1/31, BOR/3/A/IX/1/45; Chapter 2.
57 **Baltic Cottage:** as above.
58 **Shops:** ORO BOR/3/A/IX/1/44, BOR/3/A/IX/1/45; Briers, 153.
59 Fieldwork by Ruth Gibson. ***Angel*:** HAHG Rept (unpubl.) 7/5/09. **1487:** Briers, 95–6.
60 **Granaries:** e.g. ORO BOR/3/A/IX/1/12–13, BOR/3/A/IX/1/35, BOR/3/A/IX/1/159. **Perambulation:** *ibid.* BOR/3/C/VIII/1a. **Chantry House:** ORO Acc. 4443, 1/3/1–15.
61 **Inn dates:** Cottingham. **Hall at *Bear*:** Oxford Dendro Lab report (Dec. 2008).

Opening the River: Trade and Navigation 1540–1700, pp.61–72

62 Boas, FS (ed.), *The Diary of Thomas Crosfield, Fellow of The Queen's College, Oxford* (1935), 80.
63 Prior, M, 'The Accounts of Thomas West of Wallingford, a Sixteenth-Century Trader on the Thames', *Oxoniensia* 46 (1981), 73–93.
64 **West, winches, and Oxford:** *ibid.* 73–4; Prior, M, *Fisher Row: Fishermen, Bargemen, and Canal Boatmen in Oxford, 1500–1900* (1982), 112–14; Wilson, DG, *The Thames: Record of a Working Waterway* (1987), 30–2; Peberdy, RB, 'Navigation on the River Thames between London and Oxford in the Late Middle Ages: a Reconsideration', *Oxoniensia* 61 (1996), 312–13, 325–30. **1585 petition:** Thacker, FS, *The Thames Highway* (1968 edn), I, 53.
65 **Barge size:** Thacker, *Highway*, I, 53; Peberdy, 'Navigation', 330. **River:** Wilson, *Thames*, 30–2.
66 **Acts, locks and Oxford:** Act for clearing the passage by Water from London to ... Oxford, 3 Jas 1, c. 20; Act for making the River of Thames navigable from Bercot, 21 Jas I, c. 32; *VCH Oxon.* IV, 291–2; Prior, *Fisher Row*, 114–22. **1628:** Boas (ed.), *Crosfield's Diary*, 21. **Taylor:** Taylor, J, *John Taylor's Last Voyage* (1641); *New DNB*.
67 **Oxford:** *VCH Oxon.* IV, 291–2. **Culham lock and roads:** Philip, IG, 'River Navigation at Oxford during the Civil War and Commonwealth', *Oxoniensia* 2 (1937), 154, 160, 164.
68 **Later legislation:** Act to prevent exactions of the occupiers of locks and wears upon the Thames, 6 & 7 Wm III, c. 16; and see Chapter 7. **Weather:** *VCH Oxon.* IV, 292. **Bishop:** Thacker, *Highway*, I, 45–57; Prior, *Fisher Row*, 116–17; BL, Lansdowne MS 30, ff. 41–51.
69 **London imports:** Gras, NSB, *The Evolution of the English Corn Market from the Twelfth to the Eighteenth Century* (1915), 104–6, 330–2; *Cal Pat* 1558–60, 25; *Acts of Privy Council* 1586–7, 309; 1596–7, 112–13. **Slack trade:** ORO BOR3/A/V/BM/5, f. 6v (1586).
70 **Depth above Reading:** John Burton, *The Present State of Navigation on the Thames Considered* (1767 edn), 17; and see Prior, *Fisher Row*, 127.
71 **1641:** *Oxon. and North Berks. Protestation Returns and Tax Assessments 1641–2* (ORS 59, 1994), 53–7, listing 718 adult males. **1731:** SMR, PRN 5027 (doc. file, transcript from time capsule). **See also:** ORO parish reg.; TNA: PRO, E 179/255/4, part 1, ff. 127–30 (hearth tax); Whiteman, A (ed.), *Compton Census*, 242; *Visitation of Thomas Secker, 1738* (ORS 38, 1957), 78.
72 **Blome:** *Britannia* (1673), 189 (and see 38–41). **Defoe:** Cole, GDH and Browning, DC (eds), *Tour through the Whole Island of Great Britain* (1962), I, 291, 298–300. **West:** Prior, 'Accounts', 77.
73 **Wills:** ORO Henley wills and inventories, indexed in Cheyne, E and Barrett, DM, *Probate Recs of ... Oxford 1516–1732* (Brit. Rec. Soc. 93–4, 1981–5); percentages given are of the *c.*230 wills which describe occupations precisely, excluding 'gentlemen' and 'yeomen'. **1698–1706:** Dils, JA, 'Henley and the River Trade in the Pre-Industrial Period', *Oxon. Local Hist.* 2 (6) (spring 1987), 182–92; ORO parish reg. transcripts.
74 Galloway, JA, 'London's Grain Supply: Changes in Production, Distribution and Consumption during the Fourteenth Century', *Franco-British Studies* 20 (1996), 31–3; Brown, J, 'The Malting Industry', in Mingay, GE (ed.), *The Agrarian History of England and Wales*, VI (1989), 516–17.
75 **Kenton:** TNA: PRO, C2/ELIZ/A2/52; cf. *ibid.* C1/911/15–16. **Henley maltsters:** Dils, 'Henley and River Trade', 184–7; Umfreville, JH, 'The Emergence of the Malting Trade in Henley-on-Thames, 1493–1697', *Oxon. Local Hist.* 5 (2) (winter 1997–8), 12–17; Henley wills and inventories in ORO and TNA: PRO. **Grant and Elton:** ORO MSS Wills Oxon. 26/4/16, 20/4/14.
76 Plot, R, *Natural History of Oxon.* (1677), 265.
77 **Cranfield:** ORO MS Wills Oxon. 162/4/28; Dils, 'Henley and River Trade', 186–7. **Messenger:** TNA: PRO, PROB 11/327; PROB 4/11040. **West:** Prior, 'Accounts', 76–7. **Wood sales:** e.g. Spalding, R (ed.), *Diary of Bulstrode Whitelocke, 1605–75* (Recs of Social and Econ. Hist. ns 13, 1990), 117–18, 799, 803; *Cal. SP Dom.* 1672–3, 219.
78 **Bargemen:** Dils, 'Henley and River Trade', 187–90; ORO Henley wills and inventories; TNA: PRO, C2/ELIZ/A2/52 (John Gode). **Wills cited:** ORO MSS Wills Oxon. 184, f. 357v, 17/1/57, 27/1/5, 173/4/18. **Shipwrights:** Ridge, C Harold (ed.), *Records of the Worshipful Company of Shipwrights, I: 1428–1780* (1939).
79 **Oxford:** Prior, *Fisher Row*, 129–33, 170–6. **1695:** 6 & 7 Wm III, c. 16. **Corporation byelaws:** ORO BOR3/A/V/BM/5, f. 2; BOR3/A/V/BM/6, 301.

Reformation and Revolution: Henley 1540–1700, pp.73–96

80 **Wills:** ORO Henley wills and inventories; TNA: PRO, Henley PCC wills (available online). **Freeman:** ORO MS Wills Oxon. 23/1/20. **Inns:** ORO QSD V/1; Cottingham. **Quaker:** *New DNB*, Ambrose Rigge.
81 **Ravenscroft:** *New DNB*; Peters, GH, *This Glorious Henley* (1950), 25–9; Heppel and Doggett, *Chilterns*, 147; CBA Group 9, *Newsletter* 9 (1979), 128–9; HAHS *Jnl* 5 (winter 1987), 2–18; SMR, PRN 4833.
82 **Wills:** note 80. **Fairs:** ORO BOR/3/A/I/3; BOR/3/A/V/BM/7, 86; Climenson, EJ (ed.), *Passages from the Diaries of Mrs Philip Lybbe Powys* (1899), 368; *Gardner's Dir. Oxon.* (1852), 533. **Barley and malting seasons:** Mathias, P, *The Brewing Industry in England 1700–1830* (1959), 405; Naruhito, HIH Prince, *The Thames as Highway* (1989), 3–4, 88.
83 **Stevens and Michell:** ORO MSS Wills Oxon. 149/2/3, 141/1/ 39. **Servants:** e.g. *ibid.* 17/1/57, 70/2/48, 23/3/20, 8/4/ 50; TNA: PRO, PROB 11/716, f. 103.
84 **Manorial descent:** Burn, 238–84; *VCH Oxon.* XVI (forthcoming). **Whitelockes:** *New DNB*; Spalding, R (ed.), *Diary of Bulstrode Whitelocke, 1605–75* (Recs of Social and Econ. Hist. ns 13, 1990); Wortley, L, 'City Merchants' Landownership around Henley-on-Thames and the Paintings of Jan Siberechts', in Galinou, M (ed.), *City Merchants and The Arts 1670–1720* (2004), 96–7.
85 *New DNB*: Spalding (ed.), *Diary*, 59, 67–8, 112, 121–2, 166 and note 1.
86 Wortley, 'City Merchants', 96–7; 'Jan Siberechts in Henley-on-Thames', *Burlington Mag.* 149 (March 2007), 148–57; Spalding (ed.), *Diary*, 189, 219, and index refs for Hall and Lovelace.
87 **Clayton, Morris and Siberechts:** Wortley, 'City Merchants', 95–102; 'Siberechts in Henley', 148–57; *New DNB*, Sir Rob. Clayton. **Civil War:** Spalding (ed.), *Diary*, 138–9, 150–2, 159–60. **Spencer:** Burn,

241–2; ORO BOR/3/B/II/20; *New DNB*. **Freeman:** Wortley, *op. cit.*; Tyack, G, 'The Freemans of Fawley and their Buildings', *Recs of Bucks.* 24 (1982), 130.

88 **1525–6:** ORO BOR/3/A/I/3; Burn, 52; Briers, 196 sqq. **1568:** *Cal Pat* 1566–9, 154–5; ORO BOR/3/A/1/1. **Burford:** Catchpole, A, *et al.*, *Burford: Buildings and People in a Cotswold Town* (2008), 89–90.

89 **Overseers:** TNA: PRO, PROB 11/62, f. 175; ORO BOR/3/A/V/BM/6, f. 151. **Charities:** *Rep. Commissioners for Charities* (Parl. Papers 1820 (312), v), 200–17. **Almshouses:** *ibid.* 203–4, 213–14; *Parochial Collections*, II (ORS 4, 1922), 171; ORO BOR 3/A/IX/1/516a; BOR 3/A/X/CN/47a; Briers, 120, 214, 222.

90 **Early schools:** Briers, 26; Panel 4. **Grammar and Periam Schools:** Dils, J, 'The Lady Periam School, Henley-on-Thames, 1610–60', *Oxon. Local Hist.* 5 (1) (autumn 1996), 3–12; *VCH Oxon.* I, 470–2; Burn, 93–100; ORO BOR/3/A/II/1, f. 40v. **Whitelocke:** Spalding (ed.), *Diary*, 210, 693.

91 **Chilterns Lollards:** Spufford, M (ed.), *The World of Rural Dissenters, 1520–1725* (1995), 29–30, 103–63; McFarlane, KB, *John Wycliffe and the Beginnings of English Nonconf.* (1952), 183–5; Thompson, JAF, *The Later Lollards, 1414–1520* (1965), 53, 68–73, 92–3. **Henley:** Lincs. RO, reg. XX (Chedworth), ff. 57–62; Foxe, J, *Acts and Monuments*, ed. Pratt, J (*c.*1877), IV, 205, 225–8, 232, 239–40.

92 **Conservatism:** *L&P Hen. VIII*, XIV (1), 176; Briers, 228–30, refs at 262; ORO BOR/3/A/II/1, ff. 26v–28v. **Brice:** Matthews, AG (ed.), *Calamy Revised* (1934), 73; Summers, WH, *Hist. Berks., S. Bucks. and S. Oxon. Congregational Churches* (1905), 45–6, 115. **Other rectors:** *VCH Oxon.* XVI (forthcoming).

93 Clapinson, M (ed.), *Bishop Fell and Nonconf.* (ORS 52, 1980), pp. xiv–xv, xx–xxi, xl, 36–7, 40–1, 63–4, 69–70; Payne, EA, *The Baptists of Berkshire through Three Centuries* (1951), 11, 19, 33, 147; Pitt, A, *Henley Quakers: A Short History* (Henley Preparative Meeting, 1994); Summers, *Congregational Churches*, 115–24; *Calamy Revised*, ed. Matthews, 222, 339–40.

94 **Background:** *VCH Oxon.* IV, 78–85; *VCH Berks.* III, 356–61; Spalding (ed.), *Diary*, 132 sqq.; Whitelocke, B, *Memorials of the English Affairs* (1853 edn), I, 227–8, 244, 278–9; *Jnl of Sir Samuel Luke* (ORS 29, 31, 33, 1950–3); Burn, 273–8. **Harrington:** *Cal. SP Dom.* 1644–5, 145, 175, 184–5. **1643:** Turner, Capt. Samuel, *A True Relation of a Late Skirmish at Henley-upon-Thames* (London, 1643).

95 ORO BOR/3/A/V/BM/6; *Lords' Jnls* V [1642–3], 286–7; *Commons' Jnls* IV [1644–6], 435; Spalding, *Diary*, 178, 181, 184; Burn, 275; *Luke's Jnl.* III, 194.

96 **Royalist support:** *Cal Cttee for Compounding*, II, 1631; *Cal SP Dom.* 1650, 135; *Cal. Cttee for Advance of Money*, III, 1300. **Tyler:** *Cal SP Dom.* 1655, 244, 399; Turner, G Lyon (ed.), *Original Recs of Early Nonconf.* (3 vols. 1911–14), I, 259, 446. **Whitelocke:** *New DNB*. **Lovelace:** Spalding, R, *Contemporaries of Bulstrode Whitelocke, 1605–75* (1990), 180–1.

97 Burn, 279–80; Singer, SW (ed.), *Corresp. of Henry Hyde, Earl of Clarendon, with the Diary of Lord Clarendon* (1828), II, 224–5; Wortley, 'Siberechts in Henley', 156; *New DNB*, Clayton and Lovelace.

98 **1683 and Springall:** *Cal SP Dom.* July–Sept. 1683, 37–8, 68, 153; ORO BOR 3/A/V/BM/6, ff. 424v., 433, 445v–6, 461v; BOR 3/A/V/BM/7, 32–7, 40–7. **Bargemen:** Prior, M, *Fisher Row: Fishermen, Bargemen, and Canal Boatmen in Oxford, 1500–1900* (1982), 170–6.

99 **Background:** Hoskins, WG, *Provincial England* (1963), *The Making of the English Landscape*, revised by Taylor, C (1988), 115–16, 125–8; Machin, R, 'The Great Rebuilding; a Reassessment', *Past and Present* 77 (1977), 33–6; Platt, C, *The Great Rebuildings of Tudor and Stuart England* (1994), 1–9. **Buildings:** Account by G. Tyack; descriptions incorporate internal investigations by Ruth Gibson and HAHG (some unpublished reports available in NMR).

100 Harrison, W, *The Description of England*, ed. Edelen, G (1994 edn), 197, 200–1; Havinden, M A (ed.), *Household and Farm Inventories in Oxfordshire, 1550–90* (ORS 44, 1965), Henley refs (originals in ORO MSS Wills Oxon.). **Grant:** ORO MS Wills Oxon. 116/2/3. **Barretes:** Havinden, 146–8.

101 TNA: PRO, E 179/255/4, part 1, f. 127.

102 ORO Henley wills and inventories: analysis based on a random sample transcribed at time of writing. **Barnes:** ORO MS Wills Oxon. 6/2/6.

103 **Oxford House:** Tyack, G, *Oxford: An Architectural Guide* (1998), 119 ('Old Palace').

104 **Houses named:** unpublished survey work by Ruth Gibson. **Lobby entrances:** Platt, *Great Rebuildings*, 141–2, 152–3; Pilling, J, *Oxfordshire Houses: a Guide to Local Traditions* (1993), 39–41.

105 **Buildings named:** unpublished surveys by Ruth Gibson; dendro-dating (*Bear*) by Dan Miles, Oxford Dendro Lab. **Dolton and *Bear*:** ORO MS Wills Oxon. 164/1/46; Cottingham, 77–8.

106 ORO Henley inventories. ***King's Arms* barn:** HAHG Report 68/1993; dendro report in Vernacular Archit. Group *Jnl* 31 (2000). **57/9 Market Place:** *Oxon. Recorder* (Oxon. Buildings Record Newsletter) 32 (2007); 35 (2008). **Shops:** ORO MS Wills Oxon. 30/4/27; Havinden, *Inventories*, 146-8, 234-7.

107 **Lower Hernes:** HAHG Report 20 (1984/5); Bridge, M, Oxford Dendro Lab Report 2008/17. **Brickmaking:** Bond, J, Gosling, S and Rhodes, J, *Oxfordshire Brickmakers* (1980), 8–9, 12–13. **Messenger:** TNA: PRO, PROB 4/11040.

108 **Duke Street house:** see Fig. 12, projecting frontage on left of street.

109 **Fawley Court:** Tyack, 'Freemans of Fawley', 130–42. **Park Place:** Wortley, 'Siberechts in Henley', 152–3, 156–7 (disproving an assumption it was built for Archibald Hamilton). **Phyllis Court:** Burn, 267, 281; Oxf Jnl Synopsis, 6 June, 29 July 1786, 7 Apr. 1787.

The Age of Improvement: Road and River 1700–1830, pp.97–114

110 **Agricultural Revolution:** Beckett, JV, *The Agric. Revolution* (1990). **Turnpikes and coaching:** Gerhold, D, *Carriers and Coachmasters: Trade and Travel before the Turnpikes* (2005); Hepple and Doggett, chapter 9. **Canals:** Hadfield, ECR, 'The Thames Navigation and the Canals, 1770–1830', *Econ. Hist. Rev.* 14.2 (1944), 172–9; Household, H, *Thames and Severn Canal* (1969), 97–8.

111 **Background:** Gerhold, *Carriers*. **Henley coachmasters:** *ibid.*, 117, 135, 138–9, 203–4; Milne, JG, *Cat. Oxon. Seventeenth-Century Tokens* (1935), 12, 39; Cottingham, 21, 250; TNA: PRO, PROB 11/458, f. 146 (Hathaway), PROB 11/649, f. 228 (Alleway). **Whitelocke:** Spalding, R (ed.), *Diary of Bulstrode Whitelocke* (1990), 189, 638, 747.

112 Gerhold, *Carriers*, 152–5; Hepple and Doggett, 153–65; *Commons' Jnls* XVIII, 728; Turnpike Acts 9 Geo. II, c. 14; 8 Geo. III, c. 50.

113 **White Hill:** Brady, F, and Pottle, FA (eds), *Boswell in Search of a Wife, 1766–9* (1957), 168–9. **Gainsborough:** Tyler, D, 'Humphrey Gainsborough (1718–1776): Cleric, Engineer and Inventor', *Transacs of the Newcomen Soc.* 76 (1) (2006), 51–86; Kendal, R, Bowen, J and Wortley, L, *Genius and Gentility: Henley in the Age of Enlightenment* (Henley River & Rowing Museum, 2002), 20–31; *New DNB.*

114 Gerhold, *Carriers*, 156–64; *Univ. Brit. Dir.* (1791); Oxf. Jnl Synopsis, 24 Apr. 1780, 17 Mar. 1781, 22 Sept. 1787; Cottingham, 21–2.

115 **Inns mentioned:** Cottingham, 50, 56, 181–90, 249; ORO Acc. 4443, box 1, 1/3/15 (implying rebuilding at *Red Lion* before 1732). **March:** Tyack, 'Rebuilding', 71; ORO BOR/3/A/V/BM/8, pp. 476–7, 633. **Coach building and hire:** Oxf. Jnl Synopsis, 1 Jan. 1785; Climenson, EJ (ed.), *Passages from the Diaries of Mrs Philip Lybbe Powys* (1899), 359; *Univ. Brit. Dir.* (1791).

116 Cottingham, 56, 188; *Powys Diaries*, 179, 185, 190–1.

117 Mavor, W, *General View of the Agriculture of Berks.* (1813), 420, 427–37, 507, 531; *Report from Cttee into ... Improvement of the Thames* (Parl. Papers 1st ser. xiv, 1793); Griffiths, R, *Essay to prove that the Jurisdiction ... of the River Thames is Committed to the ... City of London* (1746), 158–61; Berks RO, D/EX 1457/1/130. Naruhito, *Thames as Highway* (1989), 32–3, misinterprets the total number of barges.

118 *Rept from Cttee into Improvement of the Thames* (1793), 11 and Appendices; ORO BOR/3/B/II/24/23, 46, 48–50, 57.

119 **Thames:** Acts 3 Geo. II, c. 11; 24 Geo. II, c. 8; 11 Geo III, c. 45; Vanderstegen, W, *Present State of the Thames Considered* (1794); Thacker, F S, *The Thames Highway* (1968 edn), I, 105–98. **Conway etc:** Tyler, 'Gainsborough'. **Kennet violence:** Willan, TS, 'The Navigation of the Thames and Kennet, 1600–1750', *Berks Archaeol. Jnl* 40 (1936), 151–6. **1770–4 canal proposals:** Vanderstegen, *op. cit.*, 6–7; *Gent. Mag.* 41 (1771), 56; ORO CH/N/III/i–ii.

120 Burton, J, *The Present State of Navigation on the Thames Considered* (1767); Wilson, D, *The Thames: Record of a Working Waterway* (1987), 40, 66; HIH Prince Naruhito, *The Thames as Highway* (1989), 81–4; Oxf. Jnl Synopsis, 17 Feb. 1784, 10 May 1788.

121 **Ushers:** Cottingham, 256. **Soundy:** Oxf. Jnl Synopsis, 8 Nov. 1788; *Univ. Brit. Dir.* (1791). **Smith:** TNA: PRO, PROB 11/550, f. 114 and v. **East:** Oxf. Jnl Synopsis, 11 Aug. 1774. **Mills and Langley:** ORO BOR/3/B/II/24/46; *Rept from Cttee into Improvement of the Thames* (1793), 26–7. **Sarah Jackson:** Oxf. Jnl Synopsis, 9 July 1774; TNA: PRO, PROB 11/903, ff. 284–5. **Bargemasters in 1812:** Berks RO, D/EX 1457/1/130.

122 **Bargemen:** Mavor, *Agric. Berks.* 432; TNA: PRO, PROB 11/524 (Wm Cocke); PROB 11/552 (Nic. Jennings). **Halers:** Act for Improving the Thames, 11 Geo. III, c. 45; Prior, M, *Fisher Row: Fishermen, Bargemen, and Canal Boatmen in Oxford, 1500–1900* (1982), 135–6.

123 **Fortune's:** e.g. ORO MS Wills Oxon. 162/4/28; *ibid.*, BOR/3/B/II/16/1–2; Oxf. Jnl Synopsis, 20 March 1783; Cottingham, 212–14. **Stonor wharf:** Henley River & Rowing Museum, Fawley estate map (*c.*1788), and Jan Siberechts' painting of 'Henley from the Wargrave Road' (1698). **Hart Street to New Street:** ORO BOR/3/B/II/24/23–4, 46–52, 57.

124 **Fawley Court and Park Place:** Tyack, G, 'The Freemans of Fawley and their Buildings', *Records of Bucks.* 24 (1982), 130–43; Tyler, 'Gainsborough', 55–6.

125 Sheppard, F, 'Henley Bridge and its Architect', *Architectural History* 27 (1984), 320–9; ORO BOR/3/A/V/BM/8; BOR/3/A/XIX/BB/7; BOR/3/A/XX/1; Act for Building a Bridge at Henley-on-Thames (1781), 21 Geo. III, c. 33; Doble, C E (ed.), *Remarks and Collections of Thos Hearne*, IV (OHS 34, 1898), 28.

126 Henley Bridge Acts, 21 Geo. III, c. 33; 48 Geo. III, c. 111 (Local and Personal); ORO BOR/3/A/IX/1/633; BOR/3/A/V/BM/8, *passim*; *ibid.* MS Oxf. Archd. Oxon. b 24, ff. 248–51; Henley River & Rowing Museum, Fawley estate map (*c.*1788). **Phyllis Court:** Burn, 281. **Duke Street:** Chapter 9.

127 Burn, 96–7; ORO BOR/3/B/II/24, *passim*; Henley River & Rowing Museum, Fawley estate map (*c.*1788).

The 18th-Century Town, pp.115-136

128 **Henley brewing:** Sheppard, F, *Brakspear's Brewery, Henley-on-Thames, 1779–1979* (1979); *Universal British Dir.* III (*c.*1794), 365–9. **Cluett and Brigstock:** TNA: PRO, PROB 11/735; PROB 11/804; ORO BOR 3/A/V/BM/7 (24 Sept. 1716); *ibid.* MS dd Par. Henley b 1 (1 Apr. 1728, 5 Jan. 1741/2, 13 June 1750); Cottingham, 3, 64, 196.

129 Sheppard, *Brewery*, 4–13, 36–7; *Univ. Brit. Dir.*; wills in ORO and TNA: PRO. For context: Mathias, P, *The Brewing Industry in England 1700–1830* (1959), xxi–xxv, 394, 437, 539.

130 ORO and TNA: PRO, Henley wills; *Bailey's Western & Midland Dir.* (1784); *Univ. Brit. Dir.*; *Pigot's Dir.* (1823–4); *Gardner's Dir. Oxon.* (1852). **Occupations 1841:** TNA: PRO, HO 107/874. **Blandy:** Burn, 146–7. **Banks:** Sheppard, *Brewery*, 38; Burn, 90. **1785:** Climenson, E J (ed.), *Passages from the Diaries of Mrs Philip Lybbe Powys* (1899), 219. **Travelling woman:** Oxf. Jnl Synopsis, 5 Aug. 1774.

131 Brewer, J N, *Topog. and Hist. Description of the County of Oxford* [*c.* 1813], 324–5; *Lewis's Topog. Dict.* (1840), 409–10; Chapter 1.

132 Kendal, R, Bowen, J and Wortley, L, *Genius and Gentility: Henley in the Age of Enlightenment* (2002), 8–18; *Univ. Brit. Dir.* III, 369; *VCH Berks.* III, 160–3; *New DNB*. **Grotes:** Clarke, ML, *George Grote, a Biography* (1962); Oxf. Jnl Synopsis, 17 Dec. 1785. **Caesar:** ORO Harpsden par. reg. transcript, 13 Aug. 1778.

133 **1841:** TNA: PRO, HO 107/874. **Schools:** *Univ. Brit. Dir*; Oxford Jnl Synopsis, 13 July 1782.

134 *Powys Diaries*, esp. 178–94, 217, 235, 279, 282–5, 297–9, 324–31, 362; *New DNB*, Caroline Powys; Oxford Jnl Synopsis, 22 Dec. 1777. **Austen connection:** Pibworth, J, 'The Austen Connection', *Berks. Family Historian*, 24.2 (Dec. 2000).

135 **Theatre:** Port, B, *The Well-Trod Stage* (2005); *Powys Diaries*, 361. **Gambling and pubs:** Sheppard, *Brewery*, 33–4.

136 Tyler, D, 'Humphrey Gainsborough', *Trans. of the Newcomen Soc.* 76 (1) (2006), 51–86; Tyack, G, 'The Freemans of Fawley and their Buildings', *Records of Bucks.* 24 (1982), 137–8; Sheppard, *Brewery*, 18–21; Kendal *et al.*, *Genius and Gentility*, 20–31.

137 ORO BOR/3/A/I/2; BOR/3/A/I/ 5–6; Burn, 54–6; *First Rep. of Commissioners into Municipal Corporations, App. Pt 1* (Parl. Papers 1835 [116], xxiii), 69–74.

138 **Expenditure:** *Poor Abstract, 1777*, 140; *1787*, 188; *1804*, 398–9; *1818*, 352–3; *Poor Rate Retns, 1822* (Parl. Papers 1822 [556], v), 135; *1835* (Parl. Papers 1835 [444], xlvii), 153. **Vestry and management:** ORO MS dd Par. Henley b 1 (vestry bk 1725–1816).

139 Summers, W H, *Hist. Berks., S. Bucks. and S. Oxon. Congregational Churches* (1905), 117–24; OxS, Baptism and Burial Transcripts, Independent Free Church Rotherfield Greys; Tyler, 'Gainsborough', 72–4; *Gent. Mag.* 55 (2) (1785), 931–2.

140 Pitt, A, *Henley Quakers: A Short Hist.* (Henley Preparative Meeting, 1994); Curnock, N (ed.), *Jnl of John Wesley* (1909–16), V, 45, 292, 345; Telford, J (ed.), *Letters of John Wesley* (1931), VII, 180; ORO MSS Oxf. Dioc. d 568, f. 172v; d 572, ff. 162–3; Worrall, ES (ed.), *Retn of Papists, 1767* (Cath. Rec. Soc. Occas. Publ. 2, 1989), II, 116.

141 **Church and fittings:** ORO BOR/3/A/V/BM/7, p. 84; BOR/3/A/V/BM/8, pp. 413, 611–12, 757, 785–6; *ibid.* MS Oxf. Archd. Oxon. b 24, ff. 186–281; Evans, JT, *Church Plate of Oxon.* (1928), 82. **Religious life:** visitation retns in ORO MSS Oxf. Dioc. d 556, d 559, d 562, d 566, d 568; *VCH Oxon.* XVI (forthcoming).

142 *Univ. Brit. Dir.* III, 365–6; Brewer, *Oxon.* 324 ('handsome and capacious'); Colvin, HM, 'Architectural History of Marlow and its Neighbourhood', *Records of Bucks.* 15 (1) (1947), 5–6. **Buildings:** by G. Tyack, incorporating unpublished internal investigations by Ruth Gibson.

143 Summerson, J, *The Classical Language of Architecture* (1963, revised 1980); Worsley, G, *Inigo Jones and the European Classicist Tradition* (2007), 77–8.

144 **1712 houses:** Bodl. Gough Maps 26, f. 67. **Jennings:** Burn, 308–9.

145 **Old Rectory:** Cottingham, A and Sheppard, F, 'The Old Rectory', HAHS *Jnl* (Summer 1986), 1–11; Sheppard, *Brewery*, 6; NMR record files. **Queen Anne Cottage:** Baker, GBA and Cottingham, A, 'Queen Anne Cottage', HAHG *Jnl* 17 (Summer 2002).

146 **Grey brick:** Clifton-Taylor, A, *The Pattern of English Building* (1972), 235–6; Bond, J *et al.*, *Oxfordshire Brickmakers* (1980), 10; Brunskill, R W, *Brick Building in Britain* (1990).

147 **Longlands and Countess Gardens:** reports in NMR; the dates 1768 and 1769 inscribed on bricks at Longlands seem incompatible with its stylistic character. **Pattern books:** Summerson, J, *Georgian London* (2003 edn), 49–68; Cruikshank, D and Wyld, P, *London: the Art of Georgian Building* (1975), *passim*.

148 **No. 20:** NMR report (1989). **Malthouses:** Cottingham, 297–8; *Oxon. Recorder* 35 (Summer 2008), 2–3.

149 **No. 86:** Sheppard, *Brewery*, 11.

150 ORO SL/132/3/D/5.

151 **Bradshaw and Friday Street:** ORO BOR/3/A/V/BM/8, pp. 93, 115, 118, 121, 133; *ibid.* MS dd Par. Henley b 1, 23 Apr. 1733 (almshouses); NMR report; Cottingham, 262–4. **1813:** Brewer, *Oxon.* 324. **Ann Boleyn Cottage:** survey by Ruth Gibson (correcting Buildings List).

152 ORO MS dd Par. Henley b 1, 19 May 1790; *ibid.* BOR/3/C/IV/PW/11; Colvin, H M, *Biog. Dictionary of British Architects* (1995 edn), 152–3; Alasia, V, in HAHG *Jnl* (Spring 2000). **Coleridge:** Higginbotham, P, *Workhouses of the Midlands* (2007), 81.

153 **Ownership etc:** Cottingham, 55–6, 188; Henley River & Rowing Museum, Fawley estate map (*c.*1788). **Buildings:** unpublished surveys by Ruth Gibson (superseding Cottingham's interpretation of Denmark House).

154 **New Street and Shennan:** Oxf. Jnl Synopsis, 28 Apr. 1786, 13 Dec. 1788, 27 May 1790. **Bell Street:** ORO BOR/3/B/IV/BR/22a (under 1785).

155 **Assembly rooms:** HAHG *Report* 47 (1987). **9 Northfield End and Northfield House:** information from Ruth Gibson. **Brakspear's house:** Sheppard, *Brewery*, 59.

156 ORO BOR/3/A/IX/2, no. 32; Tyack, 'Rebuilding', 72; refs at note 135.

157 **1808:** 48 Geo. III, c. 111. **Corner buildings:** Cottingham and Fisher, *Henley*, 72, 141–2. **Almshouses:** datestones; ORO BOR/3/A/X/CP/50; BOR/3/A/X/CJ/93. **Demolished houses:** Bodl. MS Top.Oxon. a 67, f. 318.

New Beginnings: Railway and Regatta 1830–1914, pp. 137–162

158 MacDermot, ET and Clinker, CR, *History of the Gt Western Railway* (1964 edn); Karau, P, *An Illustrated Hist. of the Henley-on-Thames Branch* (1982); Gardiner, J and Wenborn, N (eds), *History Today Companion to British Hist.* (1995), railways.

159 Thacker, F S, *The Thames Highway* (1968 edn), I, 181–9, 218–39.

160 **River traffic:** Wilson, D G, *The Thames: Record of a Working Waterway* (1987), 91–109; *Royal Commission into Canals and Inland Navigations, 2nd Report, Mins and Evidence* (Parl. Papers 1907 [Cd 3718], xxxiii (1)), 336 sqq. **Henley barges:** *Kelly* (1883), 581; Karau, *Henley Branch*, 21; TNA: PRO, RG13/1369 (1901 census).

161 **Coaches:** *Pigot's Dir. Oxon.* (1830); *Gardner's Dir. Oxon.* (1852); *Dutton, Allen & Co.'s Dir. Oxon.* (1863); Rowland, A, *An Independent Parson: The Autobiography of Alfred Rowland* (1924), 3. **Inns:** Cottingham, 56–7, 95–7, 188–90, 252–4.

162 **1848 petition:** *Reading Mercury and Oxf. Gaz.*, 1 July 1848 (quoted Cottingham, 23). **Population:** *Census*, 1801–1911. **Grote:** Grote, Mrs [Harriet], *The Personal Life of George Grote* (1873), 62. **Quiet town:** Rowland, *Autobiography*, 3.

163 *Oxf. Jnl* 30 Oct 1852, 6 June 1857; *Guide to Henley-upon-Thames* (1838 and later edns).

164 *Guide to Henley* (1866); Climenson, E, *Guide to Henley-upon-Thames* (1896). **1897:** Karau, *Henley Branch*, 29–31.

165 TNA: PRO, RG13/1369 (1901 census); Tyack, 'Rebuilding', 85–6; *New DNB*, Crisp, Smith.

166 Burnell, R, *Oxford and Cambridge Boat Race 1829–1953* (1954), 25–54; Burnell, R and Rickett, H R N,

Short History of Leander Club 1818 to 1968 (1968); Burnell, R, *Henley Royal Regatta: a Celebration of 150 Years* (1989); Cottingham, A, 'Beginnings of Henley Regatta', HAHG *Jnl* 11 (Summer 1996); *Oxf. Jnl*, 6 June 1829, 18 June 1831, 9 June 1837, 22 June 1839; *Times*, 26 June 1844.

167 *Oxf. Jnl*, 9 June 1837; Rowland, *Autobiography*, 3–4; Burnell, *Regatta*. **1849 petition:** Burnell, *Regatta*, 41.

168 *Guide to Henley-upon-Thames* (1850 and 1866 edns); Climenson, *Guide*, 68–72. **Pollution:** *Birmingham Daily Post*, 20 July 1886.

169 Burnell, *Regatta*, 5–6, 67–72, 87–118.

170 Climenson, *Guide*; Cottingham, 189–90; ORO MSS Oxf. Dioc. c 347, f. 210; c 356, f. 201v; Karau, *Henley Branch*, 33–4, 126–7; *Sphere*, 9 July 1900.

171 *Guide* (1838 and later edns); Climenson, *Guide*, 85–7; *Oxf. Jnl* 30 Oct 1852; Perkins, A, *The Phyllis Court Story* (1983), 80 sqq.

172 TNA: PRO, RG13/1369 (1901 census).

173 Climenson, *Guide*, 58–9; Sheppard, F, *Brakspear's Brewery* (1979), 42–85.

174 Climenson, *Guide*, 59–64; *Kelly's Dir. Oxon.* (1883 and later edns). **Silk mill:** Burn, 89; *Sale Cat, Fawley Court Estate* (1853), lot 6: copy in ORO SC 231. **New Mills:** *Guide* (1838 edn), 19–20; *VCH Oxon.* XVI (forthcoming), Rotherfield Peppard. **Stuart Turner:** *Stuart Turner Ltd: a Little Souvenir* (2006); *Berks. Mercury*, 1 Feb. 1979, 10.

175 *Gardner's Dir. Oxon.* (1852); *HS* 10 Oct. 1919 (WA Simmons' recollections: cutting in OxS, Henl 944); Peters, G H, *This Glorious Henley* (1950), 42–5. **1901 trades:** TNA: PRO, RG13/1369. **Newtown:** ORO, Rotherfield Greys tithe award and map; OS Map 6", Oxon. LIV (1883 edns).

176 Karau, *Henley Branch*, 17, 20–2, 31, 34, 39–40, 45, 82–5, 156.

177 *Guides* (1838 and later edns); Climenson, *Guide*.

178 Climenson, *Guide*, 67–8; *Royal Commission on Liquor Licensing Laws: 3rd Rept, Mins of Evidence* (Parl Pps 1898 [C 8693–4], xxxvi), 74–80; Umfreville, JH, 'The Comings and Goings of Charles Clements', *Oxon. Local Hist.* 5.5 (1998–9), 9–10.

179 **Schools:** Burn, 101–2, 107, 114; *Bp Wilberforce's Visitation Retns* (ORS 35, 1954), 70, 123; *Kelly* (1883 and later edns); Peters, *Glorious Henley*, 90–2; Cottingham, 57; ORO MSS Oxf. Dioc. d 568, f. 172; d 707, f. 82; ORO S 128/1AM2/N17; S 128/2IM/A1. **Nonconformists:** Rowland, *Autobiography*, 11–12. **Dismissal:** MS Diary of Annette Brakspear, f. 49 (photocopy in OxS, o920 BRAK).

180 **Poverty and overcrowding:** *Wilb. Visit.* 70; ORO MS Oxf. Dioc. c 332, f. 225. **Workhouse:** Alasia, V, 'Henley Union Workhouse 1834–61', *Oxon. Local Hist.* 6.1 (1999), 24–52; *Census*, 1851. **Charities etc:** *Guide* (1866 edn), 34–8; Climenson, *Guide*, 46–9. **Allotments:** *Guide* (1850 edn), 21.

181 *1st Rept of Commissioners ... into Munic. Corpns; App. pt 1* (Parl. Papers 1835 [116], xxiii), 69–74; *Guide* (1838 and later edns); Climenson, *Guide*; *Kelly* (1891). **Board:** ORO BOR/3/A/VI/LM/1–2; BOR/3/A/VI/LS/5. **Boundaries:** *Census*, 1891–1951; *Kelly* (1895); *Act to confirm Provisional Orders*, 55 & 56 Vic. c.197 (Local & Personal); OS Maps 6", Oxon. LIII–LIV (1883 and later edns).

182 Umfreville, ' Charles Clements', 3–25. **Newspapers:** *Henley Standard*, 9 Mar. 1979 (Supplement), 27 June 1986; Cordeaux, EH, and Merry, DH, *Bibliog. of Printed Works relating to Oxon.* (1955), I, 141–2.

183 **Ritual:** MS Diary of Annette Brakspear, ff. 81–2, 91, 98. **Restoration:** Burn, 117. **Rectory:** ORO MSS Oxf. Dioc. c 2196, no. 3; c 2168, no. 5. **Dissent:** Tiller, K (ed.), *Church and Chapel in Oxon. 1851* (ORS 55, 1987), 48–9, 85–6; *Kelly* (1883 and later edns); Peters, *Glorious Henley*; Pitt, A, *Henley Quakers: A Short Hist.* (Henley Preparative Meeting, 1994); Cottingham and Fisher, *Henley-on-Thames: a Pictorial Hist.* 144; *Henley Baptist Church* (centenary pamphlet, 1976); Sacred Heart website (May 2006).

184 **Buildings:** by G. Tyack. **Population:** *Census*. **1830s demand:** *Guide* (1838), 22.

185 **Greys:** ORO MS dd Par Rotherfield Greys e 7 (survey and field book, 1815); *ibid.* Greys tithe award and map (1844); *Census*. **1829:** *Berks. Chron.*, 20 June 1829. **West Street:** *Census*, 1851. **1860s houses:** abstracts of title 1886 (info. from Hilary Fisher).

186 **Owthwaite:** Snare, *Dir. Oxon.* (1847); *PO Dir. Oxon.* (1847 and later edns); ORO QSD/A/47 (Greys inclosure award, 1860). **Trinity church:** ORO MS dd Par Rotherfield Greys c 13.

187 **Phyllis Court:** Burn, 267; Perkins, A, *The Phyllis Court Story* (1983), 93. **Rotherfield Court**: Climenson, *Guide*, 93. **Oxford Villas:** *Guide* (1866), 24–5. **River Terrace:** *PO Dir.* (1869); *Sale Partics.* 19 May 1887.

188 **Simmons:** cutting in OxS, HENL/944. **Improvements:** ORO BOR/3/A/VI/LS/5; BOR3/A/III/9; BOR/3/A/V/BM/12; BOR/3/A/VI/LM/1–2; BOR/3/A/VII/2, 10 Sept 1890. **Drinking fountain:** *Kelly* (1895), 105. **Clements:** *HS* 24 Sept 1920. **Wing and Haslam:** Gold, SM, *A Biographical Dictionary of Architects at Reading* (1999), 81, 213–6.

189 **Institute:** Allen, G, *Story of Henley College* (2004), 22, 94. **Schools:** above; Cottingham and Fisher, *Henley*, 164–70. **Brooks:** Dixon, R, 'Life and Work of James Brooks' (Courtauld Institute PhD thesis 1976), 20. **Workhouse:** HAHG *Jnl* 14 (spring 2000), 2; ORO PLU4/G/2M5; Colvin, H M, *Biog. Dict. British Architects* (2008 edn), 124; *PO Dir.* (1877). **Police station:** *Oxf. Jnl* 16 May 1868. **Cemetery:** *Kelly* (1891).

190 Climenson, *Guide*, 3.

191 **Queen Street:** *Henley Advertiser*, 13, 17 Sept 1879. **Hamiltons:** ORO BOR 3/A/VI/LM/2, 14 May, 9 July 1883; A/VII/CM/2, 13 Mar., 9 Oct. 1889, 11 June 1890; A/VII/CM/3, 16 Nov. 1892 etc.; A/VII/CM/4, 21 June 1899; *HS* 25 Dec. 1931. **Gravel Hill:** datestone.

192 **Caxton Terrace:** Sheppard, F, *Henley in Old Picture Postcards* (1983), pl. 38; datestone. **Owthwaite:** ORO QSD/A/47; *Henley Advertiser*, 8 Oct. 1887. **St Mark's estate:** ORO BOR 3/A/VI/LM/2, 13 Mar. 1889; A/VII/LC/4, 26 April 1899 and *passim*; *Royal Commn on Liquor Licensing Laws* (Parl Pps 1898), 74; OS Map 6", Oxon. LIV.SW (1900 edn, revised 1897).

193 **Friar Park:** Climenson, *Guide*, 93–4; Crisp, F, *Guilde to Friar Park* (1908); Mowl, T, *Historic Gardens of England: Oxon.* (2007), 119–32. **Edwards:** information from Lydia Wilson. **Norman Ave:** *HS* 23 Aug. 1920.

194 **Royal:** Sheppard, *Postcards*, pl. 42. **Webb:** Gold, *Reading Architects*, 201–5. **Imperial:** *Builder*, 25 April 1896, 371.

195 ***Red Lion* etc.:** *HS* 13 Jan 1899; Climenson, *Guide*, 37; Cottingham and Fisher, *Henley*, 15–16; Bodl. GA Oxon. b 6, f. 36 (sale partics 1901); Cottingham, 185–9. **Boathouses:** ORO BOR 3/A/VII/CM/3, 11 Jan 1893 and *passim*; Pilling, J and Ward, L, *Henley-on-Thames Past and Present* (2000), 58. ***Little White Hart*:** Cottingham, 154–6. **Grandstand:** Whitehead, D, *Henley-on-Thames: a History* (2007), 127–8.

196 **Breweries etc:** Sheppard, *Brewery*, 74–9; Cottingham, 305–11. **Banks:** Sheppard, *Postcards*, pl. 27. **Masonic Hall:** Gold, *Reading Architects*, 149.

197 Aston, JM, *Henley-on-Thames Town Hall* (HAHG, 1975); Gray, S, *Edwardian Architecture: a Biographical Dictionary* (1985), 204–6.

Modern Henley, pp. 163–178

198 Whitehead, D, *Henley-on-Thames* (2007), 76–8; cuttings (1914–19) from Sybil Reeves scrapbook in OxS, Pamph HENL 944. **Turner:** ORO BOR3/A/VII/CM/19, p. 41. **Royal Engineers:** *HS* 7 May 1976, 5. **Regatta:** Burnell, R, *Henley Royal Regatta* (1989), 119.

199 *Kelly* (1935 edn).

200 Whitehead, *Henley*, 78–80, 82; *HS* 11 Jan. 1985, reminiscences; ORO BOR3/A/VII/CM/2, 13 Jan. 1892; ORO BOR3/A/VII/CM/20, p. 335; BOR3/A/VII/CM/21, p. 123; BOR3/A/VII/CM/22, p. 355. **Market:** *Kelly* (1935 edn); Pilling, J and Woods, L, *Henley-on-Thames Past and Present* (2000), 100.

201 *Phyllis Court Club, Henley: Plans and Partics of Enlargement* (1928); Perkins, A, *The Phyllis Court Story* (1983), 109–38; *Salter's Guide to the Thames* (1936 edn), quoted in Whitehead, *Henley*, 82–4; *Kelly* (1935); cuttings (1931–2) in OxS, Pamph HENL 944.

202 Whitehead, *Henley*, 82–5; *Kelly* (1935 edn); ORO BOR3/A/VII/CM/17–25.

203 Whitehead, *Henley*, 79–80; Pevsner, 638; Pitt, A, *Henley Quakers: A Short History* (Henley Preparative Meeting 1994).

204 Whitehead, *Henley*, 85–9; *HS* 3 April, 4 Dec. 1981, 15 June 1988.

205 **Population:** *Census*, 1911–51.

206 **Council housing:** ORO BOR3/A/VII/CM/19–22, BOR3/A/VII/HM/45; Whitehead, *Henley*, 78. **Trust:** *HS* 23 Dec. 1932; 29 May 1936; 13 April 1979, 3; ORO BOR3/A/VII/CM/22–3.

207 OS Map 6", Oxon. 54 SW (1938 edn); *New DNB*, Osbert Lancaster.

208 **Hospital:** *HS* 8 June 1923; *Programme for Laying Foundation Stone* (1922): copy in OxS. **PO:** Cottingham and Fisher, *Henley-on-Thames: a Pictorial Hist.* 147. **Pubs:** Sheppard, *Brakspear's Brewery*, 90–1; Sheppard, *Henley in Old Picture Postcards*, pl. 32. **Regal:** Moloney, C, 'Excavations and Building Survey at Bell Street, Henley-on-Thames, 1993–4', *Oxoniensia* 62 (1997), 131; *Oxf Times*, 31 Dec. 1993.

209 **Population:** *Census*, 1931–2001; Oxon. County Council, *Informal Town Map, Borough of Henley-on-Thames: Rept of Survey 1963, adjusted 1966* (copy in OxS). **Reminiscences:** *HS* 11 Jan. 1985.

210 **Planning:** *Informal Town Map* (1966); South Oxon. District Council, *Local Plan No. 4: District Plan for Henley-on-Thames, Draft Report* (Jan 1979); *Local Plan* (Dec. 1993): copies in OxS. **Stuart Turner:** *HS* 22 July 1983; *Stuart Turner: A Little Souvenir* (2006 centenary booklet). **Brakspears:** *Oxf. Mail* 6 Aug., 28 Oct. 2002; Wychwood brewery website (Jan. 2009). **Perpetual:** *HS* 15 Jan 1993.

211 **Planning:** previous note. **Disputes:** OxS, newspaper cuttings 1985–2002. **Recession:** *HS* 9 Jan. 1987, 18 Dec. 1992, 16 April 1993, 30 July 1993.

212 **Turner and Perpetual:** *HS* 22 July 1983, 15 Jan. 1993. **2009:** *HS* 2 March 2009.

213 **House prices:** 'Twenty Years of UK Housing' (Halifax Group press release 25 Jan. 2003, accessed online). **Amenities:** SODC, *Local Plan* (Dec. 1993); OxS, newspaper cuttings; Whitehead, *Henley*, 95–9.

214 Wilson, D, *The Thames: Record of a Working Waterway* (1987), 97–109; SODC, *District Plan: Henley* (Jan. 1979), 47–8, 130–5, 141–4; *Local Plan* (Dec. 1993), 193–9, 222; *HS* 18 June 1993, 10 July 1998.

215 Burnell, *Regatta*, 10, 54–65, 151–3; Whitehead, *Henley*, 100.

216 **Housing development:** Whitehead, *Henley*, 89–90; ORO BOR3/A/VII/HM/45–48; BOR3/A/VII/CM/27–29; local info. **Criticisms:** Brett, L, *Landscape in Distress* (1965), 18–23. **Friar Park:** *Reading Mercury*, 11 Feb. 1967; *New DNB*, George Harrison.

217 ***Catherine Wheel*:** Whitehead, *Henley*, 95. **Walled Garden:** *Country Life*, 10 Nov. 1960, p. 1120. **Surgery:** RIBA drawings, PB 624/3 (1–10) (extended in 1982). **Past Field:** Harwood, E, *England: A Guide to Post-War Listed Buldings* (2000). **Badgemore school:** *Building Design*, 400 (1978), 8.

218 Whitehead, *Henley*, 91. **Malthouses:** *HS* 27 April 1984, 21 Feb. 1986. **College:** Allen, G, *Henley College* (2004), 108, 121. **Tesco:** *HS* 19 March 1993. **Perpetual House and station:** *HS* 14 May, 28 May, 8 Aug. 1993; Pilling and Woods, *Henley*, 83.

219 **Regatta HQ:** *Building*, 25 April 1986, 10–11; *Building Design*, 2 May 1986, 20–1. **Museum:** *Architectural Design* 69 (1999), 112; *Country Life*, 17 Sept. 1998, 106–7.

Further Reading and Sources

The following is a selective list of the most important sources for the history of Henley and the Thames. A more general guide to recent work on towns, vernacular buildings, and other urban themes is available in our EPE book on the Oxfordshire town of Burford (*Burford: Buildings and People in a Cotswold Town*), and on the Oxfordshire EPE website. The Victoria County History has published accounts of numerous towns and cities, including (in Oxfordshire) Banbury, Bicester, Deddington, Witney, Woodstock and Oxford itself. A VCH volume on Henley and the surrounding area is in preparation.

BOOKS AND ARTICLES
Henley and Related Topics

Burn, JS, *A History of Henley-on-Thames* (1861)
Burnell, R, *Henley Royal Regatta: a Celebration of 150 Years* (1989)
Burnell, R, and Rickett, HRN, *A Short History of Leander Club, 1818 to 1968* (1968)
Campbell, BMS, Galloway, JA, Keene, D and Murphy, M, *A Medieval Capital and its Grain Supply: Agrarian Production and Distribution in the London Region* c.*1300* (Hist. Geog. Research Series 30, 1993)
Clarke, ML, *George Grote, a Biography* (1962)
Cottingham, A, *The Hostelries of Henley* (2000)
Cottingham, A, and Fisher, H, *Henley-on-Thames: a Pictorial History* (1990)
Dils, JA, 'Henley and the River Trade in the Pre-Industrial Period', *Oxon. Local Hist.* 2.6 (Spring 1987), 182–92
Dils, J, 'The Lady Periam School, Henley-on-Thames, 1610–60', *Oxon. Local Hist.* 5.1 (Autumn 1996), 3–12
Durham, B, 'Henley, St Anne's Bridge', *South Midlands Archaeol.* 19 (1989), 52; 16 (1986), 101
Galloway, JA, Keene, D, and Murphy, M, 'Fuelling the City 1290–1400', *Econ. Hist. Review* 49 (1996), 447–72
Galloway, JA, 'London's Grain Supply: Changes in Production, Distribution and Consumption during the Fourteenth Century', *Franco-British Studies* 20 (1996), 23–34
Gras, NSB, *The Evolution of the English Corn Market from the Twelfth to the Eighteenth Century* (1915)
Harvey, PDA, *A Medieval Oxfordshire Village: Cuxham 1240 to 1400* (1965)
Hearn, K, 'Merchant Clients for the Painter Jan Siberechts', in Galinou, M (ed.), *City Merchants and The Arts 1670–1720* (2004), 83–92
Henley Archaeological & Historical Group *Journal* (1984–): *passim*
Hepple, LW and Doggett, AM, *The Chilterns* (1994 edn)
Hollingworth, G, *The Story of Henley* (1983)
Karau, P, *An Illustrated History of the Henley-on-Thames Branch* (1982)
Kendal, R, Bowen, J and Wortley, L, *Genius and Gentility: Henley in the Age of Enlightenment* (Henley River & Rowing Museum, 2002)
Moloney, C, 'Excavations and Building Survey at Bell Street, Henley-on-Thames, 1993–4', *Oxoniensia* 62 (1997), 109–33
Perkins, A, *The Phyllis Court Story: 14th Century Manor to 20th Century Club* (1983)
Peters, GH, *This Glorious Henley* (1950)
Pilling, J, and Ward, L, *Henley-on-Thames Past and Present* (2000)
Pine, J, 'Excavation of Medieval and Post-Medieval Features at the Rear of 42c Bell Street, Henley, Oxfordshire', *Oxoniensia* 64 (1999), 255–73
Pitt, A, *Henley Quakers: A Short History* (Henley Preparative Meeting, 1994)
Port, B, *The Well Trod Stage [of the Kenton Theatre]* (2005)
Shaida, M, *Views of Henley-on-Thames* (1984)
Sheppard, F, *Brakspear's Brewery, Henley-on-Thames, 1779–1979* (1979)
Sheppard, F, *Henley in Old Picture Postcards* (1983)
Sheppard, F, 'Henley Bridge and its Architect', *Architectural History* 27 (1984), 320–9
Spalding, R, *The Improbable Puritan: a Life of Bulstrode Whitelocke 1605–75* (1975)
Spalding, R, *Contemporaries of Bulstrode Whitelocke, 1605–75* (1990)
Spufford, M (ed.), *The World of Rural Dissenters, 1520–1725* (1995)
Steane, J and Andrews, J, 'Henley-on-Thames Bridge', *South Midlands Archaeol.* 15 (1985), 77–9
Summers, WH, *History of the Berkshire, South Buckinghamshire and South Oxfordshire Congregational Churches* (1905)
Tiller, K (ed.), *Benson: A Village Through its History* (1999)
Tomalin, GHJ, *The Book of Henley-on-Thames* (1975)
Tyack, G, 'The Freemans of Fawley and their Buildings', *Recs of Bucks.* 24 (1982), 130–43
Tyack, G, 'The Rebuilding of Henley-on-Thames, 1780–1914', *Oxon. Local History* 3.2 (spring 1989), 67–89

Tyler, D, 'Humphrey Gainsborough (1718–1776): Cleric, Engineer and Inventor', *Transacs of the Newcomen Soc.* 76 (1) (2006), 51–86
Umfreville, JH, 'The Emergence of the Malting Trade in Henley-on-Thames, 1493–1697', *Oxon. Local Hist.* 5.2 (winter 1997–8), 12–17
Umfreville, JH, 'The Comings and Goings of Charles Clements', *Oxon. Local Hist.* 5.5 (1998–9), 3–25
Whitehead, D, *Henley-on-Thames: a History* (2007)
Wortley, L, 'City Merchants' Landownership around Henley-on-Thames and the Paintings of Jan Siberechts', in Galinou, M (ed.), *City Merchants and The Arts 1670–1720* (2004), 95–102
Wortley, L, 'Jan Siberechts in Henley-on-Thames', *Burlington Mag.* 149 (March 2007), 148–57

Navigation and the Thames

Ackroyd, P, *Thames: Sacred River* (2007)
Blair, J (ed.), *Waterways and Canal-Building in Medieval England* (2007)
Davis, RHC, 'The Ford, The River and the City', *Oxoniensia* 38 (1973), 258–67
Hadfield, ECR, 'The Thames Navigation and the Canals, 1770–1830', *Econ. Hist. Review* 14.2 (1944), 172–9
Household, H, *The Thames and Severn Canal* (1969)
Lewis, MJT, Slatcher, WN and Jarvis, PN, 'Flashlocks on English Waterways: A Survey', *Industrial Archaeol.* 6 (1969), 209–53
Marsden, P, *Ships of the Port of London: 12th to 17th Centuries AD* (1996)
Naruhito, HIH Prince, *The Thames as Highway* (1989)
Peberdy, RB, 'Navigation on the River Thames between London and Oxford in the Late Middle Ages: a Reconsideration', *Oxoniensia*, 61 (1996), 311–40
Philip, IG, 'River Navigation at Oxford during the Civil War and Commonwealth', *Oxoniensia* 2 (1937), 152–65
Prior, M, *Fisher Row: Fishermen, Bargemen, and Canal Boatmen in Oxford, 1500–1900* (1982)
Prior, M, 'The Accounts of Thomas West of Wallingford, a Sixteenth-Century Trader on the Thames', *Oxoniensia* 46 (1981), 73–93
Thacker, FS, *The Thames Highway* (1968 edn, 2 vols)
Willan, TS, 'The Navigation of the Thames and Kennet, 1600–1750', *Berks Archaeol. Jnl* 40 (1936), 146–56
Wilson, DG, *The Thames: Record of a Working Waterway* (1987)

Miscellaneous

Beresford, MW, *New Towns of the Middle Ages* (1967)
Blair, J, *Anglo-Saxon Oxfordshire* (1994)
Gerhold, D, *Carriers and Coachmasters: Trade and Travel before the Turnpikes* (2005)
Henig, M and Booth, P, *Roman Oxfordshire* (2000)
Mathias, P, *The Brewing Industry in England 1700–1830* (1959)
Rodwell, K (ed.), *Historic Towns in Oxfordshire* (1974)

Unpublished theses

Briers, PM, 'The Medieval Borough of Henley' (Oxford Univ. B.Litt thesis 1935)
Peberdy, RB, 'The Economy, Society, and Government of a Small Town in Late Medieval England: A Study of Henley-on-Thames from *c.*1300 to *c.*1540' (Leicester Univ. PhD thesis 1994)

PRINTED SOURCES (EXCLUDING MAPS)

Bailey's Western & Midland Dir. (1784)
Blome, R, *Britannia* (1673)
Briers, PM (ed.), *Henley Borough Records: Assembly Books 1395–1543* (ORS 41, 1960)
Brewer, JN, *Topographical and Hist. Description of the County of Oxford* (1819)
Burton, J, *The Present State of Navigation on the Thames Considered* (1767 edn)
Calendars of Charter Rolls; Close Rolls; Patent Rolls etc (HMSO; Record Commission)
Climenson, EJ, *Guide to Henley-upon-Thames* (1896)
Climenson, EJ (ed.), *Passages from the Diaries of Mrs Philip Lybbe Powys* (1899)
Crisp, F, *Guide to Friar Park* (1908)
Defoe, D, *Tour through the Whole Island of Great Britain*, ed. Cole, GDH and Browning, DC (1962)
Foxe, J, *Acts and Monuments*, ed. Pratt, J (*c.*1877)
Gardner's Directory of Oxfordshire (1852)
Griffiths, R, *Essay to prove that the Jurisdiction ... of the River Thames is Committed to the ... City of London* (1746)
Guide to Henley-upon-Thames and its Vicinity (1826 and later edns)
Harvey, PDA (ed.), *Manorial Records of Cuxham c.1200–1359* (ORS 50, 1976 for 1974)
Havinden, MA (ed.), *Household and Farm Inventories in Oxfordshire, 1550–90* (ORS 44, 1965)
Kelly's Directory of Oxfordshire (1883–1939)
Kingsford, CL (ed.), *The Stonor Letters and Papers 1290–1483* (Camden 3rd series 29–30, 1919)
Mavor, W, *A General View of the Agriculture of Berkshire* (1813 edn), esp. 427–37
Midgley, LM (ed.), *Ministers' Accounts of the Earldom of Cornwall* (Camden 3rd ser. 66–7, 1942–5)
Oxfordshire Record Society publications: *passim*

Plot, R, *Natural History of Oxfordshire* (1677)
Post Office Directory of Oxfordshire (1847–77)
Rowland, A, *An Independent Parson: The Autobiography of Alfred Rowland* (1924)
Sale Cat, Fawley Court Estate (1853) (copy in ORO, SC 231)
Sharpe, RR (ed.), *Calendar of Wills proved and enrolled in the Court of Husting, London* (2 vols, 1888–90)
Singer, SW (ed.), *Correspondence of Henry Hyde, Earl of Clarendon, with the Diary of Lord Clarendon* (1828), II, 224–5
Spalding, R (ed.), *Diary of Bulstrode Whitelocke, 1605–75* (Records of Social and Econ. Hist. ns 13, 1990)
Stuart Turner Ltd: a Little Souvenir (2006)
Taylor, J, *John Taylor's Last Voyage* (1641)
Thomas, AH (ed.), *Calendar of Plea and Memoranda Rolls ... of the Corporation of the City of London at the Guildhall, 1323–64* (1926)
Turner, Capt. Samuel, *A True Relation of a Late Skirmish at Henley-upon-Thames* (London, 1643)
Universal British Dir. III (*c.*1794), 365–9
Vanderstegen, W, *The Present State of the Thames Considered* (1794)
Weaver, JRH and Beardwood, A (eds), *Some Oxfordshire Wills* (ORS 39, 1958)

Newspapers

E.g. *Henley Advertiser; Henley Standard; (Jackson's) Oxford Journal; Reading Mercury*. Some are searchable online through the British Library's 19th-Century Newspapers Online website, available from some libraries.

Parliamentary Papers and Acts

Act for Clearing the Passage by Water from London to and beyond the City of Oxford (1604), 3 James 1, c.20
Act for making the Thames navigable from Burcot to Oxford (1623), 21 Jas I, c.32
Act to prevent exactions of the occupiers of locks and wears upon the Thames (1695), 6 & 7 Wm III, c.16
Act for repairing the Roads from Henley Bridge to ... Magdalen Bridge (1735), 9 Geo. II, c.14
Act for regulating the navigation of the River Thames (1751), 24 Geo. II, c.8
Act for Repairing the Road from Reading to Hatfield (1768), 8 Geo. III, c.50
Act for Improving the Navigation of the River Thames (1771), 11 Geo III, c.45
Act for Building a Bridge at Henley-on-Thames (1781), 21 Geo. III, c. 33 (with amendments 35 Geo. III, c.79, 48 Geo. III, c.111 (Local and Personal), 6 Wm IV, c.40 (Local and Personal))
Report from Committee into ... Improvement of the Thames (Parl. Papers 1st ser. xiv, 1793)
First Report of Commissioners into Municipal Corporations, Appendix Part 1 (Parl. Papers 1835 [116], xxiii), 69–74
Royal Commission on Liquor Licensing Laws: 3rd Report, Minutes of Evidence (Parl. Papers 1898 [C 8693–4], xxxvi), 74–80
Royal Commission into Canals and Inland Navigations, 2nd Report, Minute and Evidence (Parl. Papers 1907 [Cd 3718], xxxiii (1)), 336 sqq

Planning Reports

Oxon. County Council, *Informal Town Map, Borough of Henley-on-Thames: Report of Survey 1963, adjusted 1966* (typescript, copy in OxS)
South Oxfordshire District Council, *Local Plan No. 4: District Plan for Henley-on-Thames, Draft Report* (January 1979)
South Oxfordshire District Council, *Local Plan* (December 1993)
South Oxfordshire District Council, *Local Plan 2011, adopted Jan. 2006* (available online)

MAPS

Henley was one of the few towns surveyed by the Ordnance Survey at the very large scale of 1:500 (Oxfordshire sheets LIV.9, 1878–9). The area was also covered at the more usual 1:2500 and at six inches to the mile (see OS *Area Book*, 1879). Earlier printed maps showing the Henley area include: J Rocque, *Map of the County of Berkshire* (1761); T Jefferys, *The County of Oxford* (1767); R Davis, *A New Map of the County of Oxford* (1797); and 1" Ordnance Survey, 1st edn (sheet 13, 1830).

The earliest estate map is that of Strickland Freeman's Fawley estate (*c.*1788) in Henley River & Rowing Museum, which shows Henley in outline (see Figure 81). The tithe map of 1843 in Oxfordshire Record Office shows the parish's rural parts in detail, but the town again only in outline; the area south of Friday Street is included in more detail in the Rotherfield Greys tithe map of 1844. A detailed estate map of the Badgemore estate in 1788 is in the Bodleian Library (MS Top. Oxon. a 3)

UNPUBLISHED COLLECTIONS

Oxford, Oxfordshire Record Office. Holds Henley's voluminous Borough Records (BOR 3), containing a wealth of material from the Middle Ages to the 20th century; for partial listings, see Access to Archives (www.nationalarchives.gov.uk/a2a). Also holds important collections for particular properties and businesses, and records relating to Thames navigation (CH/N). Other relevant collections include wills and inventories; quarter sessions records (including victuallers' recognizances for Henley's inns); diocesan and other church records (including visitation returns); parish records (including parish registers and vestry minutes); and nonconformist records.

Oxford, Oxfordshire Studies. Extensive newspaper cuttings, pamphlets, sales catalogues, and printed ephemera, along with Ordnance Survey and earlier printed maps, transcripts of parish and Congregationalist registers, copies of census returns, and extensive photographic collections. Also holds a copy of Annette Brakspear's unpublished 19th-century diary. The collections (including the photographs) are partly searchable online through Heritage Search, accessible from the Oxfordshire County Council website at www.oxfordshire.gov.uk.

Oxford, Historic Environment Record. Archaeological and some buildings data for the county, including the Henley area; partly searchable online through Heritage Search.

Oxford, Bodleian Library. Includes topographical drawings by JC Buckler and others (eg MS Top. Oxon. a. 65), and printed and manuscript maps including that of Badgemore in 1788 (above).

Aylesbury, Buckinghamshire Record Office. Papers of the Mackenzie family of Fawley Court (AR 1/93 and AR 41/94), many of them relevant to Henley.

Gloucester, Gloucestershire Record Office. Papers of the Freeman family of Fawley Court (D1245/FF), many of them relevant to Henley.

Henley Library. Newspapers, sale catalogues, directories, photographs and printed ephemera complementing the collections in Oxfordshire Studies; also copies of the censuses.

Henley River & Rowing Museum. Extensive collections for the history of the town as well as of the river, including photographs, drawings, paintings, and artefacts. Jan Siberechts' painting of Henley from the Wargrave Road is on public display; so is a large-scale reproduction of the Fawley estate map of *c.*1788.

Henley Town Hall. Miscellaneous borough and other records in the custodianship of Henley Archaeological & Historical Group (some in the process of transfer to Oxfordshire Record Office).

London, The National Archives (Public Record Office). Best searched through its online catalogue, which is not fully comprehensive. Important sources include taxation records (in E 179), wills proved in the Prerogative Court of Canterbury (PROB 11, available online), and national censuses (1841–1911).

London, British Library. Relevant material includes topographical drawings (e.g. Add. MS 36373, ff. 80b–100), and to a lesser extent the papers of Sir Bulstrode Whitelocke and Caroline Powys. Lansdowne MS 30 includes some of John Bishop's petitions concerning Thames locks in 1580.

Reading, Berkshire Record Office. Records of the Thames Navigation Commissioners and Thames Conservancy; miscellaneous collections relevant to Henley.

Swindon, National Monuments Record (English Heritage). Extensive buildings and photographic collections for Henley and elsewhere.

WEBSITES

www.englandspastforeveryone.org.uk

The England's Past For Everyone (EPE) interactive website is making available a wide range of historical and educational material from EPE projects across the country, including (in Oxfordshire) the Burford and Henley projects. Material for Henley will include census and wills transcripts, buildings information, and schools materials arising from the Oxfordshire schools project with Henley River & Rowing Museum and Mabel Prichard school in Oxford.

www.victoriacountyhistory.ac.uk/Oxfordshire

The VCH Oxfordshire website includes work in progress on Henley and neighbouring parishes, earmarked for publication in VCH Oxfordshire 16 (Henley and Environs).

www.oxfordshire.gov.uk (Heritage Search)

www.imagesofengland.org.uk (Listed Buildings)

www.nationalarchives.gov.uk/a2a (Access to Archives)

http://thames.me.uk (guide to the Thames)

Index

NOTE: Entries relate to Henley except where stated. *Italics* refer to a picture or picture caption.

Picture Credits

The authors and publishers wish to thank the following for permission to reproduce their material. Any infringement of copyright is entirely accidental: every care has been taken to contact or trace all copyright owners. We would be pleased to correct in future editions any errors or omissions brought to our attention. References are to page numbers except where stated.

Ashmolean Museum, Oxford, 70 (Fig. 44)
Berkshire Record Office, 63
Bibliothèque Nationale de France, Paris, 38
Bodleian Library, Oxford, 23, 54 (Fig. 31), 62, 81 (Fig. 53), 93, 112, 115, 118, 127
James Bond, 23
Paul Brakspear, 117 (Fig. 83)
British Library, 9, 22, 33, 65
Christ Church, Oxford (by permission of the Governing Body), 83
Martin Cook, 174
Ann Cottingham, 14 (Fig. B)
John Eade, 143
English Heritage (Karen Guffogg), 32; (Derek Kendall), 58, 60, 82, 132 (bottom)
English Heritage (NMR), 140, 148 (Fig. 110), 176
Hilary Fisher, 17, 107, 108 (Fig. A), 142, 154 (Fig. 113), 161, 164-5
Ruth Gibson, 5, 14 (Fig. A), 49 (Figs D-E), 52-3, 55 (drawing), 56 (Fig. 33 right) 59 (Figs B and D), 94 (Fig. 66), 132 (top), 169
Gloucestershire Record Office, 85, 123
Linda Hall, 48 (Fig. B)
Peter Higginbotham, 124
Hume & Son (K.F. Hume), 59 (Fig. C)
Jersey Heritage Trust (courtesy of the Jersey Heritage Trust Collection, PW/52), 120 (Fig. 86)
John Leighfield, 99
The National Archives: Public Record Office, 149 (Fig. A)
The National Gallery of Ireland, 105 (Fig. 76)
National Media Museum/SSPL, 138
The National Portrait Gallery, 73, 77
Nottingham City Museums and Galleries, 79 (Fig. C)
Oxfordshire County Council Photographic Archive, 8, 16, 25, 27, 64, 136, 144-6, 157 (Fig. 117)
Oxfordshire Record Office (images Simon Townley), 19 (top), 40, 69, 80, 89, 105 (Fig. 77)
Oxfordshire Studies (Oxford Central Library), 166
River & Rowing Museum, Henley, 15, 50 (Fig. 29), 68, 70 (Fig. 43), 88, 97, 100 (Fig. 73), 111, 113, 125, 178 (Fig. 136)
John Steane, 48 (Fig. A)
Tate Gallery, London (all images ©Tate, London 2009), 71, 78, 79 (Fig. B), 108 (Fig. B)
Derek Toms, 130-1 (except Fig. B)
Geoffrey Tyack, 177
University of London (Matthew Bristow), 101, 163, 172; (Stephen Mileson), 2; (Simon Townley), x, 19 (bottom), 20, 49 (Fig. C), 50 (Fig. 30 right), 55 (right), 56 (Figs 33 left, 34), 57, 76, 84, 91-2, 94 (Fig. 67), 95, 103, 120 (Fig. 87), 128-9, 131 (Fig. B), 133-5, 154 (Fig. 114), 156, 157 (Fig. 118), 159-60, 162, 168, 178 (Fig. 135)
V&A Images/Victoria and Albert Museum, London, 75
Victoria Art Gallery, Bath and North East Somerset Council/Bridgeman, 122
Wadham College, Oxford (by courtesy of the Warden and Fellows; image Studio Edmark , Oxford), 87

The following maps are by Cath D'Alton, ©University of London: Figs 4, 6, 9, 10, 18, 20, 21, 23, 25, 72, 112. Figs 9-10 and 112 superimposed on Ordnance Survey maps of 1899 and 1938; Figs 20, 23 and 25 from originals ©R.B. Peberdy (1994); Figs 18, 20-1 and 72 from originals cited in captions.